AF659329

Political Violence in ASSAM

Political Violence in ASSAM

Sanghita Das

CENTRUM PRESS
NEW DELHI-110002 (INDIA)

CENTRUM PRESS
H.O.: 4360/4, Ansari Road, Daryaganj,
New Delhi-110002 (India)
Tel: 23278000, 23261597, 23255577, 23286875
B.O.: No. 1015, Ist Main Road, BSK IIIrd Stage,
IIIrd Phase, IIIrd Block, Bangalore-560085 (INDIA)
Tel: 080-41723429
Email: centrumpress@gmail.com
Visit us at: www.centrumpress.com

Political Violence in Assam

© Reserved

First Edition, 2011

ISBN 978-93-80921-66-2

PRINTED IN INDIA

Printed at Tarun Offset Printers, Delhi-110053

Contents

Contents

Preface

This book is an attempt to describe the prevailing political violence in Assam. The objective of the book is to trace the root cause of violence in the state. We have given the detailed introduction of the state enabling the readers to understand the various aggressive and violent activities in the state. We have also included the chapter on ethnic conflict and attempted to give detailed major incidents of terrorist violence in Assam, during 1990 to 2010. All the major organizations, ULFA, SULFA and BODO, accounted for the conflicts in the state have also been dealt in detail. In addition to it many other issues such as external influences, role of media and report of Amnesty Internationals have also been presented in detail.

The book also gives an insight to the economic fall of the state due to violence. Underdevelopment has been associated with the violence and its different aspects have been dealt with utmost objectiveness.

This book will not only make the readers aware about the violence prevailed in the state, but it has also endeavored to assess the present condition of the state. The language of book is very easy, lucid and interactive.

Hope the book would certainly will be of immense use for the readers.

Author

1

Assam: An Introduction

LOCATION

Assam is northeastern state of India with its capital at Dispur in the city of Guwahati. Located south of the eastern Himalayas, Assam comprises the Brahmaputra and the Barak river valleys along with the Karbi Anglong and the North Cachar Hills with an area of 30,285 square miles (78,438 km^2). Assam is surrounded by six of the other *Seven Sister States*: Arunachal Pradesh, Nagaland, Manipur, Mizoram, Tripura and Meghalaya. Popularly the Northeatern part of India is also called "The Unexplored Paradise".

These states are connected to the rest of India via a narrow strip in West Bengal called the Siliguri Corridor or "Chicken's Neck". Assam also shares international borders with Bhutan and Bangladesh; and cultures, peoples and climate with South-East Asia—important elements in India's Look East policy.

Assam became a part of India after the British occupied the region following the First Anglo-Burmese War of 1824-1826. It is known for Assam tea, large and old petroleum resources,Assam silk and for its rich biodiversity. Assam has successfully conserved the one-hornedIndian rhinoceros from near extinction, along with the tiger and numerous species of birds, and it provides one of the last wild habitats for the Asian elephant. It is becoming an increasingly popular destination for wildlife tourism, and Kaziranga and Manas are bothWorld Heritage Sites. Assam was also known for its Sal tree forests and forest products, much depleted now. A land of high rainfall, Assam is endowed with lush greenery and the mighty river Brahmaputra, whose tributaries and oxbow lakes provide the region with a unique hydro-geomorphic and aesthetic environment.

ETYMOLOGY

Assam was known as Pragjyotisha in the Mahabharata; and Kamarupa in the 1st millennium. "While the Shan invaders called themselvesTai, they came to be referred to as *Asam, Asam* and sometimes as *Acam* by the indigenous people of the country. The modern Assamese word *Ahom* by which the Tai people are known is derived from *Asam* or *Asam*. The epithet applied to the Shan conquerors was subsequently transferred to the country over which they ruled and thus the name Kamarupa was replaced by Asam,which ultimately took the Sanskritized form *Asama,* meaning 'unequalled, peerless or uneven'. The British province after 1838 and the Indian state after 1947 came to be known as*Assam*. On 27 February 2006, the Government of Assam started a process to change the name of the state to *Asom* or *Axom*, a controversial move that has been opposed by the people and political organizations.

Assam and its Environs: As per the plate tectonics, Assam is in the eastern-most projection of the Indian Plate, where the plate is thrusting underneath the Eurasian Plate creating a subduction zone and theHimalayas. Therefore, Assam possesses a unique geomorphic environment, with plains, dissected hills of the South Indian Plateau system and with the Himalayas all around its north, north-east and east.

Geomorphic studies conclude that the Brahmaputra, the life-line of Assam is an antecedent river, older than the Himalayas. The river with steep gorges and rapids in Arunachal Pradesh entering Assam, becomes a braided river (at times 10 mi/16 km wide) and with tributaries, creates a flood plain (Brahmaputra Valley: 50–60 mi/80–100 km wide, 600 mi/1000 km long). The hills of Karbi Anglong, North Cachar and those in and close to Guwahati (also Khasi-Garo Hills) now eroded and dissected are originally parts of the South Indian Plateau system. In the south, the Barakoriginating in the Barail Range (Assam-Nagaland border), flows through the Cachar district with a 25–30 miles (40–50 km) wide valley and enters Bangladesh with the name Surma.

Assam is endowed with petroleum, natural gas, coal, limestone and other minor minerals such asmagnetic quartzite, kaolin, sillimanites, clay and feldspar. A small quantity of iron ore is available in western districts. Discovered in 1889, all the major petroleum-gas reserves are in Upper parts. A recent USGS estimate shows 399 million barrels (63,400,000 m^3) of oil, 1,178 billion cubic feet (3.34×10^{10} m^3) of gas and 67 million barrels (10,700,000 m^3) of natural gas liquids in the Assam Geologic Province.

With the "Tropical Monsoon Rainforest Climate", Assam is temperate (summer max. at 95–100 °For 35–38 °C and winter min. at 43–46 °F or 6–8 °C) and experiences heavy rainfall and high humidity. The climate is characterized by heavy monsoon downpours reducing summer temperatures and affecting foggy nights and mornings in winters. Thunderstorms known as*Bordoicila* are frequent during the afternoons. Spring (Mar-Apr) and Autumn (Sept-Oct) are usually pleasant with moderate rainfall and temperature.

Assam is one of the richest biodiversity zones in the world and consists of tropical rainforests, deciduous forests, riverine grasslands,bamboo orchards and numerous wetland ecosystems; Many are now protected as national parks and reserved forests. The Kaziranga, home of the rare Indian Rhinoceros, and Manas are two UNESCO World Heritage Sites in Assam.

The state is the last refuge for numerous other endangered species such as the Golden Langur (Presbetis geei), White-winged Wood Duck or *Deohanh* (Cairina scutulata), Bengal Florican, Black-breasted Parrotbill, Pygmy Hog, Greater Adjutant and so on. Some other endangered species with significant population in Assam are the Tiger, Elephant, Hoolock Gibbon, Jerdon's Babbler and so on to name a few. Assam is also known for orchids. The region is prone to natural disasters with annual floods and frequent mild earthquakes. Strong earthquakes are rare; three of which were recorded in 1869, 1897 (8.1 on the Richter scale); and in 1950 (8.6).

HISTORY

Assam and adjoining regions have evidences of human settlements from all the periods of the Stone ages. The hills at the height of 1500–2000 feet (460 to 615 m) were popular habitats probably due to availability of exposed doleritic basalt useful for tool-making. According to the Kalika Purana (c.17th–18th AD), written in Assam, the earliest ruler of Assam was Mahiranga followed by Hatak, Sambar, Ratna and Ghatak; Naraka removed this line of rulers and established his own Naraka dynasty. It mentions that the last of the Naraka-bhauma rulers, Narak, was slain by Krishna. Naraka's son Bhagadatta, mentioned in the Mahabharata, fought for the Kauravas in the battle of Kurukshetra with an army of *kiratas, chinas* and *dwellers of the eastern coast*. Later rulers of Kamarupa frequently drew their lineage from the Naraka rulers. However, there are lots of evidences to say that Mahayana Buddhism was prominent in ancient Assam. After Huen Shang's visit Mahayana Buddhism came to Assam. Relics of Tezpur, Malini Than, Kamakhya and Madan Kam Dev Temple are the evidences of Mahayana Buddhism.

ANCIENT AND MEDIEVAL

The Ahom Kingdom, c.1826. Ancient Assam, known as Kamarupa was ruled by powerful dynasties: the Varmanas (c.350–650 AD), the Salstambhas (*Xalostombho*, c.655–900 AD) and the Kamarupa-Palas (c.900–1100 AD). In the reign of the Varman king, Bhaskaravarman (c.600–650 AD), the Chinese traveller Xuan Zangvisited the region and recorded his travels. Later, after weakening and disintegration (after the Kamarupa-Palas), the Kamarupa tradition was somewhat extended till c.1255 AD by the Lunar I (c.1120–1185 AD) and Lunar II (c.1155–1255 AD) dynasties. Two later dynasties, the Ahoms and the Koch left larger impacts. The Ahoms, a Tai group, ruled Assam for nearly 600 years (1228–1826 AD) and the Koch, a Tibeto-Burmese, established sovereignty in c.1510 AD The Koch kingdom in western Assam and present North Bengal was at its zenith in the early reign of Naranarayana (c.1540–1587 AD). It split into two in c.1581 AD, the western part as a Moghul vassal and the eastern as an Ahom satellite state. Since c.13th AD, the nerve centre of Ahom polity was upper Assam; the kingdom was gradually extended till Karatoya River in the c.17th–18th AD It was at its zenith during the reign of Sukhrungpha or Sworgodeu Rudra Simha (c.1696–1714 AD). Among other dynasties, the Chutiyas ruled north-eastern Assam and parts of present Arunachal Pradesh and the Kacharis ruled from Dikhow River to central and southern Assam. With expansion of Ahom kingdom, by c.1520 AD the Chutiya areas were annexed and since c.1536 AD Kacharis remained only in Cachar andNorth Cachar more as an Ahom ally then a competing force. Despite numerous invasions, mostly by the Muslim rulers, no western power ruled Assam until the arrival of the British. The most successful invader Mir Jumla, a governor of Aurangzeb, briefly occupied Garhgaon(c.1662–63 AD), the then capital, but found it difficult to control people making guerrilla attacks on his forces, forcing them to leave. The decisive victory of the Assamese led by the great general Lachit Borphukan on the Mughals, then under command of Raja Ram Singha atSaraighat (1671) had almost ended Mughal ambitions in this region. Mughals were finally expelled in c.1682 AD from lower Assam.

BRITISH ASSAM

A map of the British Indian Empire in 1909 during the partition of Bengal (1905–1911), showing British India in two shades of pink (coral and pale) and the princely states in yellow. *The Assam Province* (initially as the Province of Eastern Bengal and Assam) can be seen towards the north-eastern side of India Ahom palace intrigue and political turmoil due to the Moamoria rebellion aided the Burmese to invade Assam and install Chandra Kanta Singh as a puppet king in 1817.

In 1821, Singh switched his allegiance to the British, leading the Burmese to invade again. The Burmese defeated the Assamese army in 1822, and made Assam a Burmese province under a military governor-general. With the Burmese having reached the East India Company's borders, the First Anglo-Burmese War ensued in 1824. The war ended under the

Treaty of Yandabo in 1826, with the Company taking control of Lower Assam and installing Purander Singh as king of Upper Assam in 1833. The arrangement lasted till 1838 and thereafter the British gradually annexed the entire region. Initially Assam was made a part of the Bengal Presidency, then in 1906 it was a part of Eastern Bengal and Assam province, and in 1912 it was reconstituted into a Chief Commissioners' province. In 1913, a Legislative Council and in 1937 the Assam Legislative Assembly was formed in Shillong, the erstwhile capital of the region. The British tea planters imported labour from central India adding to the demographic canvas. After few initial unsuccessful attempts to free Assam during the 1850s, the Assamese since early 20th century joined and actively supported the Indian National Congress against the British. At the turn of the 20th century, British India consisted of eight provinces that were administered either by a Governor or a Lieutenant-Governor. *The Assam Province* was one amongst those major eight provinces of British India. The following table lists their areas and populations (but does not include those of the dependent Native States): During the partition of Bengal (1905–1911), a new province, *Assam and East Bengal* was created as a Lieutenant-Governorship. In 1911, *East Bengal* was reunited with Bengal, and the new provinces in the east became: Assam, Bengal, Bihar and Orissa.

Table. Below Shows the Major Original Provinces During British India that Includes The Assam Province:

Province of British India	Area (in thousands of square miles)	Population (in millions of inhabitants)	Chief Administrative Officer
Burma	170	9	Lieutenant-Governor
Bengal	151	75	Lieutenant-Governor
Madras	142	38	Governor-in-Council
Bombay	123	19	Governor-in-Council
United Provinces	107	48	Lieutenant-Governor
Central Provinces and Berar	104	13	Chief Commissioner
Punjab	97	20	Lieutenant-Governor
Assam	49	6	Chief Commissioner

In 1947, Assam including the present Arunachal Pradesh, Nagaland, Mizoram and Meghalaya became a state of the Union of India (princely states, Manipur and Tripura became Group C provinces) and a district of Assam, Sylhet chose to join Pakistan.

POST BRITISH

Assam till 1950s; The new states of Nagaland, Meghalaya and Mizoram formed in the 1960-70s. From Shillong, the capital of Assam was shifted to Dispur, now a part ofGuwahati. After the Indo-China war in 1962,Arunachal Pradesh was also separated out. Since 1947, with increasing economic problems in the region, separatist groups began forming along ethnic lines, and demands for autonomy and sovereignty grew, resulting into fragmentation of Assam.

Since the mid-20th century, people from present Bangladesh have been migrating to Assam. In 1961, the Government of Assam passed a legislation making use of Assamese languagecompulsory. It had to be withdrawn later under pressure from Bengali speaking people in Cachar. In the 1980s the Brahmaputra valley saw a six-year Assam Agitation triggered by the discovery of a sudden rise in registered voters on electoral rolls. It tried to force the government to identify and deport foreigners illegally migrating from neighbouring Bangladesh and changing the demographics. The agitation ended after an accord between its leaders and the Union Government, which remained unimplemented, causing simmering discontent.

The post 1970s experienced the growth of armed separatist groups like United Liberation Front of Asom (ULFA) and National Democratic Front of Bodoland (NDFB). In November 1990, the Government of India deployed the Indian army, after which low-intensity military conflicts and political homicides have been continuing for more than a decade. In recent times, ethnicity based militant groups (UPDS, HPDC, etc.) have also mushroomed. Regional autonomy has been ensured for Bodos in Bodoland Territorial Council Areas (BTC) and for the Karbis in Karbi Anglong after agitation of the communities due to sluggish rate of development and aspirations for self-government.

TEA HISTORY

This 1850 engraving shows the different stages in the process of making tea in Assam. After discovery of Camellia sinensis (1834) in Assam followed by its tests in 1836–37 in London, the British allowed companies to rent land since 1839. Thereafter tea plantations mushroomed in Upper Assam, where the soil and the climate were most suitable. Problems with the imported laborers from China and hostilities of native Assamese resulted into migration of forced laborers from central-eastern parts of India.

After initial trial and error with planting the Chinese and the Assamese-Chinese hybrid varieties, the planters later accepted the local Camellia assamica as the most suitable one for Assam. By 1850s, the industry started seeing some profits. Industry saw initial growth, when in 1861, investors were allowed to own land in Assam and it saw substantial progress with invention of new technologies and machinery for preparing processed tea during 1870s. The cost of Assam tea was lowered down manifold and became more competitive than its Chinese variant. Despite the commercial success, tea laborers continued to be exploited, working and living under poor conditions. Fearful of greater government interference, the tea growers formed The Indian Tea Association in 1888 to lobby to retain the status quo. The organization was very successful in this, and even after India's independence conditions of the laborers have improved very little.

SUBDIVISIONS

Assam is divided into 27 administrative districts. More than half of these districts were carved out during 80s and 90s from original 1. Lakhimpur, 2. Jorhat, 3. Karbi Anglong, 4. Darrang, 5. Nagaon, 6. Kamrup, 7. Goalpara, 8. North Cachar and 9. Cachar districts, delineated by the British. Earlier, during 70s, Dibrugarh was separated out from original Lakhimpur district.

These districts are further sub-divided into 49 "Sub-divisions" or Mohkuma. Every district is administered from a district head quarter with the office of the District Collector, District Magistrate, Office of the District Panchayat and usually with adistrict court. The districts are delineated on the basis of the features such as the rivers, hills, forests, etc. and majority of the newly constituted districts are sub-divisions of the earlier districts. For the present districts of Assam and their location, refer the attached map.

The local governance system is organised under the jila-parishad (District Panchayat) for a district, panchayat for group of or individual rural areas and under the urban local bodies for the towns and cities. Presently there are 2489 village panchayats covering 26247 villages in Assam. The 'town-committee' or nagar-xomiti for small towns, 'municipal board' or pouro-xobha for medium towns and municipal corporation or pouro-nigom for the cities consist of the urban local bodies.

For the revenue purposes, the districts are divided into revenue circles and mouzas; for the development projects, the districts are divided into 219 'development-blocks' and for law and order these are divided into 206 police stations or thana.

Population Growth Trend from 1901 to 2001

Assam has many ethnic groups and the People of India projecthas studied 115 of these. Out of which 79 (69%) identify themselves regionally, 22 (19%) locally, and 3 trans-nationally. The earliest settlers wereAustroasiatic, followed by Tibeto-Burman, Indo-Aryan speakers, and Kradai speakers. Forty-five languages are spoken by different communities, including three major language families:Austroasiatic (5), Sino-Tibetan (24) and Indo-European (12). Three of the spoken languages do not fall in these families. There is a high degree of bilingualism.

RELIGIONS

According to the 2001 census, there are 17,296,455 Hindus, 8,240,611 Muslims, 986,589Christians, 22,519 Sikhs, 51,029 Buddhists, 23,957 Jains and 22,999 belonging to other religious communities. The latter includes Animism (Khamti, Phake, Aiton etc. communities).

HINDUISM

The Hindus of Assam perform several dances to practice their devotion to their Gods. One category of them is the Sattriya Dances. Kamakhya, dedicated to Goddess Durga is the eastern-most pilgrimage of Hinduism. Popular forms of God in Assam are Durga, Shiva, Krishna and Narayana, although several tribes practice devotion to local deities as well.

Brahmo Samaj: Assam is the home of Kalicharan Mech, a Bodo Hindu who stopped the British Christian missionaries, spread ahimsa and vegetarianism. He was deeply influenced by theBrahmo Samaj. He later became known as "Gurudev Kalicharan Brahmachari" or "Guru Brahma". His principles were established as the Brahma Dharma. Perhaps his teachings can be summarized by his given phrase, "Chandrama Surya Narayans Jyoti", meaning, *"the light (jyoti) from the sun is capable from dispelling darkness and taking people to Brahma (Narayans)."*

From the teachings of Guru Brahma, the "Bodo-Brahmas" (the Bodos of this sect) have boycotted alcohol and heavy dowry as well as meat-eating.

This sect is written by scholars to be Vedic and Upanishadic. As per Vedic rituals, the priests perform Horn Yajna, which was begun by Guru Brahma to organize the Bodos. While the Bodo Christians today are laying stress on adopting a Roman script for the Bodo community, the Bodo-Brahmas prefer the traditional Bengali-Ahomi script.

ISLAM

Muslims constitute the second largest religious group in Assam with 8,240,611 persons. In 16th century Ajan Fakir, a Islamic saint from Baghdad had come to Assam.Assam stands in third position in Indian provinces to have Muslims on the basis of proportion after the Union Territory Of Lakshadweep Islands and the state of Jammu and Kashmir. The only female Chief Minister of Assam was a Muslim.

CHRISTIANITY

The Bible was translated into Assamese in the year of 1819. In 1827, an attempt was made to start a Baptist church in Guwahati, but it made no permanent converts in the area. Later the American Baptist Foreign Missionary Society was able to make some headway in Guwahati. Although these earliest Christian missionary endeavros which were focused in the north-east of India, were in Modern Assam, the great success of Protestant missionaries in North-East India which they achieved in late 19th and the 20th Centuries, was primarily in areas such as Nagaland, Mizoram and Meghalaya which are not part of Assam anymore.

As of 1991 only Tripura of the seven eastern states of India had a lower percentage of Christians than Assam. There were more Christians in Assam than in Mizoram even though Mizoram was the second most Christian state in India at the time. Besides the Protestants there are also Catholics. There is a Roman Catholic Archdiocese in Shillong.

SIKHISM

Gurdwara Sri Guru Tegh Bahadur Sahib main building

The first prophet of the Sikhs,Guru Nanak Dev had visited Kamrup (Assam) in the 1505 as recorded in the his first visit in Purantan Janam Sakhi (the historical papers related to the visits and daily recorded activities of the Guru). Guru Nanak had met Srimanta Sankardeva(the founder of the Mahapuruxiya Dharma) as the Guru travelled from Dhaka to Assam. But no sangat or historical shrine dedicated to him survives as to date. Ninth Guru or prophet of Sikhs Guru Tegh Bahadur visited Assam in 1668. This place is also famous for the Sikh Gurdwara Thara Sahib or Gurdwara Damdama Sahib which was constructed in memory atop the hillock place of meditation of the Guru in Dhubri, Kamrup.

The historical site and places of interest of the Gurdwara are many times referred to as Gurdwara Sri Guru Tegh Bahadur Sahib situated in Dhubri (Assam) by the banks of the Brahmaputra. The grateful Ahom King invited Guruji to the Kamakhya shrine, where he was honoured with great respect.

In the year 1820, few hundred Sikh soldiers went to Assam at the initiative of Maharaja Ranjit Singh to help Ahom rulers in a war. Their descendants are mostly concentrated in Lanka in Nagaon district of Assam. Sikhs have been living in Assam for approximately two hundred years.

BUDDHISM

The religion is practised by 51,029 persons in Assam. Among them are the Chakma and Boruas.The Chakmas of Assam are loacted mostly in Chachar and Karbi Anglong with very lesser presence in Nagaon district. Guwahati has lots of Buddhist temples,the most prominent being the Bamunimaidan Buddhist temple.

CULTURE AND ITS EVOLUTION

Culture of Assam is traditionally a hybrid one developed due to assimilation of ethno-cultural groups in the past. Therefore, both local elements or the local elements in Sanskritised forms are distinctly found.

The major milestones in evolution of Assamese culture are:

- Assimilation in the Kamarupa Kingdom for almost 700 years (under the Varmans for 300 years, Salastambhas and Palas for each 200 years).
- Establishment of the Ahom dynasty in the 13th century AD and assimilation for next 600 years.
- Assimilation in the Koch Kingdom (15th–16th century AD) of western Assam and Kachari Kingdom (12th–18th century AD) of central and southern Assam.

DAKHINPAT SATRA OF MAJULI

Presenting 'Gayan Bayan' in Majuli, the Neo-Vaishnavite Cultural heritage of Assam

- Vaishnava Movement led by Srimanta Sankardeva (*Xonkordeu*) and its contribution and cultural changes.Vaishanav Movement, the 15th century religio-cultural movement under the leadership of great Srimanta Sankardeva (Xonkordeu) and his disciples have provided another dimension to

> Assamese culture. A renewed Hinduisation in local forms took place, which was initially greatly supported by the Koch and later by the Ahom Kingdoms. The resultant social institutions such as *namghar* and *sattra* (the Vaishnav Monasteries) have become part of Assamese way life. The movement contributed greatly towards language, literature and performing and fine arts. It is also noticed that many a times, Vaishnav Movement attempted to introduce alien cultural attributes and modify the way of life of common people. *Brajavali* a language specially created by introducing words from other Indian languages had failed as a language but left its traces on the Assamese language. Moreover, new alien rules were also introduced changing people's food habits and other aspects of cultural life. This had a greater impact on alienation of many local ethno-cultural and political groups in the later periods.

Historically, it is not difficult to understand that on one hand, during the strong politico-economic systems under stronger dynasties, greater cultural assimilations created common attributes of Assamese culture, while on the other during smaller politico-economic systems or during political disintegration, more localised attributes were created with spatial differentiation. Time-factor for such integrations and differentiations has also played extremely important role along with the position of individual events in the entire series of sequential events.

With rich traditions, the modern culture is greatly influenced by events in the British and the Post-British Era. The language was standardised by the American Baptist Missionaries such as Nathan Brown, Dr. Miles Bronson and local pundits such as Hemchandra Barua with the form available in the Sibsagar (*Sivasagar*) District (the ex-nerve centre of the Ahom Kingdom). A renewed Sanskritisation was increasingly adopted for developing Assamese language and grammar. A new wave of Western and northernIndian influence was apparent in the performing arts and literature.

Increasing efforts of standardisation in the 20th century alienated the localised forms present in different areas and with the less-assimilatedethno-cultural groups (many source-cultures). However, Assamese culture in its hybrid form and nature is one of the richest, still developing and in true sense is a 'cultural system' with sub-systems. It is interesting that many source-cultures of Assamese cultural-system are still surviving either as sub-systems or as sister entities, for *e.g.* Bodo or Karbi or Mishing. It is important to keep the broader system closer to its roots and at the same time to focus on development of the sub-systems.

Some of the common and unique cultural traits in the region are peoples' respect towards areca-nut and betel leaves, symbolic clothes (Gamosa, Arnai, etc.), traditional silk garments and towards forefathers and elderly. Moreover, great hospitality and Bamboo culture are common.

SYMBOLISM

A pair of areca nuts, betel leaves and a *Gamosa* in a *Xorai*; this represents cultural symbolism of respect towards the recipient by the person presenting it.

A decorative Assamese *Jaapi* laid over a Gamosa Symbolism is an ancient cultural practice in Assam and is still a very important part of Assamese way of life. Various elements are being used to represent beliefs, feelings, pride, identity, etc. *Tamulpan,Xorai* and *Gamosa* are three important symbolic elements in Assamese culture. *Tamulpan* (the areca nut and betel leaves) or*guapan* (gua from *kwa*) are considered along with the Gamosa (a typical woven cotton or silk cloth with embroidery) as the offers of devotion, respect and friendship.

The Tamulpan-tradition is an ancient one and is being followed since time-immemorial with roots in the aboriginal Austro-Asiatic culture. *Xorai* is a traditionally manufactured bell-metal article of great respect and is used as a container-medium while performing respectful offers. Moreover, symbolically many ethno-cultural groups use specific clothes to portray respect and pride.

There were many other symbolic elements and designs, but are now only found in literature, art, sculpture, architecture, etc. or in use today for only religious purposes. The typical designs of *assamese-lion, dragon, flying-lion,* etc. were used for symbolising various purposes and occasions. The archaeological sites such as the Madan Kamdev (c. 9th–10th AD) exhibits mass-scale use of lions, dragon-lions and many other figures of demons to show case power and prosperity. The Vaishnava monasteries and many other architectural sites of late medieval period also showcase use of lions and dragons for symbolic effects.

LANGUAGES

See also: Assamese language, Assamese literature, Bodo language, Sylheti language, and Bishnupriya Manipuri language. Assamese and Bodo are the major indigenous and official languages while Bengali holds official status in the three districts in the Barak Valley and is the second most widely spoken language of the state (27%). Traditionally Assamese was the language of the commons (of mixed origin—Austroasiatic, Tibeto-Burman, Magadhan Prakrit) in the ancientKamarupa and in the medieval kingdoms of Kamatapur, Kachari, Chutiya, Borahi, Ahom and Koch. Traces of the language is found in many poems by Luipa, Sarahapa, etc. in Charyapada (c.7th–8th AD).

Modern dialects Kamrupi, Goalpariya, etc. are the remnant of this language. Moreover, Assamese in its traditional form was used by the ethno-cultural groups in the region as lingua-franca, which spread during the stronger kingdoms and was required for needed economic integration. Localised forms of the language still exist in Nagaland, Arunachal Pradesh. The form used in the upper Assam was enriched by the advent of Tai-Shans in the 13th century.

A page from Charyapada: 7th–8th century specimen of Assamese literature Linguistically modern Assamese traces its roots to the version developed by the American Missionaries based on the local form in practice near Sibsagar (Xiwoxagor) district. Assamese (*Oxomeeya*) is a rich language due to its hybrid nature with its unique characteristics of pronunciation and softness. Assamese literature is one of the richest. Bodo is an ancient language of Assam. Spatial distribution patterns of the ethno-cultural groups, cultural traits and the phenomenon of naming all the major rivers in the North East Region with Bodo-Kachari words (*e.g.* Dihing, Dibru, Dihong, D/Tista, Dikrai, etc.) reveal that it was the most important language in the ancient times. Bodo is presently spoken largely in the Lower Assam (Bodo Territorial Council area).

After years of neglect, now Bodo language is getting attention and its literature is developing. Other native languages of Tibeto-Burman origin and related to Bodo-Kachari are DEORI Mishing, Karbi, Dimasa, Rabha, Tiwa, etc. Rajbongshi also known as Kamatapuri/Goalpariya is also widely spoken by the people of western Assam. Nepali is also spoken in almost all parts of the state.

There are smaller groups of people speaking Tai-Phake, Tai-Aiton, Tai-Khamti, Tai-Khamyang etc., some of the Tai languages. The Tai-Ahom language (brought by Sukaphaa and his followers), which is no more a spoken language today is getting attentions for research after centuries long care and preservation by the Bailungs (traditional priests). There are also small groups of people speaking Manipuri, Khasi,Garo, Hmar, Kuki, Zeme Naga etc. in different parts.

Bengali is the official language in Barak Valley, although the widely spoken language is Sylheti, a dialect of Bengali. Bengali is also largely spoken in the western districts of Dhubri, Barpeta, and Goalpara. Santali or Santhali is also spoken widely by the tribal population in the tea garden districts of Assam. these people who were initially brought as tea estate labourers by the British to Assam have now made it their home state. Bishnupriya Manipuri language is also spoken by a small minority of people in Barak Valley.

FESTIVALS

There are several important traditional festivals in Assam. Bihu is the most important and common and celebrated all over Assam. Durga Puja is another festival celebrated with great enthusiasm.Muslims celebrate two Eids with much eagernes in all over Assam.

Bihu is a series of three prominent festivals. Primarily a non-religious festival celebrated to mark the seasons and the significant points of a cultivator's life over a yearly cycle. Three Bihus, *rongali*or *bohag*, celebrated with the coming of spring and the beginning of the sowing season; *kongali* or*kati*, the barren bihu when the fields are lush but the barns are empty; and the *bhogali* or *magh*, the thanksgiving when the crops have been harvested and the barns are full. Bihu songs and Bihu dance are associated to *rongali* bihu. The day before the each bihu is known as 'uruka'. The first day of 'rongali bihu' is called 'Goru bihu' (the bihu of the cows), when the cows are taken to the nearby rivers or ponds to be bathed with special care. In recent times the form and nature of celebration has changed with the growth of urban centres.

TRADITIONAL CRAFTS

Bell metal made xorai and xophura are important parts of culture; offerings with respect are made using these during festivals and religious ceremonies and are seen as respectable items. Assam has a rich tradition of crafts; presently, Cane and bamboo craft, bell metal and brass craft,silk and cotton weaving, toy and mask making, pottery and terracotta work, wood craft, jewellerymaking, musical instruments making, etc. remained as major traditions.

Historically, Assam also excelled in making boats, traditional guns and gunpowder, ivory crafts, colours and paints, articles of lac, agarwood products, traditional building materials, utilities from iron, etc. Cane and bamboo craft provide the most commonly used utilities in daily life, ranging from household utilities, weaving accessories, fishing accessories, furniture, musical instruments, construction materials, etc. Utilities and symbolic articles such as *Xorai* and *Bota* made from bell metal and brass are found in every Assamese household. Hajo and Sarthebari (*Xorthebaary*) are the most important centres of traditional bell-metal and brass crafts.

Assam is the home of several types of silks, the most prestigious are: Muga—the natural golden silk, Pat—a creamy-bright-silver coloured silk and Eri—a variety used for manufacturing warm clothes for winter. Apart from Sualkuchi (*Xualkuchi*), the centre for the traditional silk industry, in almost every parts of theBrahmaputra Valley, rural households produce silk and silk garments with excellent embroidery designs. Moreover, various ethno-cultural groups in Assam make different types of cotton garments with unique embroidery designs and wonderful colour combinations.

Moreover, Assam possesses unique crafts of toy and mask making mostly concentrated in the Vaishnav Monasteries, pottery and terracotta work in lower Assam districts and wood craft, iron craft, jewellery, etc. in many places across the region.

Fine Arts

The archaic Mauryan Stupas discovered in and around Goalpara district are the earliest examples (c. 300 BC to c. 100 AD) of ancient art and architectural works. The remains discovered in Daparvatiya (*Doporboteeya*) archaeological site with a beautiful doorframe in Tezpur are identified as the best examples of art works in ancient Assam with influence of Sarnath School of Art of the late Gupta period.

Many other sites also exhibit development of local art forms with local motifs and sometimes with similarities with those in the Southeast Asia. There are currently more than forty discovered ancient archaeological sites across Assam with numerous sculptural and architectural remains. Moreover, there are examples of several Late-Middle Age art and architectural works including hundreds of sculptures and motifs along with many remaining temples, palaces and other buildings. The motifs available on the walls of the buildings such asRang Ghar, Joydoul, etc. are remarkable examples of art works. Painting is an ancient tradition of Assam. Xuanzang (7th century AD) mentions that among theKamarupa king Bhaskaravarma's gifts to Harshavardhana there were paintings and painted objects, some of which were on Assamese silk. Many of the manuscripts such as Hastividyarnava(A Treatise on Elephants), the Chitra Bhagawata and in the Gita Govinda from the Middle Ages bear excellent examples of traditional paintings. The medieval Assamese literature also refers to chitrakars and patuas.

There are several renowned contemporary artists in Assam. The Guwahati Art College in Guwahati is a government institution for tertiary education. Moreover, there are several art-societies and non-government initiatives across the state and the Guwahati Artists Guild is a front-runner organisation based in Guwahati.

ECONOMY

In the 1950s, per capita income in Assam was little higher than that in India. In 2000–01, in Assam it was INR 6,157 at constant prices (1993–94) and INR 10,198 at current prices; almost 40% lower than that in India. According to the recent estimates, per capita income in Assam has reached INR 6756 (1993–94 constant prices) in 2004–05, which is still much lower than India's. A tea garden in Assam: tea is grown at elevations near sea level, giving it a malty sweetness and an earthy flavour, as opposed to the more floral aroma of highland (*e.g.* Darjeeling, Taiwanese) teas.

MACRO-ECONOMY

Economy of Assam today represents a unique juxtaposition of backwardness amidst plenty.Despite its rich natural resources, and supplying of up to 25% of India's petroleum needs, growth rate of Assam's income has not kept pace with that of India's; differences increased rapidly since 1970s. Indian economy grew at 6% per annum over the period of 1981 to 2000, the same of Assam was only 3.3%. In the Sixth Plan period Assam experienced a negative growth rate of 3.78% when India's was positive at 6%. In the post-liberalised era (after 1991), the differences widened further.

According to recent analysis, Assam's economy is showing signs of improvement. In 2001–02, the economy grew (at 1993–94 constant prices) at 4.5%, to fall to 3.4% in the next financial year. During 2003–04 and 2004–05, the economy grew (at 1993–94 constant prices) more satisfactorily at 5.5% and 5.3% respectively. The advanced estimates placed the growth rate for 2005–06 at above 6%. Assam's GDP in 2004 is estimated at $13 billion in current prices. Sectoral analysis again exhibits a dismal picture. The average annual growth rate of agriculture, which was only 2.6% per annum over 1980s has unfortunately fallen to 1.6% in the 1990s.Manufacturing sector has shown some improvement in the 1990s with a growth rate of 3.4% per annum than 2.4% in the 1980s. Since past five decades, the tertiary sector has registered the highest growth rates than the other sectors, which even has slowed down in the 1990s than in 1980s.

AGRICULTURE

Accounts for more than a third of Assam's income and employs 69% of workforce. Assam's biggest contribution to the world is tea. It produces some of the finest and expensive teas and has its own variety *Camellia assamica*. Assam also accounts for fair share of India's production of rice,rapeseed, mustard seed, jute, potato, sweet potato, banana, papaya, areca nut and turmeric. It is also a home of large varieties of citrus fruits, leaf vegetables, vegetables, useful grasses, herbs,spices, etc. Assam's agriculture yet to experience modernisation in real sense. With implications to food security, per capita food grain production has declined in past five decades. Productivity has increased marginally; but still lower comparing to highly productive regions. For instance, yield of rice (staple food of Assam) was just 1531 kg per hectare against India's 1927 kg per hectare in 2000–01 (which itself is much lower than Egypt's 9283, US's 7279, South Korea's 6838,Japan's 6635 and China's 6131 kg per hectare in 2001). On the other hand, after having strong domestic demand, 1.5 million hectares of inland water bodies, numerous rivers and 165 varieties of fishes, fishing is still in its traditional form and production is not self-sufficient.

The Assam Agriculture University is located at Jorhat, Assam. It is the only agricultural university for the Seven Sisters.

INDUSTRY

Apart from tea and petroleum refineries, Assam has few industries of significance. Industrial development is inhibited by its physical and political isolation from neighbouring countries such asMyanmar, China and Bangladesh and from other growing Southeast Asian economies; ultimately leading to neglect by the federal government in regards to development—a key motivation for separatist groups. The region is landlocked, situated in the eastern periphery of India and is linked to the mainland by a flood and cyclone prone narrow corridor, known as the Siliguri Corridor or Chicken's Neck, with weak transport infrastructure that have remained undeveloped since independence.

The international airport in Guwahati is yet to find airlines providing direct international flights. The Brahmaputra suitable for navigation does not possess sufficient infrastructure for international trade and success of such a navigable trade route will be dependent on proper channel maintenance and diplomatic and trade relationships with Bangladesh.

Processed Assam Tea

Assam is a major producer of crude oil and it accounts for about 15% of India's crude output, exploited by the Assam Oil Company Ltd., and natural gas in India and is the second place in the world (after Titusville in the United States) where petroleum was discovered. Asia's first successful mechanically drilled oil well was drilled in Makum (Assam) way back in 1867.

Most of the oilfields are located in the Upper Assam region. Assam has four oil refineries located in Guwahati, Digboi, Golaghat (Numaligarh) and Bongaigaon with a total capacity of 7 Million metric tonnes (7.7 million short tons) per annum. Despite its richness in natural resources, the benefits have yet to improve the lives of the people of Assam. Although having a poor overall industrial performance, several other industries have nevertheless been started, including a chemical fertilizer plan at Namrup, petrochemical industries at Namrup and Bongaigaon, paper mills at Jagiroad, Panchgram and Jogighopa, sugar mills at Barua Bamun Gaon, Chargola, Kampur, cement plant at Bokajan and Badarpur, cosmetics plant (HLL) at Doom Dooma, etc. Moreover, there are other industries such as jute mill, textile and yarn mills, silk mill, etc. Unfortunately many of these industries are facing loss and closure due to lack of infrastructure and improper management practices.

EDUCATION

Cotton College in Guwahati initiated modern tertiary education and research in Assam and has been continuing classical and high-educational standards for more than hundred years; many of the buildings in the college are excellent examples of Assamese architecture with colonial flavours.

Academic Complex of IIT Guwahati

- Assam has several institutions for tertiary education and research.
- *The major institutions are*: Gauhati University, Guwahati,Dibrugarh University, Dibrugarh; Assam University, Silchar; Tezpur University, Tezpur; Silchar Medical College, Silchar; Assam Agricultural University, Jorhat;Indian Institute of Technology Guwahati and National Institute of Technology, Silchar etc.

Cities and Towns

A view of Guwahati; the city known as Pragjyotishapura (city of eastern light) in the ancient times has a past extended to more than two thousand years. History of urban development goes back to almost two thousand years in the region. Existence of ancient urban areas such as Pragjyotishapura (Guwahati), Hatapesvara (Tezpur), Durjaya, etc. and medieval towns such as Charaideu, Garhgaon, Rongpur, Jorhat, Khaspur, Guwahati, etc. are well recorded. Guwahati is the largest urban centre and a million plus city in

Assam. The city has experienced multifold growth during past three decades to grow as the primate city in the region; the city's population was approximately 900,000 (considering GMDA area) during the census of 2001.Population-wise and area-wise Silchar is the second largest and important city in the state.

It is the economic gateway to the state of Mizoram, Manipur and Tripura. The town of Silchar has tremendous commercial importance. It consequently, witnesses the settlement of a sizeable population of traders from distant parts of India. The other important urban areas are Dibrugarh, Jorhat, Golaghat, Tinsukia (Tinicukiya), Sibsagar (Sivasagar), Tezpur, Nagaon, North Lakhimpur, Bongaigaon, etc.Nalbari, Rangia, Mangaldoi, Karimganj, Hailakandi, Barpeta, Kokrajhar, Goalpara, Diphu, Dhubri (Dhubury), Haflong etc. are other towns and district head quarters. On the other hand Duliajan, Digboi, Namrup, Moran, Bongaigaon, Numaligarh, Jogighopa Rangia, etc. are major industrial towns. Currently, there are around 125 total urban centres in the state.

TOURISM IN ASSAM

Assam is the central state in the North-East Region of India and serves as the gateway to the rest of the Seven Sister States. For the purposes of tourism there are wildlife preserves like the Kaziranga National Park, Manas National Park etc. The climate is sub-tropical. Assam experiences the Indian monsoon and has one of the highest forest densities in India. The winter months are the best time to visit. It has a rich cultural heritage going back to the Ahom Dynasty which governed the region for many centuries before the British occupation.

Main Destinations

- *Brahmaputra*: The only male river in India, this is both a source of sorrow and sustenance for the people of Assam.There is cruise facility to enjoy the beauty of the river.
- *Guwahati*: One of the key urban centres of Assam and

the biggest city in North-East India, this serves as the major gateway to the whole region. This is the primary hopping point for accessing Shillong, the hill station.

- *Majuli*: The largest freshwater island in South Asia on the Brahmaputra River.
- *Kaziranga National Park*: This is one of the few places covered as a World Heritage Site and the main habitat of the Great Indian One-horned Rhinoceros. Also check out Orang National Park and Nameri National Park.
- *Jatinga*: The mystery of the bird suicides in Jatinga in the North Cachar Hills.
- *Tezpur*: Small town steeped in history and culture. Check out Usha Pahar, Agnigarh, Mahabhairav Temple, etc...
- *Sivasagar*: Seat of the Ahom Kingdom. Check out Rang Ghar, Talatal Ghar, Sivadol, Kareng Ghar ofGarhgaon etc...
- *Hajo*: Hajo is a small township situated to the northwest of Guwahati across the river Brahmaputra. Hajo is a remarkable example of communal harmony. This is an ancient pilgrimage centre for three religions Hinduism, Islam and Buddhism.
- *Dibru-Saikhowa National Park*: Dibru-Saikhowa National Park is a beautiful National Park situated in Tinsukia district. There are few Eco lodges situated here to enjoy the beauty of this park.
- *Goalpara*: Goalpara is also a major tourist spot in Assam.It has a numerous tourist spots and temples like Sri Surya Pahar,Tekreshwari Pahar,Paglartek in Pancharatna,Pir Babas Mazar in Joleshwar, Naranarayan Setu (Bridge) connecting northern Assam districts like Kokrajhar, Bongaigaon, Dhubri etc. to Goalpara,Guwahati and major part of Meghalaya.
- *Dibrugarh*: Business hub in upper Assam. Serves as gateway to Nagaland.Naharkatiya is a place here which is famous for a Buddhist monastery. There are numerous temples, ruins of palaces, etc.

2

Political Violence in Assam: Three Trends

The trend of rising violence in India 's North East demonstrates that Kashmir 's violence is minor compared to what is possible in this region. It is not Kashmir but Tripura which tops the country in terms of civilian casualties due to insurgency-related violence in the last four years. It is a sobreing thought that easy availability of small arms India's North East has resulted in a disproportionate and indiscriminate use of illegal weapons by insurgents/civilians/ 'unidentified assailants' who can target any person or institution anywhere across the region at any time. But even more dangerous is the fact that this has led to a subversion of democratic processes, criminalization of civil society and subversion of electoral processes leading to a serious crisis of governance in India 's North East.

The rising incidents of political violence in Assam illustrate that it is fast becoming one of the most dangerous places in the country to live in.

These incidents of political violence over the last three months reveal some significant trends in the state:

- A series of 'secret killings' of the family members and relatives of ULFA cadres by 'un-identified assailants';
- Violence and 'Quit Assam' notices served on the Hindi-speaking communities living in Assam;
- Mass killings of 'soft targets' like Bhutanese petty tradesmen and people of marginalised communities by random insurgent groups;

The frequency and intensity of the secret killings' in Assam have been on the rise in the past three months. It is a matter of speculation as to who are the real perpetrators of such crimes. The fact that these 'secret' killings have remained unresolved tends to support the popular thesis of the state's covert aquiescence in a bid to discredit the ULFA and force it to the negotiating table in a 'Punjab-style' offensive.

Apart from the violence against the ULFA by pro-government former militants referred to as SULFA (Surrendered-ULFA), and the government's counter-insurgency operations merged to create a messy political situation. While some analysts see the hand of the ISI in these killings, others suggest they are done at the behest of the government and carried out by its retainers, the gun-toting 'rehabilitated' SULFA, to gain mileage in the forthcoming Assembly elections.

Lawlessness has reached such a state in Assam that the gunman do not need an issue. The urge to settle scores, to win an election, to 'manage' a government contract or even play-back an evening show of 'Mission Kashmir' because he had missed the first few reels, is good enough reason to incite serious acts of violence.

That the popularly elected government in Dispur has completely failed to stop these 'secret' killings and acts of violence is irrevocably established. While the 'official' statements blame the ULFA, the banned outfit has yet to claim responsibility for such acts.

Most opposition parties have come joined to demand President's Rule in Assam and handing over of the murder inquiries to the CBI. With the police, armed forces and the para-military forces strategically positioned across the state, it is surprising that not one 'unidentified assailant' has been successfully nabbed. Again, since 1992, some 6,000 SULFAs have been brought 'back into the mainstream' and yet the law and order situation has not shown any improvement.

The rural youth of Assam continue to join the ULFA. This has led to a further criminalisation of civil society by introducing a new culture of violence by the pro-government group SULFA who frequently use their 'legal' weapons to commit acts of violence in pursuit of their 'new' occupations of organised crime, racketeering, extortion and becoming government informers.

That the political masters have turned a blind eye to such acts but have actively engaged them in anti-insurgency initiatives and criminalising electoral politics sets a dangerous precedent. It makes armed violence and criminal activities an acceptable route to accumulating wealth or gaining political mileage. What makes this danger real is that while the ULFA largely remained an entity 'outside' the civil society, the SULFAs functions from within and as a part of civil society to openly pursue their illegitimate activities 'legitimately'.

The recent murder of some 100 Hindi-speaking people in Assam also appears to be politically motivated, not an ethnic-cleansing offensive, to discredit the ruling government just before the Assembly elections. The murder of 14 Bhutanese petty traders in lower Assam has put an end to any hopes the Indian government may have had of a Bhutanese military offensive against the Assamese militants hiding in Bhutan.

All in all, it seems quite clear that Assam will experience more violence in the coming months leading upto the Assembly elections in April.

A CRITIQUE OF THE OFFICIAL APPROACH TOWARDS CONFLICT RESOLUTION

The present approach of the GOI towards a negotiated settlement with the ULFA does not give much scope to commend it. The word 'talks' in MHA lexicon means withdrawal, undeclared if necessary, of the demand for secession. As with the GOI-NSCN-IM talks, the priority seems to be that ULFA should renounce its secessionist demand, not its armed activities.

This is evident in the case of the peace-process with the NSCN-IM, which has merrily continued using the threat of weapons against the common public while maintaining a temporary silence on the aim of secession. While officials may construe the apparent 'neutralising' of secessionist forces as a success, the civil society continues to suffer from the continuance of armed activity by insurgents, who become more of a menace after cessation of CI operations against them following a cease-fire with the GOI. To reach a permanent solution, the Indian state shall have to change its mindset. The common people, who are in overwhelming majority against armed insurgency, will have to be taken into confidence. The need of the hour is mutual trust and confidence between the people of the region and the Indian state.

The Northeast has long suffered due to the imposition of certain special Acts, like the Disturbed Areas Act, 1955, and the Armed Forces Special Powers Act, 1958, 37 admittedly necessitated by abnormal situations. Suspicion amongst the Assamese about the Centre's antipathy towards the State precedes the appearance of the ULFA's secessionist insurgency. The ULFA has only been cashing in on the general discontentment prevalent in society against perceived injustices. The vitiated democratic environment, inevitable after arming the State police and other security forces, including the Army, with quasi-judicial powers, has been a fertile ground for the growth of secessionism amongst the Assamese in general and armed secessionism amongst the Assamese youth in particular.

The common people, though coerced into silence by extra-constitutional exercise of state power, develop sympathy for the armed insurgents as a reaction to this arm-twisting by the state. The insurgents have been extracting full advantage of this harmful situation and the irresponsible utterances by certain MHA officials exhibiting disdain for Assamese sentiments have not been particularly helpful. While it is correct that underdevelopment preceded insurgency in Assam, it is equally true that the continuance of insurgent violence has led to an outflow of scarce capital from the State. The resultant stagnation in economic development has, in turn, created a vast horde of unemployed youth, which is a potential source of fresh recruits into the insurgent ranks.

Thus, Assam has entered a full circle of under development leading to insurgency, which in turn leads to more underdevelopment. This vicious cycle has to be broken to liquidate insurgency from the State. It is obvious that if the ready cause of the perceived 'exploitation and neglect by Delhi' had not been easily available, the ever-increasing pool of frustrated youth-power in Assam would have discovered other 'causes' to serve as an excuse for embarking on a career in illegal armed activities. Without going into statistical details, one can say, on the basis of first hand knowledge and experience, that more than 90 per cent of the present ULFA cadre consists of educational drop-outs hailing from a rural poor background. Gone are the days when well-educated boys and girls of all economic segments of the Assamese society were attracted to the romantic notion of becoming a 'rebel with a cause'.

The real threat to life has undone the earlier romantic appeal of being an ULFA cadre, and only the really desperate among these join the ULFA now. Unfortunately, with a stagnating economy and no scope for earning a livelihood, there is no dearth of desperate youngsters opting for an alternative career. It would not be off the mark to say that ULFA, and for that matter, the various ethnic insurgent outfits cropping up in Assam and in the entire Northeast region actually serve as an arena for alternative employment. Those who could have earned a decent living without becoming insurgents are a fast disappearing species among the underground cadres now. The dismal economic scene, coupled with popular disenchantment against the state, has created an ideal environment for the growth and sustenance of collective armed activity in the name of secessionist insurgency.

At the same time, consequent to the fading of the initial admiration for 'our boys' amongst the common people, the insurgents have replaced voluntary support with coerced co-operation. In rural areas, where the state is not omnipresent and omnipotent, people have to continue cooperating with the armed ULFA cadres under the threat of the gun, normally discreet or implicit but, if necessary, openly expressed. If they resist the ULFA, when asked for shelter, food and other services, they risk being harmed by the cadres.

On the other hand, if they acquiesce to the demands, they are punished by the security forces for 'supporting' ULFA. Though this situation has alienated the people from the ULFA, insofar as genuine support and sympathy is concerned, it has also not endeared the state and its agencies to the common people, who perceive the latter as a malevolent punitive authority, rather than a benevolent benefactor.

The urban segment of the society has its own problems. The insurgent gun, unchecked by legal or constitutional constraints, is feared and the rebel diktat is surreptitiously obeyed, though, vocally, loyalty is proclaimed to the state. A section of the intelligentsia, however, uses the insurgent influence as a shortcut to secure personal objectives and fame. It is not a rare exception in Assam to find a respected intellectual advocating the insurgent cause, of course from a safe distance and carefully balancing constitutional restrictions and revolutionary babble. Many among the more sobre intellectuals in Assam prefer to maintain a deliberate silence on the issue. The most harmful effect comes from the general criticism of the Union government, which is a common refrain amongst the Assamese intelligentsia.39 The insurgents and their supporters amongst the intelligentsia have to merely increase the tone of this general criticism by a few notches to convert it into rebel propaganda. Many Assamese intellectuals thus unconsciously provide propaganda material to the insurgents by openly condemning the Union government for its perceived negative attitude towards the State.

From personal experience gathered while interacting with the MHA, this author, however, holds the opinion that the lack of a proper attitude amongst some officers of the Union government has more to do with an individual lack of sensitivity and administrative efficiency, rather than a deliberate government policy.

The prevailing mistrust between the GOI and the Assamese, which has been stirred up over a period of time, leads to a negative interpretation of most of GOI's activity vis-à-vis Assam. This brings us back to the earlier refrain that 'justice should also appear to be done.'

SUGGESTIONS ON CONFLICT RESOLUTION

It is hoped that the preceding discussion has been able to specifically characterise the problem arising out of ULFA's secessionist-insurgency in Assam. Within the context of this analysis, it is felt that an unbiased approach to 'secessionist insurgency'-a political problem-and 'terrorism'-a heinous method of registering protest and conducting insurgency-is needed to tackle the problem of violence in the forms currently prevailing in Assam. Romantic and idealistic youth with a rebellious inclination and lumpen elements with criminal and terrorist tendencies co-habit the insurgent camp. It is certain that the insurgent, whose priority lies in the ends rather than the means, would accept a peaceful and easier method of propagating secessionism.

The terrorists, for whom the goal of secession is just an excuse to indulge in inhuman violence, would be effectively isolated and denied any popular sympathy. Though secessionism itself is harmful to the concept of a united India or India as a nation, the pan-Indian nationalism preferred and propagated by the Indian state is more a matter of winning hearts than imposing constitutional restrictions on freedom of speech. It should be remembered that though freedom of speech may be partially suppressed by statutory restrictions, no power on earth can suppress freedom of thought, unexpressed though it might be. Whispers and murmurs carry ideas as effectively as open discussions.

The continued existence of democracy and a democratic state ultimately depend on the freedom of speech and expression, in practice as well as in theory. The restrictive clauses applied to the freedom of speech and expression as enshrined in the Indian Constitution have provided a valid excuse for all secessionists to practice armed rebellions which have, more often than not, degenerated into terrorism.

While the practice of terrorism has effectively unmasked the secessionist-insurgent organisations as unworthy leaders, the people of the affected areas have not been provided with an unambiguous method of expressing a convincing verdict on the worthiness of the goal itself. This has led to the revival of the insurgent movements like the mythical phoenix, and has in turn led to certain areas of the country being permanently labelled as unsafe places for investment.

Tottering along second-generation economic reforms, India can ill-afford a disgruntled populace. Rebellions start in the weakest moments of the state. And a succession of such weak moments is a strong possibility before India can successfully complete the process of its economic reforms.

It is sensible to remove disgruntlement among the people to the extent that this is practicable, rather than to expend the nation's resources in quelling rebellions after they occur. Very few areas of India actually have a population that desires secession. It is the lack of a convincing democratic apparatus to gauge public sentiments that has deprived the Indian state of the means to effectively project the microscopic support actually enjoyed by the separatists in most cases of secessionist-insurgencies. Unadulterated freedom of speech, including the right to peaceful and democratic propagation of secession, would effectively liquidate the excuse to take up arms for secessionism. While, in all probability, this might boost the morale of the Kashmiri separatists in the Kashmir Valley, it can be confidently assumed that, it would only be an exception to the general rule of rejection of secessionism by the majority in States like Assam and Punjab.

The process of bringing in a proposed change in the constitutional law of India could begin by repealing the sixteenth amendment to the Constitution of India,40 which brought in the so-called 'reasonable restrictions' to the freedom of speech and expression, as also to the freedom of association laid out in Article 19, clause 1, sub clause 'a' through 'c'. Such a repeal cannot be deemed a radical change, as it only restores the Constitution to its original form as envisaged by its founders in the Constituent Assembly.

In plain language, the law of the state should be suitably rectified to make peaceful and democratic propagation of political ideas, including secession, a legal exercise, without the provision of any punitive reaction by the state. The recalcitrant rebels who cling to their guns and lumps of RDX after the availability of democratic and peaceful means of propagating their professed cause, would lose the last remnants of any goodwill or sympathy they may have among their own people.

There is, of course, the theoretical possibility of the populace of a particular area expressing its desire to secede through the means newly made available to them, but this cannot be something that the Indian state should be intimidated by. This proposal, most probably, would have to run the gauntlet of hostility from many quarters. But the exploration of every probable avenue of conflict resolution is an unavoidable necessity to arrive at a suitable solution. Holding man-made concepts and laws as sacrosanct has the same affect as that of putting pre-conditions before negotiations. Every concept should be clinically analysed before retaining or discarding it. In fact, a logically explained repudiation of the proposal proffered here would itself contribute in strengthening Indian democracy. The plurality of India necessitates an open mind on the part of its intelligentsia. Loyalty extracted from convinced minds is always a better option than coerced allegiance. It would be immensely beneficial if this debate could be taken further.

ASSAM INSURGENCY AND THE DISINTEGRATION OF CIVIL SOCIETY

This paper proposes to focus more on the 'decline' of the United Liberation Front of Asom (ULFA) and less on either its emergence in 1979 or its development through the 1980s. While I have had earlier occasion of dealing with ULFA's emergence and development, I have written almost nothing till date on its much-touted 'decline' in the 1990s.

The monograph I wrote in 1994 covered the period between 1979 and 1991 and only briefly hinted at some of the very early signs of its disintegration. My otherwise longish essay on ULFA written for a Bengali journal in 1999 was not only published much later but also meant for a limited audience. Although right from the days of the monograph's publication, many scholars—both from India and abroad, have joined issue with me, I have not felt sufficiently provoked to respond to them. My Bengali essay sought to put across the argument that ULFA has brought to the fore a unique political critique, which its adversaries will find difficult to simply wish away or for that matter, wipe out by force and coercion. If ULFA *appears to have* deserted the critique (or the 'cause') it had produced and so fervently brought to the fore over the years, its adversaries have squarely to be blamed for making it desert what once was so dear to it.

As the critique deserts itself, ULFA does not make itself felt any longer through the power of a discourse. It is thus *forced* to clutch on to various non-discursive forms of power. The political critique *per se* has not lost its validity. It has only outlived one of its most powerful agents. In many ways, this paper is a continuation of the same argument. But it marks a departure on at least two counts: First, my earlier paper took a romantic view of the political critique or the discourse that ULFA produced and brought to the fore.

The critique in question is not something that can be deserted and left in the cold in this manner or, for that matter, be subsequently reactivated and represented by any other political force at its own sweet will. The critique does not so much require the mediation of an agent to articulate it, but very much a conjunction of forces within which it gains its currency. The conjunction of forces gives it a site where it articulates and circulates itself—a site where the terms of the critique are debated, exchanged and transacted—in short, acquire its meanings and thereby produces and reproduces itself. We describe this site as a discourse. This paper, in short, proposes to move away from an agent-centric view of the critique to a view that focuses on what Foucault calls, 'the relations peculiar to a discourse'. The agent-centric view only indulges in what I prefer to call 'a blame game'. My Bengali essay was not altogether free from this game.

Analyses on ULFA today seem to have approached a blind alley within this context: On the one hand, commentators like, Jaideep Saikia accuse ULFA of having provoked the government into 'a counter-insurgent over-reaction'. As he argues: Counter-insurgency measures by the state are mostly stimulus responses. This is true primarily for the State of Assam where counter-insurgency operation has largely been limited to a military option.

Very few cases have been recorded whereby the government forces... have taken a proactive role in order to neutralize ULFA. Referring to the extraordinarily high and rising level of political violence in the State, Harin Mahanta, on the other hand argues, "the government that has decided to answer the (voice of) reason only through gun has given birth to terrorism." Even as late as in 1998, Mukul Mahanta argues that if 'muscle power has gained in importance' it is the Indian army that has 'taught' it.

In other words, if ULFA has turned 'terrorist' it is the government that has pushed it in this direction. The problem with the agent-centric view of discourse is that it has the inherent tendency of finding fault with either of the adversaries involved in a conflict situation.

Second, the irony is that there is nobody to celebrate the 'decline' of ULFA. This degeneration does not give the ULFA's adversaries any reason whatsoever to celebrate. Even a very rough estimate made by official agencies suggests that more than 500 security force personnel lost their lives in course of their encounters with the militants in Assam during the 1990s. Moreover, the people by now have become used to the huge presence of security forces—especially troops all over the State. As Wasbir Hussain observes:

Today, the Army has lost its psychological edge due to its prolonged use in internal security duties, because the people see the troops everywhere, in the towns and cities, guarding bridges on the national highways, patrolling rivers, checking vehicles and so on.

Some of the country's top policemen, with enviable records of successfully handling insurgencies—whether in the northeast or in the northwest (*e.g.* Punjab and Kashmir)—are also aware of the limits of counter-insurgency operations. As a scholar argues in a somewhat general vein: "... there is a latent awareness in many of those directly engaged in fighting terrorism that state violence has its limits and by itself cannot solve the problem of terrorism." On the other hand, what is trumpeted as widespread public disenchantment with ULFA also involves many complexities. It is true that there have been reports of ULFA cadres being beaten and subsequently turned over to the security forces by villagers in upper Assam. Examples of a cross-section of people taking out processions against alleged 'ULFA atrocities' are by no means rare. But ULFA's loss of public sympathy does not seem to signify any gain for the Indian state. As Udayon Misra observes:

The excesses committed by the State alienated it further from the people and its moral authority was severely eroded. The collapse of the moral authority of the State actually helped the proponents of *Swadhin Asom*. Consequently, though there may have been a noticeable decline in public sympathy for ULFA's recent activities, people by and large seem to be against any kind of 'stern' action being taken against them. *Prantik*—an Assamese biweekly, had conducted an opinion poll amongst its readers drawn from as many as 19 districts of Assam and parts of Arunachal Pradesh on the eve of the Legislative Assembly elections in May 2001.

The respondents, among the many other segments of the reading public covered by the Survey, included a disproportionately large section of middle-class professionals. While 60 per cent of respondents believed that 'terrorism of the militants' would be an issue in the then approaching elections in Assam, only six per cent actually asked for 'stern measures' against them. In the writings of such analysts as Jaideep Saikia, the fact of erosion of public sympathy is blown out of proportions, often at the expense of ignoring this dilemma that characterizes the public psyche in contemporary Assam. My Bengali essay indicated, but paid only inadequate attention to, this dilemma.

This dilemma to my mind is extremely significant: First of all, its presence demonstrates that the critique implicit in ULFA's theoretical and political practice is still not dead or fully destroyed. What I call the critique is, according to Jaideep Saikia, 'adequate for the purpose of examining the genesis of the (ULFA) movement'. If one assumes now that ULFA 'began to careen out of control', does this necessarily mean that the critique has lost its adequacy? The fact that an organization has supposedly deserted the 'cause' that it had once so steadfastly upheld and brought to the fore does not imply that the 'cause' has been realised or rejected, or that it has, consequently, lost all its relevance for the society.

Further, the ULFA's course of development and decline also points to the continuing necessity of nurturing and developing the critique through such social and political institutions that are essential for the development of the cause, and certainly not through the kind of violence that the insurgents and counter-insurgents are found to have unleashed and perpetrated against each other.

The ensemble of institutions that helps the critique and the discourse enveloping it is called 'civil society'. It is at this point that we choose to pitch in our plea for a vibrant civil society in Assam. Unfortunately, the decline of ULFA has also been accompanied by a certain disintegration of civil society institutions in Assam.

Accordingly, this paper is divided into three rather unequal parts: In the first part, we propose to examine the reported decline of ULFA. The second part takes us back to what we describe as ULFA's critique, and it seeks to draw attention to some of the questions posed by the critique relating to nationalism in Assam that are considered crucial, but that nevertheless seem to remain unresolved. The third part takes note of the factors that are responsible for the disintegration of civil society institutions in Assam.

ULFA'S DECLINE

The decline of the ULFA has received some—though very sketchy attention in scholarly circles. Its decline first of all refers to its growing inability to pursue the 'cause' that once formed part of its revolutionary political agenda. According to Udayon Misra, ULFA was never conceived as an organization capable of pursuing a revolutionary agenda: "... right from the beginning the ULFA was organized as a militaristic organization where the political wing occupied a subsidiary status."

It is well known that a five-member team consisting of Golap Baruah (General Secretary), Robin Neog (Chief Instructor), Kalpajyoti Neog (Foreign Secretary), Siddhartha Phukan (Convenor, Publicity Cell) and Sobhan Saikia (Member) signed a 'Letter of Intent' (*Pratisruti Patra*) on January 12, 1992, as a step towards holding talks with the Government of India.

They promised:

- To have accepted the Constitution of India;
- Expressed their willingness to solve all their demands within the Constitution of India; and
- To abandon the violent path by surrendering arms at their disposal.

In exchange, they requested the Government to:

- Stop military operations and arresting its cadres;
- Withdraw the Armed Forces Special Powers Act and also the ban slapped on ULFA;
- Expedite the proceedings against all those who were held in police custody;
- Free all supporters and sympathizers of ULFA who had committed no 'serious offence';
- Free its members who were still in prisons.

Paresh Baruah—ULFA's Commander-in-Chief, immediately scotched the idea by expressing his 'dissatisfaction' with 'the unilateral surrender of arms' and 'one-sided acquiescence to the Constitution of India'.

The domination of the military wing over the political wing was also responsible for the erosion of what Udayon Misra calls, 'inner-party democracy'. Way back in September 1990, Sanat Duara, one of ULFA's sergeants who underwent training in Kachin territory, surrendered before the police and admitted that "the individual member at the lower rungs has hardly any right to express his opinions—thanks to ULFA's very tough rules in this regard." The more the organization throttles inner-party democracy, the more its revolutionary agenda is subordinated to the interests of a handful of self-seeking leaders. The violence it takes resort to is often deployed in order to settle 'personal scores': The fight of United Liberation Front of Assam is gradually losing its importance in terms of values and ideologies. In such situations the members of the group exploit the situation to settle personal scores. Similarly, the funds in ULFA coffers, acquired by whatever means and through whatever justifications, are never subjected to the rigours of financial discipline. Jaideep Saikia has 'put on record' the ULFA Budget of 2001-2002 'made available to the author by a reliable source'.

The problem with his analysis is that he does not seem to recognize that the reliability of the source is not the same as reliability of the information. Moreover, he appears to be privy to sources, which are simply inaccessible to the general scholar, and the information flowing from them remains not only unverified but also unverifiable. Notwithstanding these problems, his otherwise scathing observation that "the lion's share of the ULFA coffer is being operated without the knowledge of the organization's cadres" may contain some truth. This is reflected in the reportedly lavish life-styles of ULFA's top leadership, so much so that they have already earned the disrepute of being 'silver-screen' rebels. In sum, one finds that the top leadership has been successful in monopolizing its control, both over arms and finance, the two key resources of an insurgent organization.

ULFA's organizational metamorphosis has been responsible not only for its reported digression from the revolutionary agenda but also what is termed, mostly in journalistic circles, as its 'terrorist' transformation. In other words, its public activities appear only to be a reflection of its deeper organizational decay.

All the contemporary writings on the decline of the ULFA appear to be centred on what I call an *inside-out narrative*. The malady that afflicts its organization also has its ramifications for the politics it initiates or is involved in. There are at least three major trends that are highly visible in ULFA's politics through the 1990s. One, insofar as military and financial power becomes concentrated in the hands of a few leaders, the organization starts closing in increasingly on itself, alienating, in the process, the public support and sympathy that it had hitherto enjoyed.

The argument is that ULFA never took any active measures to boost its public image and whatever support and sympathy it enjoyed were conferred on it by the general public (*raij*) more out of their own disenchantment with the prevailing political system than out of any affirmation of its politics.

The public, the argument goes, read their disenchantment into its politics. While a good deal of such support and sympathy came from a widespread sense of disenchantment that had gripped the society in Assam, there were, nevertheless, some very significant and positive initiatives on ULFA's part to reach out to the masses, not only to communicate what they intended to accomplish, but also to receive precious feedback from the public.

The problem with the inside-out narrative is that it does not take note of these initiatives: First of all, there is reason to believe that even in the early 1990s, ULFA took notice of the public criticisms levelled against it, and felt it necessary to respond to them. *Budhbar* would carry a column on public opinion (*janmat*) through which the Publicity Secretary of ULFA was in regular correspondence with the reading public.

Secondly, the nature of the activities undertaken by the *Jatiya Unnayan Bahini*—believed to be one of ULFA's overground organizations, may also be mentioned in this connection. These activities were geared more to the objective of being in constant touch with the people at large and making them self-reliant, so much so that they would develop the capacity to reject the dependency on the state in undertaking development projects to address their own grievances. As a member of its Central Publicity Cell in one of the interviews pointed out: We do not think that we can give some relief by constructing a road here or a school there. We do it in order to associate the people with all activities and with the objective of making them actively participate (in them) so that they become aware of their power and capability. We do these activities in order to awaken (in us) the feeling that we can be self-reliant. The enthusiastic participation of the people for establishing socialism is absolutely necessary. Everybody will have to work for the construction of the future society.

Last but not the least, ULFA's attempts since the middle of 1992 at reorganizing the district committees and unplugging them from the hitherto firm and tightening grip of the central headquarters, may also be regarded as an initiative in reaching out to the people. According to Sanjib Baruah, these attempts did not, of course, bear any instant fruit and "a battle is on today for the hearts and minds of the people." To remain oblivious to these developments, however, betrays a one-sided and incomplete reading of ULFA's organizational history.

Secondly, ULFA's reportedly indiscriminate and random use of violence has been a subject of frequent scholarly discussion and is believed to be responsible for its allegedly 'terrorist' transformation. Terrorist violence, according to Hiren Gohain, cannot be the 'essence' of revolution.

For it has the tendency of creating anarchy and chaos, which unless coordinated and directed to "the objective of freedom from economic exploitation and oppression" will only make people feel "incompetent and powerless." While 'purposelessness' has been one of the most spectacular characteristics of ULFA's resort to violence, it has largely been accused of having brought in what is often described as a 'gun culture' into Assam. It is true that ULFA has taken great pains to absolve itself of any responsibility for the massacre of Hindi-speaking civilians in upper Assam in late-2000, but the organisation continues to be blamed for these excesses. We do not have any independent means of verifying the actual facts, but what is interesting to note in this connection is that, if we assume that ULFA has a hand in masterminding and organizing these killings, then they also show the inherent limits of such violence—in the inability to publicly own up to them and to back them with any kind of discursive justification acceptable to others.

This had never been the case in ULFA's earlier history. In other words, the recent spate of violence allegedly masterminded and organised by ULFA, has also robbed it of the intellectual means of justification. 'Terrorist' transformation imposes limits on the organisation's attempts at couching its political practice within the terms of its discourse.

Thirdly, and as a corollary to the second, we know that the operations of a revolutionary organization are necessarily subordinate to its ideological requirements. Its terrorist transformation, on the other hand, turns the table around by subordinating ideological considerations to operational requirements. The plea for constantly learning from practice, and thereby continuously enriching the theory one subscribes to, is not the same as subordinating theory to the requirements of practice. The concept of 'theoretical practice' is intended to take care of the complex interplay between theory and practice.

ULFA is explicitly accused of having subordinated its ideology to what Jaideep Saikia calls, 'operational requirements'. Thus, the shift in its stance on the question of immigrants from Bangladesh in 1992 is explained in terms of the organisation's need to secure safe hideouts in a foreign country at a time when the Indian security forces have successfully turned the pressure on it.

In an otherwise long pamphlet entitled 'Asombasi Purbabangeeya Janagoshthiloi ULFAr Ahvan' (ULFA's Call to the groups from East Bengal living in Assam), ULFA redefines the concept of 'the Assamese' (*Asomiya*) as "a people of all communities, the mixture of people who are determined to work for all-round progress of Assam". Thus the scope of the concept no longer remains restricted to those who speak Assamese as their mother tongue. Obviously, the immigrants from Bangladesh being the largest group of immigrants are 'an indispensable part' of the revised notion of *Asomiya*. Jaideep Saikia has accused ULFA of having made the turnaround at the instance of its operational requirement of securing a safe haven in Bangladesh, from where it can mastermind and organize all its activities while escaping the Indian security dragnet.

The insurgents, Saikia argues, have scant respect for strong Assamese sentiments against the alarmingly high rate of immigration from across the borders threatening their language and culture. Thus, in Saikia's words, the dream of a '*Swadhin Asom*' (Independent Assam) may soon turn into a nightmare of a '*Brihat Bangla*' (Greater Bengal), were ULFA to continue its hobnobbing with external espionage agencies.The advent of terrorism, in other words, marks the transformation of ULFA's ideology from an end into a mere means. Nowhere is this sharper than, perhaps, in Subir Ghosh's observation:

A frustrated, cornered insurgent is a dangerous liability for society. He becomes out-and-out a terrorist. He does not care for changing the means to achieve his ends. The means are ends in themselves. He does not care what he is supposed to be fighting for. He lives to kill and he kills to live. And he does not care whom he kills and how many he has to kill so that he can live. That has been the tragedy of the ULFA.

ULFA, in short, is now accused of being unfaithful to its ideology almost to the point of forgetting it. The more it invokes the ideology as a means of justifying the apparently senseless and macabre violence that it is often charged with perpetrating—and finds difficult to disown—the more it exposes its political and ideological bankruptcy.

THE UNRESOLVED QUESTIONS

As we have argued, ULFA's gradual transformation into a 'terrorist' organization in the 1990s and its growing inability to represent the critique it had once brought to the fore have neither resolved the critique, nor made it redundant. Some of the questions thrown open by the critique remain unresolved till date and what is interesting to note in this connection is that their resolution is still central to the articulation and further elaboration of 'nationalism' in Assam. The alleged decline of ULFA as one of the most powerful representatives of this critique has not reduced—but indeed exacerbated—the necessity of its representation. This section proposes to review only three of these questions underlying ULFA's critique.

First, given that society in Assam is of a composite and multi-ethnic nature, how are the relations between diverse ethnic communities ('nations' and 'nationalities' in ULFA's parlance) to be conducted? At one extreme, there are scholars who assume that cultural assimilation in a society like Assam is an 'objective historical fact' that cannot be altered or, for that matter, reversed at anyone's sweet will, at least in the foreseeable future.

Amalendu Guha, for one, argues that the assimilation of different tribal and caste groups and minorities into regional identities and, subsequently, the assimilation of these regional identities into the 'Indian great nation' (*Bharatiya Mahajati*) have always been a 'slow' process.

Monirul Hussain, too, describes this as an 'irreversible' process. I have elsewhere argued that such a simple and linear narrative of the formation of regional identity and the Indian nation smacks of a highly positivist reading of Assam's society and history.

At the other extreme, there are those who seem to argue that the society in Assam is held together only at the cost of wresting away from the communities, especially the minorities, their respective right to cultural self-determination. There has emerged a whole new literature on how Assamese language and culture came to acquire a dominant position in the otherwise composite Assamese society, so much so that, in many cases, it led to the displacement of the autochthonous tribal languages and cultures. The writings of such scholars as Hiren Gohain, Shivanath Barman, Indibar Deuri and others bear ample testimony to this trend.

It is in the context of this larger debate that ULFA's intervention becomes relevant: On the one hand, its attachment to the territoriality of Assam as it existed on April 7, 1979, that is to say, the day when it actually came into being, is by now well-known. While Assam has been subjected to several consecutive rounds of surgical operations, ULFA is now opposed to any further fragmentation of the State.

It takes the territoriality of Assam as it existed on its foundation day as both given and unalterable. Its stiff opposition to the attempts at extending the Naga cease-fire beyond the territorial limits of Nagaland issues from the apprehension that this might serve as a prelude to the formation of 'Greater Nagaland' (*Nagalim*) by including the

Naga-inhabited areas of North Cachar Hills and Karbi Anglong. On the other hand, it considers the question of self-determination of the ethnic communities as only secondary to the question of establishing a '*Swadhin Asom*' by way of liberating her from 'the colonialism of New Delhi'. In this perspective, the prevailing ethnic divisions within the society have only prevented her from posing a unified and concerted challenge to such 'colonialism'.

Thus, unless the communities that are the victims of this 'internal colonialism' come together and fight a battle against the 'colonial rule', the prospects of their becoming successful in the quest for self-determination are quite bleak. The word 'Unified' in its self-designation focuses on ULFA's realization of the immediate necessity of fighting a unified battle against what it considers to be its enemy.

ULFA seems to make a distinction between the immediate objective of establishing an 'Independent Asom' and the ultimate objective of positioning diverse ethnic communities within it in a manner that will not privilege any one or a particular group of these. But these two objectives are not absolutely separate from each other.

The organisation feels the necessity of fighting an internal battle against all such historically followed acts of privileging (the Assamese community), while battling against the external domination of 'colonial New Delhi'. In other words, the nucleus of the future society is formed in the course of the collective struggle. Even ULFA took time to recognise the dangers involved in the thesis of 'de-nationalisation' (*nirjatikaran*) that it once had propounded with much enthusiasm.

As late as in 1990, Siddhartha Phukan, ULFA's then Publicity Secretary, strongly advocated 'de-nationalization'. The thesis contains two key elements: one, the variegated ethnic mosaic in the northeast is posing an obstacle to the people's unified struggle against the 'colonialism of New Delhi'. Their ethnic differences are at times so strong that these literally prevent them from coming together and forging a revolutionary unity.

The first element reflects ULFA's understanding of the definite historic conjuncture existing at the time when it propounded the thesis. Secondly, and as a corollary to the first, ULFA also believes that it is only 'the economic identity' that is capable of binding the people together, in the sense that the perception of being the victims of the same 'internal colonialism' is likely to prevail over that of variegated ethnic or nationalistic identities.

There is reason to believe that, what Phukan calls, 'economic identity' is identical to what, in Classical Marxism, is known as class identity. In simple terms, ethnic consciousness is dismissed as 'false consciousness.' Phukan for instance, prefers to describe the tea garden people as 'tea labourers' rather than 'tea tribes'. While the latter emphasizes their tribal identity and treats them as a category separate from others—both tribals and non-tribals—ULFA's accent on their identity as 'labourers' should be read as an attempt at placing them under the generic category of 'labourers', irrespective of their ethnic differences.

As Phukan observes: "Economic identity should be emphasized more than ethnic identity, tea garden people instead of becoming tea tribes should become tea labourers." If anyone feels that Classical Marxism has been insensitive to the question of ethnicity or nationality, then ULFA will also be accused of the same insensitivity. The whole idea was to make the people conscious of their class identity through a rigorous regime of cultural indoctrination to weld them together in their battle against the common 'enemy'. ULFA viewed itself as a vanguard and, most importantly, as a microcosm in which ethnic differences were deliberately sought to be done away with. ULFA's thesis of 'de-nationalisation' drew flak both from within the region as well as from without. For one thing, it was accused of being too 'abstract'. It was apprehended that, in the name of obliterating ethnic differences, it would actually promote and patronise the hegemony of the already entrenched ethnic communities.

Even if the revolutionary struggle was expected to take on a non-ethnic/nationalistic character, the rhetoric of this struggle could not be internationalist either. ULFA's international overtures were not issued from the imperative necessity of forging a wider class-based unity on an international scale. For another, it was feared that any rapid implementation of this policy would elicit hysteric reactions from the minorities in general and the smaller tribal groups in particular. The United Reservationist Minority Council of Assam (URMCA), for example, argued that the thesis was 'anti-tribal' in character.

In short, the question is rather one of evolving appropriate mechanisms for bringing the otherwise heterogeneous population under the banner of a common nationality. The realisation of this necessity led ULFA to revisit its thesis of 'de-nationalization'. By May 1992, the organisation showed signs of decisively moving away from the thesis. While acknowledging that ULFA had not been successful in obtaining 'unflinching support' from all the ethnic communities of Assam—thanks to some 'wrong policies' adopted by it—Biplab Hazarika, one of its top ranking leaders, introduced the principle of 'equal rights and equal dignity'.

The only way by which such a principle can be established is to make the communities parts of a common struggle by way of preserving 'their own language and culture'. An Eleven Point Statement was issued on behalf of ULFA at about the same time, forming the basis of the rejection of its earlier thesis.

More negatively stated, this unambiguously denounced any form of 'hegemonism' of one community over another. Positively, it pointed out that ULFA "will give recognition to the right to self-determination of all ethnic groups and religious communities on the basis of equal rights and equal dignity in Independent Assam."

This formulation replaced the hitherto prevailing designation of 'Assamese nationalism' (*Asomiya jatiyatabad*) by a new one of 'combined nationalism of all the exploited peoples of Assam' (*Asomar samuh soshit raijar sanmilit jatiyatabad*). It called for 'free self-development' of each nationality in 'Independent Assam'. Next was the question whether 'internal colonialism' was the be-all-and-end-all of nationalism in

Assam? Contrary to the commonplace belief, ULFA's objective of putting an end to 'the colonialism of New Delhi' is not at all unrelated to the ethnic or nationality question. While branding ULFA as a 'terrorist' organization, Walter Laquer for example, observed:

> Like other states, the Assam radicals felt neglected by the capital; little patronage came their way, and they established yet another liberation front, the United Liberation Front of Assam (ULFA).
>
> The initiative came from radical elements at the Universities, and ethnic and religious factors have figured very little in the movement, but it is very difficult to clearly distinguish between religious and non-religious motivation among terrorists in Assam and in other parts of India.

The argument that the politics of ULFA is driven more out of a sense of 'neglect' than out of strong nationalist sentiments implies that the best way to handle this sense of 'neglect' is to undertake and implement appropriate economic reforms and development projects sensitive to the region's specific requirements. I think, the problem with this argument is that it reduces the entire ULFA-phenomenon to a statement of relative deprivation.

For ULFA, the sense of 'neglect' is only secondary to its assertion that 'Assam was never a part of India, nor shall she ever be.' What is at issue is not so much the nature of economic neglect that Assam has been subjected to since the beginning of colonial rule way back in 1826, and that continued unabated even after 1947, but very much the *externality* of the rule being established over her. Contrary to what Laquer says, ULFA's intervention has to do more with the autonomy that Assam supposedly enjoyed throughout the greater part of her history, and less with 'neglect'.

To collapse the former into the paradigm of economic development is to miss the whole point. ULFA's critique has brought to the fore the question of whether economic development is at all possible in a situation where ethnic or 'national' divisions coincide with the dichotomy between the colonisers and the colonised.

Such an argument on ULFA's part has led it to invent the difference, literally to bring it into existence, and to make it a part of its 'social imaginaire'. Parag Kumar Das's *Swadhinatar Prastab* is an interesting text that seems to have been inspired by the single-point agenda of driving home the point that the Assamese have always been *ethnically different* from the rest of India. It is the principle of difference that also articulates them as a separate 'nation' (*jati*). We may note here in passing that Parag Kumar Das was for long associated with *Budhbar* and is often regarded as one of the finest theoreticians of the ULFA, who reportedly fell prey to the bullets of the Surrendered militants of the ULFA (popularly known as SULFA).

The Assamese, according to him, are closer to their 'Mongolian brothers', rather than part of the 'Indian socio-cultural ethos'. Das identifies certain anthropological traits of the Assamese and shows how they are different from those of the 'Indians'. Thus, to cite an instance, Sankaradeva was not part of the 'Indian socio-cultural ethos' as he was a fish-eater. While *Swadhinatar Prastab* is often accused of being 'simplistic' and 'selective' in drawing our attention to these 'anthropological traits', it seeks to celebrate the principle of difference as a means of establishing the community.

The allusions to so-called physical and cultural traits—however naive and flimsy they may appear to us—signify their *priority* over the phenomenon of 'internal colonialism'. They have been 'colonised' because they are different. They are not different because they are 'colonised'. 'Internal colonialism' is only an adjunct to the principle of difference. ULFA's critique, of course, is much broader than a simple political economy critique of the Indian state. It is embedded in the site where the differences between communities are acted upon, interrogated and negotiated on an everyday basis.

Thirdly, ULFA's critique also draws our attention to one of the fundamental questions of Indian democracy: What if the Constitution itself stifles democracy in a country like India? What if democracy refuses to be bound by the Constitution and oversteps it? Is the Constitution the be-all-and-end-all of our democracy? ULFA's contribution lies in the fact that it has unsettled the hitherto settled connection between democracy and the Constitution.

It shows how, in a multi-ethnic context, the rule of the majority has a tendency of coinciding with that of the dominant ethnicity; and how the ethnic minorities of the 'far-off areas' or periphery always stand to lose because of their numerical weakness. The so-called democratic set up cannot but be discriminatory towards the ethnic minorities and insensitive to their particular demands. This discrimination is built into a democratic set up governed by the principle of majority rule—a euphemism for 'Delhi-ism' (*Dillibad*). While the ethnic minorities feel closeted within this inherently discriminatory set up, the Constitution does not give them the right to secession.

This right would have guaranteed them the right to opt out of it and establish a political system that they would consider to be their own, and in which they would not feel intimidated by the 'colonial rule' of the dominant ethnicity.

According to ULFA, the only way to free oneself from the clutches of this 'colonial rule' is to exercise the right to secession. One notices the distinct influence of the socialist notion of federalism in ULFA's argument. In the former Soviet Union, the right to secession was, at least theoretically, considered to be an integral part of the entire federal set up.

ULFA's argument seems to draw itself from the republican theory of popular sovereignty, according to which people are considered to be sovereign, so much so that the Constitution they craft is taken to be secondary to their will. The Constitution of India too has been 'adopted, enacted and given to themselves' by 'we, the people' and, according to this argument, the people as a sacrosanct body have the right to make and break it. So if, at some point, they consider it necessary to include this right in the Constitution, no democracy can prevent them from doing so. Harin Mahanta raises the same question when he argues:

If the Constitution was written in order to reflect the will of the people after taking oath in the name of the people, then why do many people want to violate it? ... From where did the Constituent Assembly receive the right to take oath in the name of the people? Who is to be blamed for not complying with the Constitution ... the people or the Constitution that has led to the birth of the proposal for Independence *(Swadhinatar Prastaw)*? From where did the Constitution get the right to wrest power from the people? Which dictum of democracy makes the articles obstructing the discussion of people's own will acceptable?

We may recall that ULFA is persistent in making secession one of our Fundamental Rights through a Constitution Amendment Act and stipulates it as one of the preconditions of conducting talks with the Government of India. It is true, also, that its efficacy as an intermediate political institution has been a subject of frequent political debate in the society. Democracy in India cannot avoid these questions. Our Constitution, as we know, is precariously perched between the rival notions of popular sovereignty and Constitutional sovereignty. What will happen if these two notions conflict between themselves? For how long can we afford to postpone our choice?

DISINTEGRATION

ULFA's contribution lies in raising these rather unsettling questions, and certainly not in providing any definitive answers to them. Its contribution lies in stirring up our minds rather than in soothing them with any quick fix solutions. Since we are jolted by some questions to which we do not have any easy and definitive answers, the necessity of engaging ourselves in some sort of a collective discourse has become all the more acute. A collective discourse of this nature is contingent on the development of civil society institutions in a society like Assam. But the problem is that the decline of ULFA has also been accompanied by a certain disintegration of civil society institutions in Assam. Certainly, ULFA alone is not to be blamed for this plight.

The purpose of this paper, as we have already said, is not to apportion blame, but to examine the tragic irony that the decline of ULFA has led to in recent years. Although Sanjib

Baruah recognises the crucial role played by such organizations as All-Assam Students' Union, Asom Sahitya Sabha and most importantly, ULFA, in articulating and elaborating what he calls, 'Assamese micro-nationalism', he seems to accept this as an unproblematic process. In this section we draw attention to the travails that the processes of articulation and elaboration have been faced with in recent years. First of all, if civil society is regarded as the space where people explore various 'truth alternatives' and arrive at a consensus about what the truth is, then the cult of violence has resulted in a certain externalisation of 'truth'. In simple terms, it has actually *excised truth* from the civil society agenda by making it dependent on the power of the gun.

Truth in such circumstances ceases to be an object of deliberation. Deliberation, as the procedural principle of truth, is integral to the writings of Jurgen Habermas, who notes that finding truth is a question of organising civil society in a manner that will cancel out 'the fallible results'. When external violence establishes the power of truth, truth ceases to be regarded as truth as soon as violence refuses to back it, and the agency holding it aloft loses its grip over the instruments of violence. This is the opposite of what Foucault describes as 'the regime of truth'. When power is exercised through the 'regime of truth' one is produced, as it were, as its effect and truth becomes internal to one's own self. Thus the self is posited not as the opposite of power but as its very effect. But this is seldom the case when violence becomes external to truth. ULFA's much-reported writ concerning the observance of 'Rangali Bihu' in what it considers to be 'the traditional way' in 1990 serves as a case in point.

Similarly directives sent to the Press from time to time regarding its prescribed 'code of conduct' also illustrates the same point. Sanjib Baruah accuses ULFA of being the self-styled 'custodian of Assamese interests on the pattern of more mainstream organisations such as the All-Assam Students' Union and Axom Xatiya Xabha'. When an organisation arrogates to itself the power of determining the culture of a community, it not only contributes to an escalation of violence in society, but also wipes out the other possible alternatives and disciplines, the other possible cultural forms, with a single, pre-defined type. It is, however, at the same time true that such attempts often help in stemming the rot by eliminating those alternatives that, in the name of providing alternatives, are seen to commit excesses.

Secondly, and as a corollary to the above, institutions of civil society depend on the free and unfettered circulation of truth alternatives, and hence militate against any kind of monopolistic closure. The exploration of truth is a public activity, and when people are afraid of harbouring and exploring truth alternatives in full 'public glare', civil society exists only in whispers and the people do not feel safe to publicly express and articulate their opinions. The tragedy in today's Assam is not so much that ULFA has declined, but very much that, with its decline, the entire edifice of civil society institutions has crumbled as well. An earlier draft of this paper was presented to the Seminar on 'National Security Issues: Special Emphasis on Northeastern India' organized by the Omeo Kumar Das Institute of Social Change and Development in Guwahati, Assam on April 22-4, 2002.

3

Root Causes of Violence in Assam

POLITICAL UNREST

Some of the issues in Assam have acquired such a dimension that seeking a solution has become akin to chasing a mirage. Events of the last two decades have shown that the gentle surface of the region belies the simmering bitterness, alienation and conflict that abounds. Conflicts of ethnic interests, charges of exploitation by New Delhi, linguistic disturbances, border disputes and the hillman?s suspicion of the plains people as exploiters have plagued the area.

To add fuel to the fire, the issue of illegal migrants from Bangladesh and the agitation against this influx have devastated social cohesion. Insurgencies and militant groups battle the Indian state and it appears unlikely that things will normalise on this front in the near future. As a result, the economy has been in a shambles, despite generous Central aid over the years. There has been a decline in the human living index and in overall social, financial and industrial areas. The United Liberation Front of Asom (ULFA) and the National Democratic Front of Boroland (NDFB) are the major militant groups. operating in the state. Further, despite the six-year-long agitation by the All Assam Students? Union (AASU) (1979-1985) over the illegal foreign nationals issue little tangible success has been achieved.

The attitude of the authorities in tackling the illegal influx continues to create fear that the local people will eventually be reduced to a minority, thus leading to a sense of widespread insecurity.

After Nagaland, Assam is the most volatile state in the region. Beginning 1979, the indigenous people of Assam demanded that the illegal immigrants who had emigrated from Bangladesh to Assam be detected and deported. The movement lead by All Assam Students Union began non-violently with satyagraha, boycotts, picketing and courting arrests. Those protesting frequently came under police action. In 1983 an election was conducted which was opposed by the movement leaders. The election lead to widespread violence. The movement finally ended after the movement leaders signed an agreement (called Assam Accord) with the central government in 15 August 1985.

Under the provisions of this accord, anyone who entered the state illegally between January 1966 and March 1971 were allowed to remain but were disenfranchised for ten years, while those who entered after 1971 faced expulsion. A November 1985 amendment to the Indian citizenship law allows non citizens who entered Assam between 1961 and 1971 to have all the rights of citizenship except the right to vote for a period of ten years. New Delhi also gave special administration autonomy to the Bodos in the state. However, the Bodos demanded for a separate Bodoland which led to a clash between the Bengalis, the Bodos and the Indian military resulting in hundreds of deaths.

There are several organizations which advocate the independence of Assam. The most prominent of which is the United Liberation Front of Asom (ULFA). Formed in 1979, the ULFA has two main goals, the independence of Assam and the establishment of a socialist government. The ULFA has carried out several terrorist attacks in the region targeting the Indian Military and non-combatants. The group assassinates political opponents, attacks police and other security forces, blasts railroad tracks, and attacks other infrastructure facilities. The ULFA is believed to have strong links with *Nationalist Socialist Council of Nagaland (NSCN)*, Maoists and the Naxalites.

It is also believed that they carry out most of their operations from the Kingdom of Bhutan. Because of ULFA's increased visibility, the Indian government outlawed the group in 1986 and declared Assam a troubled area. Under pressure from New Delhi, Bhutan carried a massive operation to drive out the ULFA militants from its territory.

Backed by the Indian Army, Thimphu was successful in killing more than a thousand terrorists and extraditing many more to India while sustaining only 120 casualties. The Indian military undertook several successful operations aimed at countering future ULFA terrorist attacks, but the ULFA continues to be active in the region. In 2004, the ULFA targeted a public school in Assam killing 19 children and 5 adults. Assam remains the only state in the northeast where terrorism is still a major issue. The Indian Military was successful in dismantling terrorist outfits in other areas, but have been criticized by human rights groups for allegedly using harsh methods when dealing with terrorists. On 18 September 2005, a soldier was killed in Jiribam, Manipur, near the Manipur-Assam border by members of the ULFA.

THE PROBLEM OF INSURGENCY IN ASSAM: AS A POLITICAL PHENOMENA

The problem of insurgency in Assam is often discussed as political phenomena. But a few people have tried to get to the root cause of the problem. Ethnic identity crisis can be considered as the root cause of terrorism in Assam.

Though There are lots of reasons for the decades-old insurgency in Assam, the main cause can be traced to the ethnic identity crisis. The problem of insurgency in Assam is often discussed as political phenomena. But a few people have tried to get to the roots of the problem. Assam is considered as the land of several tribes and communities having different cultural and social thoughts and beliefs. There are lots of linguistic differences as well as religious differences. So, there are differences of opinions as to how these differences can be a major factor for the growth of terrorism.

As in the process of formation of Assamese nationality, most of the tribes have lost their ethnic identity. But major political developments or changes have compelled them to think about their ethnic identity. There is a threat to the identity of various ethnic tribes and communities in Assam. The threat to the existence of most of these communities has been translated in the form of several agitations.

First of all is the decades-old agitation of the Bodo community, still in the hunt for its existence in Assam. Bodos, it may be mentioned, is an indigenous tribe of Assam, mainly confined to the Brahmaputra Valley. They still have their own cultural and linguistic identity. But in the process of Assamese nationality formation, some of them have lost their ethnic identity. The Bodo movement in Assam, somehow, brings some revivalistic tendencies among them. It is believed that most of the insurgent groups have taken advantage of these kinds of revivalistic tendencies. Insurgent groups are always hijacking the minds of the youths. This may well be seen as the root cause in the increase of the number of militant groups over the years.

After the historic Bodo Accord was signed in 2003, Bodo leaders, especially cadres of the now-disbanded Bodo Liberation Tigers (BLT), entered the political spectrum. However, the fight for an independent Bodoland continues, with another Bodo millitant group, the National Democratic Front of Bodoland (BDFB) still staging a war against India in the name of freedom. They are somehow trying to show their strength through subversive activities, particularly through blasts and killings. It leads to devastating ethnic movements in other tribes and communities of Assam too. In this regard, we can also discuss the ethnic isolation of several groups as a root cause of insurgency in Assam. It is often discussed that most of the ethnic groups are deprived by the government with regards to socio-economic development.

And almost all the major insurgent groups are taking advantage in so far as recruiting new cadres from such communities. Various political parties are not interested in solving the insurgency issue since it is an issue through which electoral gains can be made. The recent developments in the region are also depicting the same thing. But still we can discuss the ongoing peace process in the region. Some of the rebel groups have already come to the mainstream, abjuring violence and surrendering arms. There are still several ceasefire rebel groups extending their efforts towards restoration of peace. But with the government yet to consider initiating formal peace talks with urgency, there are chances of the law-and-order situation deteriorating in Assam.

TRIBAL UNREST IN ASSAM

Tribal unrest is a prominent part of the political culture of the state of Assam. One group of tribes, concentrated in the remaining hill areas of the state in the Karbi Anglong district and North Kachar Hills district, demanded the creation of a self- governing unit within Assam. The second, a much larger group of tribes within which the largest are known as Bodos, are plains tribals living in the heartland of Assam by and large on the northern bank of the Brahmaputra River, but with some on the southern bank as well.

Like other tribal peoples in another place in the northeast and in other parts of India, Bodo leaders complained that they had lost lands to non tribal peoples, that they were educationally backward, and that their language was not taught in schools to their own children. Language issues are inseparably connected to the question of jobs.

Nearly all Bodos know and use Assamese in their every day lives, but the few Bodos who do receive secondary or higher education face hard competition for public sector jobs, from the dominant Assamese Hindu castes, who have also benefited in their competition with Bengalis by the establishment of Assamese as the one and only official language of the state. The natural step for the Bodos in this state of affairs, as a result, is to demand acknowledgment for their language and the creation of a separate state in which their language and culture would be recognized.

Tribal unrest is a prominent part of the political culture of the state of Assam. One group of tribes, concentrated in the remaining hill areas of the state in the Karbi Anglong district and North Kachar Hills district, demanded the creation of a self- governing unit within Assam. The second, a much larger group of tribes within which the largest are known as Bodos, are plains tribals living in the heartland of Assam by and large on the northern bank of the Brahmaputra River, but with some on the southern bank as well.

Like other tribal peoples in another place in the northeast and in other parts of India, Bodo leaders complained that they had lost lands to non tribal peoples, that they were educationally backward, and that their language was not taught in schools to their own children. Language issues are inseparably connected to the question of jobs.

Nearly all Bodos know and use Assamese in their every day lives, but the few Bodos who do receive secondary or higher education face hard competition for public sector jobs, from the dominant Assamese Hindu castes, who have also benefited in their competition with Bengalis by the establishment of Assamese as the one and only official language of the state. The natural step for the Bodos in this state of affairs, as a result, is to demand acknowledgment for their language and the creation of a separate state in which their language and culture would be recognized. Tribal unrest is a prominent part of the political culture of the state of Assam. One group of tribes, concentrated in the remaining hill areas of the state in the Karbi Anglong district and North Kachar Hills district, demanded the creation of a self- governing unit within Assam.

The second, a much larger group of tribes within which the largest are known as Bodos, are plains tribals living in the heartland of Assam by and large on the northern bank of the Brahmaputra River, but with some on the southern bank as well. Like other tribal peoples in another place in the northeast and in other parts of India, Bodo leaders complained that they had lost lands to non tribal peoples, that they were educationally backward, and that their language was not taught in schools to their own children. Language issues are inseparably connected to the question of jobs.

Nearly all Bodos know and use Assamese in their every day lives, but the few Bodos who do receive secondary or higher education face hard competition for public sector jobs, from the dominant Assamese Hindu castes, who have also benefited in their competition with Bengalis by the establishment of Assamese as the one and only official language of the state.

The natural step for the Bodos in this state of affairs, as a result, is to demand acknowledgment for their language and the creation of a separate state in which their language and culture would be recognized

THE ARMED FORCES (SPECIAL POWERS) ACT, 1958: INTRODUCTION

Violence became the way of life in north-eastern States of India. State administration became incapable to maintain its internal disturbance. Armed Forces (Assam and Manipur) Special Powers Ordinance was promulgated by the President on 22nd May of 1958. In which some special powers have been given to the members of the armed forces in disturbed areas in the State of Assam and Union Territory of Manipur. Later the Ordinance was replaced by the armed Forces Special Powers Bill.

STATEMENT OF OBJECTS AND REASONS

An ordinance entitled the Armed forces (Assam and Manipur) Special Powers Ordinance, 1958, was promulgated by the President on the 22nd May, 1958. Section 3 of the Ordinance powers the Governor of Assam and the Chief Commissioner of Manipur to declare the whole or any part of Assam or the Union territory of Manipur, as the case may be, to be a disturbed area. On such a declaration being made in the Official Gazette, any Commissioned Officer, Warrant Officer, non-commissioned officer or any other person of equivalent rank in the armed forces may exercise, in the disturbed area, the powers conferred by section 4 and 5 of the Ordinance. The Bill seeks to replace the Ordinance –See Gazette of India, 11-8-1958, Pt. II-Sec. 2, Ext. p.714 (No.26).

ACT 28 OF 1958

The Armed Forces (Special Powers) Bill was passed by both the Houses of Parliament and it received the assent of the President on 11th September, 1958. It came on the Statute Book as The Armed Forces (Special Powers) ActCT, 1958 (28 of 1958).

List of Amending Acts:

- The State of Mizoram Act, 1986 (34 of 1986).
- The State of Arunachal Pradesh Act, 1986 (69 of 1986).
- The Armed Forces (Assam and Manipur) Special Powers (Amendment) Act, 1972 (7 of 1972).
- The Armed Forces Special Powers (Extension to Union Territory of Tripura) Act, 1970.
- The Repealing and Amending Act, 1960 (58 of 1960).

THE ARMED FORCES (SPECIAL POWERS) ACT, 1958 (28 of 1958) [11th September, 1958] An Act to enable certain special powers to be conferred upon members of the armed forces in disturbed areas in the State of [Arunachal Pradesh, Assam, Manipur, Meghalaya, Mizoram, Nagaland and Tripura].

Be it enacted by Parliament in Ninth Year of the republic of India as follows:

- *Short title and extent*:
  - This act may be called. The armed Forces (Special Powers) Act, 1958.
  - It extends to the whole of the State of [Arunachal Pradesh, Assam, Manipur, Meghalaya, Mizoram, Nagaland and Tripura].
- *Definitions*: In this Act, unless the context otherwise requires-
  - "Armed forces' means the military forces and the air forces operating as land forces, and includes other armed forces of the Union so operating;
  - 'Disturbed area' means an area which is for the time being declared by notification under section 3 to be a disturbed area';
  - All other words and expressions used herein, but not defined and defined in the Air Force Act, 1950 (45 of 1950), or the army Act, 1950 (46 of 1950) shall have the meanings respectively to them in those Acts.
- Powers to declare areas to be disturbed areas—If, in

relation to any state or Union Territory to which this act extends, the Governor of that State or the administrator of that Union Territory or the Central Government, in either case, if of the opinion that the whole or any part of such State of Union territory, as the case may be, is in such a disturbed or dangerous condition that the use of armed forces in aid of the civil power is necessary, the Governor of that State or the Administrator of that Union Territory or the Central Government, as the case may be, may by notification in the Official Gazette, declare the whole or such part of such State or Union territory to be a disturbed area.

- *Subs*: By Act 69 of 1986,sec.43 for "Assam, Manipur, Megahalya, Mizoram, Nagaland and Tripura and the Union territory of Arunachal Pradesh" (w.e.f. 20.2.1987.)
- Subs by Act 7 of 1973, sec. 3 for 'the armed forces (Assam and Manipur) special Powers Act, 1958" (w.e.f 5.4.1972).
- Subs by Act 7 of 1972, sec. 4 (w.e.f 5.4.1972).
- Subs by Act.69 of 1986,sec. 43 for 'Assam, Manipur, Meghalaya, Mizoram, Nagaland and Tripura and the Union Territory of Arunachal Pradesh'(w.e.f 20.2.1987). Sec 5 The Armed Forces (Special Powers) Act, 1958.

COMMENTS

- The Governor is empowered to declare any area of the State as "disturbed area'. It could not be arbitrary on ground of absence of legislative guidelines; *Inderjit Barua v.State of Assam,* AIR 1983 Del. 514.
- Section 3 cannot be construed as conferring a power to issue a declaration without any time limit. There should be periodic review of the declaration before the expiry of six months; *Naga People's Movement of Human Rights v. Union of India,* AIR 1998 SC 431.
- Special Powers of the armed forces—Any

commissioned officer, warrant officer, non-commissioned officer or any other person of equivalent rank in the armed forces may, in a disturbed area,-

- If he is of opinion that it is necessary so to do for the maintenance of public order, after giving such due warning as he may consider necessary, fire upon or otherwise use force, even to the causing of death, against any person who is acting in contravention of any law or order for the time being in force in the disturbed area prohibiting the assembly of five or move persons or the carrying of weapons or of things capable of being used as weapons or of fire-arms, ammunition or explosive substances;
- If he is of opinion that it is necessary so to do, destroy any arms dump, prepared or fortified position or shelter from which armed attacks are made or are likely to be made or are attempted to be made, or any structure used as a training camp for armed volunteers or utilized as a hide-out by armed gangs or absconders wanted for any offence;
- Arrest, without warrant, any person who has committed a cognizable offence or against whom a reasonable suspicion exists that he has committed or is about to commit a cognizable offence and may use such force as may be necessary to effect the arrest;
- Enter and search without warrant any premises to make any such arrest as aforesaid or to recover any person believed to be wrongfully restrained or confined or any property reasonably suspected to be stolen property or any arms, ammunition or explosive substances believed to be unlawfully kept in such premises, and may for that purpose use such force as may be necessary.

- Arrested persons to be made over to the police –Any person arrested and taken into custody under this Act shall be made over to the officer in charge of the nearest police station with the least possible delay, together with a report of the circumstances occasioning the arrest.
  In case of arrest of any person, army authority is duty bound to handover to the officer-in-charge of the nearest police station with least possible delay: *Horendi Gogoi v. Union of India,* (1991) Gau CR 3081.
- Protection to persons acting under Act—No prosecution, suit or other legal proceeding shall be instituted, except with the previous sanction of the Central Government, against any person in respect of anything done or purported to be done in exercise of the powers conferred by this Act.
- *Repeal and Saving*: Repealed by Amending and Repealing Act, 1960 (58 of 1960),First Schedule, sec.2 (26.12.1960.

4

Assam: Ethnic Conflict

INDIA'S north-east is "an anthropologist's delight and an administrator's nightmare", notes Sanjoy Hazarika, author of several books about the region. Its 39m people divide into 350 ethnic groups, many of whom feel estranged from the Indian "mainland" and uneasy about each other. This unease can quickly turn to violence. From October 3rd to 7th, members of Assam's largest tribe, the Bodo (pronounced Boro), fought bitterly with local Muslims, before troops and paramilitaries sent by the central government quelled the violence. By then, 53 people had died, 25 of them shot by the police, and 150,000 people had sought shelter in camps.

The motives behind the attacks are disputed. Most press accounts blamed anti-immigrant sentiment, which runs deep in Assamese politics. The state's border with overcrowded Bangladesh is impossible to police. Illegal migrants, who find jobs as rickshaw-pullers, brickmakers and house-servants, may number as many as 2m in Assam, thinks Mr Hazarika.

Under the Assam Accord of 1985, the government promised to identify and deport people who had crossed the border since the creation of Bangladesh in 1971. But the government lacks the ability to fulfil this pledge; it may also lack the inclination. Assam's employers benefit from Bangladeshi labour and its political parties court their votes.

In July the north-east's High Court ordered the removal of 49 Bangladeshis, some of whom had registered to vote in the state. An intemperate judge described the influx of migrants as a "cancerous growth" and called for "political will" and "public activism" to fight it.

It is tempting to view the latest violence as an example of such activism run amok. But the Bodos' antagonists were not principally Bangladeshis, points out Bibhu Prasad Routray of the Institute for Conflict Management, a think-tank in Delhi. They were instead Indian Muslims settled in the state before 1971, who were ready to fight back. The Bodos, among the earliest settlers in the Assamese plains, resent any outsider who encroaches on their tribal homelands. They do not make subtle legal distinctions between them.

The bloodshed may serve larger political ambitions, Mr Routray argues. In four districts where the Bodos are in the majority the tribe is governed by the Bodoland Territorial Council, which enjoys considerable autonomy under India's supple constitution. Some members of the tribe may be keen to create more Bodo-majority areas, by driving everyone else out. These territories might then be allowed to fall under the authority of the council. This autonomy was the fruit of a 2003 peace deal between India's government and the Bodo Liberation Tigers, who had waged a seven-year insurgency demanding a state of their own. Their leaders were quick to blame the four days of violence on a rival guerrilla group called the National Democratic Front of Bodoland, which has yet to make peace. But Mr Routray doubts the Front had much to do with it. Since it agreed to a ceasefire in 2005, many of its rank-and-file members have moved to camps, closely supervised by the government. And the group's leadership has no quarrel with Muslims. Indeed, they have found sanctuary in Bangladesh.

ASSAM: ETHNIC CLASHES THREATEN PROSPECT OF PEACE

Just when the northeastern Indian state of Assam was hoping for peace after the largest rebel group, ULFA agreed for peace talks, the prospect of return to normalcy in the state suffered a huge setback with the outbreak of violence between two tribal communities who inhabit the district of Karbi Anglong. On first site, the violence appears to have ethnic colour but a deeper probe indicates that there are other socio, political and economic issues involved. This also highlights the fact that a piecemeal approach to the northeast insurgency would not work and a solution to the various problems prevailing in the area would have to be found if a lasting peace has to be established.

LONG HISTORY OF BITTER STRUGGLE [H[

India's northeast, comprising seven states, is home to more than 200 tribes and ethnic groups and is circled by China, Bhutan, Bangladesh and Myanmar. The region has been racked by separatist and tribal insurgencies for more than 50 years. One of the important states of northeast, Assam is home to more than 30 major tribes and feuds between militias claiming to represent them over conflicting homeland demands are fairly common. In the Karbi Anglong district, the majority Karbis and Dimasas have been engaged in a bitter turf war for many years and the situation has been turning violent in recent weeks with armed militants of both tribes attacking rival community members. The outlawed United Democratic People's Solidarity (UPDS), a rag-tag rebel group fighting for a Karbi tribal homeland, and the Dima Halom Daoga (DHD), a militant group fighting for a Dimasa homeland, are suspected to be behind the recent attacks.

The two groups are operating ceasefires with New Delhi- the UPDS has been observing a truce since 2002 and the DHD entering into a ceasefire in 2003. Under the ceasefire agreements, cadres of the two rebel groups are allowed to retain their weapons although they are expected to stay within the periphery of designated camps allotted to them by the state authorities. DHD has an estimated 450 armed cadres and the UPDS some 300 rebel fighters.

OUTBREAK OF RECENT VIOLENCE

The ethnic violence in the district was triggered on September 26 when three Dimasa auto-rickshaw drivers were hacked to death by unidentified persons at Tissom village in the Diphu police station area. Diphu is the headquarters of Karbi Anglong, a district dominated by the Karbi tribe.

In retaliation, five members of a Karbi family were hacked to death at Hemari Terang village on October 2 followed by killing of another three Karbis at Upper Dikrong two days later under the same police station. On October 8 at Borsingbe village six Dimasas were killed in retaliation to which eight Karbis were killed the next day at Langsoliet village.

Then five more Dimasas were killed at Kheroni village the day after. On October 12 a Dimasa woman was hacked to death. Four bodies were recovered on October 16 from Karbi villages Hojaipur, Bokolia, Jamunapar and Sing Teron area where five people were also reported missing. On October 17, 36 Karbi villagers were killed in three separate attacks. The victims included 22 bus passengers who were hacked to death by DHD rebels. The very next day, at least seven more Karbi tribals were massacred by militants. These attacks took place in Doyangmukh village of Karbi Anglong district. The rebels set ablaze at least 50 homes before leaving the village.

The toll in current spell of ethnic violence neared 90 when nine Karbi militants were killed on October 21 by the rival Dimasa tribe, in Tamulbari in Upper Assam. According to the police, a group of Karbi extremists after torching 12 houses at Kakubasti and seven at Kisiri Bongaon villages in interior areas of a reserve forest headed for Tamulbari. Dimasa guerillas ambushed them as they were about to enter Tamulbari and shot dead nine of them.

FAILURE OF THE STATE ADMINISTRATION TO COMPREHEND THE SITUATION

The state authorities were totally clueless in the first few weeks when trouble broke out. The law enforcement officials admit that such developments in far-flung districts often go unnoticed, but the situation in Karbi Anglong has long been highly volatile. Confusing it with the regular law and order problem resulted into large-scale violence.

POLITICAL PARTIES INDULGE IN BLAME GAME

The intensifying violence in Karbi Anglong district started a bitter blame game among the political parties of the state.

They accused each other of being involved in the violence. Opposition parties like the Bharatiya Janata Party (BJP) and the regional Asom Gana Parishad (AGP) accused the ruling Congress of failing to control the escalating violence. The AGP president Brindaban Goswami demanded the resignation of the state government. The BJP also accused the local Communist Party of India-Marxist-Leninist (CPI-ML) leaders like Jayanta Rongpi of instigating the clashes. It sent a team led by S S Ahluwalia to assess the situation. Criticizing the state government the CPI (M) also demanded Centres intervention saying the state government had failed to comprehend the gravity of the situation.

ASSAM GOVERNMENT ACCUSING OPPOSITION PARTIES FOR THE VIOLENCE

Assam government accused the former MP and CPI-ML (Liberation) leader Jayanta Rongpis Red Army of involvement in the ethnic violence in Karbi Anglong district. According to the state government, it was the Red Army who triggered the whole crisis by indiscriminately attacking both Dimasa and Karbis. This infuriated the respective militants groups of Karbis and Dimasas, the UPDS and DHD, who then launched an all out attack against each other, leading to a series of violence.

However, the CPI(ML) leader Jayanta Rongpi alleged that the Congress was trying to escape responsibility of Karbi violence by creating a non-entity. Rongpi claimed that there was nothing called Red Army in Karbi Anglong. He also dared the state government to arrest him, if he was involved in the violence.

LATE RESPONSE OF THE ASSAM GOVERNMENT

The large-scale violence raised concern prompting the Centre to ask the Assam Government to use the police and paramilitary forces and also take some political steps to bring the ethnic violence in Karbi Anglog district under control. Home Minister Shivraj Patil said, "We have told the Chief Minister, who is the Chairman of the Unified Command, to use these forces; not only use these forces but also take some political steps to see that it does not happen (again)." He also stated that the state government was well equipped to deal with this situation.

ARMY CALLED IN

The authorities decided to call in the army on October 18 as shoot-at-sight order and curfew failed to contain ethnic violence in Karbi Anglong district. The decision to deploy troops was taken at a high-level meeting in Guwahati of the Unified Command Structure administrative head and chief secretary, S Kabilan, operational commander and 4 Corps GoC Lt-Gen. HS Lidder and DGP PV Sumant, as part of a special strategy mooted by Assam chief minister Mr Tarun Gogoi.

But due to late deployment of the army, casualties increased and the crisis was prolonged. In a confidential report to the President APJ Abdul Kalam, the Assam governor, Ajai Singh alleged that the state government should have acted faster to bring the ethnic clashes under control. The governor, Lt Gen Singh, says the state government did not crack down on the militants of the Dimasa and Karbi tribes when trouble began on 26 September. The governor felt that the army should have been deployed in the trouble-torn Karbi Anglong district when the clashes began. A large number of lives were lost because of the late deployment. The governor also suggested that the militants of both tribes who have signed a ceasefire agreement with the Indian government should be kept within designated camps and should not be allowed to move around freely with weapons. He pointed out that both the groups were responsible for the mayhem with each using the opportunity provided by the loose ground rules of the ceasefire. They used the weapons they carried with them on a normal course to create violence against the other community. He also suggested that both these groups should be disarmed if necessary.

VIOLENCE LEADING TO MISERIES

In the month long violence, 91 persons80 Karbi tribals, eight Dimasas, one Bodo and one Nepali have died. The Karbis bore the brunt in the recent attacks as most of the people killed belong to that tribe. Over 45,000 tribals, both Karbis and Dimasas, have fled their villages and taken shelter in 53 relief camps as the situation in the district continues to be volatile. The violence has left most of the tribals in the region without homes. For the homeless villagers, relief camps set up by the administration could now mean home for years to come. Many villagers are too scared to return to their homes.

FOCUS ON SYSTEM GLITCHES

An all party Assam Assembly team led by the Speaker Prithvi Majhi toured the strife torn district. This team has strongly recommended the restructuring of Karbi Anglong administrative system. Majhi suggested that Assams largest district should be broken into three administrative blocks with Diphu, Hamren and Bokajan as the headquarters to facilitate efficient monitoring. Decentralisation has become imperative, given the size of the district and the difficult terrain.

The Speaker made a case for more police outposts in the far-flung areas of the district, saying that inadequate security was one of the reasons for the situation in Karbi Anglong spiralling out of control. He said a single administrative unit could not be expected to do an efficient job of governing a district as large and with such undulating and inaccessible terrain as Karbi Anglong. After the visit the assembly team felt that the arson and killing spree were the result of feuding between the two dominant militant outfits of the Karbi and the Dimasa tribes the United Peoples Democratic Solidarity (UPDS) and the Dima Halam Daoga (DHD).

The Speaker supported the UPDS demand to shift the DHDs designated camp in Dhansiri out of the district. He said the genesis of the feud between the two groups was the presence of the camp. Both the UPDS and the Karbi people are of the view that the presence of a DHD camp within Karbi Anglong could legitimise the Dimasa communitys demand for the inclusion of Dhansiri and some other parts of Karbi Anglong in the proposed state of Dimaraji. However, Majhi denied the alleged involvement of a CPI (M-L) red army in the ethnic clashes. Authorities also say what first appeared to be ethnic strife is now clearly insurgent violence. Local police believes that It has arisen from a ego fight between two militant groups who are on ceasefire and have declared war on each other on certain issues, like establishment of a designated camp here of one of the groups.

The local administration believes that the strife is not just about ethnicity or militancy, but it's also about control of land and jungles. On many occasions this struggle over resources is given ethnic colour. The long-term solution to these problems lie in the management of forest and land of the district. Though several militant groups are active in the countrys largest district, Karbi Anglong, the security presence across the district is very thin. The district has only six police stations with 500 policemen. Both the militant groups involved in current spell of violence have two factions one pro-talks and the other anti-talks. And like the NSCN(IM) and NSCN(K) or the Bodo outfits even the pro-talks factions living in designated camps are violating the ceasefire ground rules.

The violence has also prompted the home ministry to take a decision in favour of disarming the two tribal rebel groups. The authorities in Assam were given orders to seize weapons from all militants belonging to the United People's Democratic Solidarity (UPDS) and the Dima Halam Daogah (DHD).

ETHNIC VIOLAECE IN NC HILLS AND KARBI ANGLONG

The two hill districts of Assam, North Cachar Hills and Karbi Anglong, are fascinating because these territories together are a microcosm of the larger ethnic profile of Northeast India. The indigenous peoples inhabiting this small area have tribal affiliations with far-flung groups in the surrounding hill states. They are Karbi (most dominant numerically), Dimasa, Jeme Naga, Kuki, Hmar, Lushai, Rangkhol, Khasi, Jaintia, Bodo and Tiwa.

It is no wonder that the effects of the multiple insurgencies going on in the vicinity-Nagaland, Manipur, Tripura and plains of Assam-have gradually but inevitably spilled over into the two hill districts. This has become more likely given the rise of better communications in recent years. These so called "autonomous" hill districts of Assam are the least developed, kind of a forgotten backyard for the dominant Assamese who are not native to this area, being plainspeople of the Brahmaputra and Barak valleys. The latter is, however, dominated by ethnic Bengalis of East Pakistan origins.

The Dimasas are an indigenous people of Assam and due to the tribulations of history have their present day home in the North Cachar Hills District. There are also a few Dimasa villages in Karbi Anglong and Cachar Districts. Dimasa organized militancy started with the Dimasa National Security Force, but lacking fizzle, its members surrendered en masse to the government. Subsequently, the Dima Halam Daogah (DHD) was formed in 1995, which is still a force to be reckoned with today.

The DHD is premised on the ideology of carving out a separate Dimasa homeland "Dimaraji Kingdom" comprising the Dimasa inhabited areas of North Cachar Hills, Karbi Anglong, parts of Nowgaon district, and parts of Dimapur district of Nagaland. However, internal dissensions have led to the DHD's split into two outfits, one led by 'commander' Dilip Nunisa and the other by 'former commander' Jewel Gorlosa. The latter group has an alias, 'The Black Widow'. The other most dominant militant group is the United Peoples Democratic Solidarity (UPDS) of Karbi Anglong. Formed in 1999, the UPDS is a rebel group fighting for a separate Karbi homeland outside of Assam. The two insurgent groups have been engaged in a bitter turf battle for years, with violent clashes killing hundreds and rendering many more homeless in the villages dotting the hilly terrain of the two districts.

According to a report by the Asian Centre for Human Rights, as a result of the ongoing conflict, nearly 44,016 ethnic Karbis and Dimasas have been displaced till October 2005 in Karbi Anglong, North Cachar Hills and Hojai sub-division of Nowgaon district. What makes matters worse is that these two groups lay claim to the same piece of land, especially in the Karbi Anglong district, which is largely dominated by the

Karbi tribe. The Government of India had entered into a cease-fire with the UPDS effective from August 1, 2002, extended periodically till July 31, 2007, and with the DHD since January 1, 2003, extended periodically till December 31, 2006. However, violence broke out on September 26, 2005 when three Dimasa autorickshaw drivers were murdered at Tissom village near Diphu, the district headquarters of Karbi Anglong.

In retaliation, five members of a Karbi family were killed at Hemari Terang village on October 2, 2005. Such retaliatory attacks continued throughout the later part of 2005. Most gruesome was the killing of 34 Karbi villagers on October 17, 2005 in Doyangmukh village of Karbi Anglong district. The DHD and UPDS rebels also set fire to 50 houses in the village. In this context, the villagers expressed anguish that they are increasingly becoming victims of armed clashes between the two rebel groups to neither of which they extend support nor have ethnic affinity.

The anti-talk faction of the DHD, the Gorlosa faction, carried out an ambush in the North Cachar Hills on a railway team in October 2006, killing 11 persons, including seven Railway Protection Special Force (RPSF) personnel. Earlier in February 2006, 30 cadres of the Hmar People's Convention (Democratic) entered the North Cachar Hills from Manipur and set up camp in Jinam Valley, 80 km southeast of Haflong, the district headquarters. In connivance with the Hmar People's Convention, the Gorlosa faction made an attempt on the life of Dilip Nunisa, leader of the pro-talk DHD.

The repeated killings of members of so-called rival ethnic groups are gradually vitiating the cordial atmosphere of concord that had existed between the two communities in the not too distant past. As usual, the state authorities are being taken unawares by the spate of violence and appear to be lacking the logistical requisites to launch a rescue and relief operation. The inaccessible nature of the terrain, crisscrossed by hills and rivers and dense forest, demands a counter-force equipped with sophisticated skills of mountain warfare in countering such hill-based ethnic insurgencies. Moreover, besides being a law and order problem, the conflict is between two ethnic rebel groups inhabiting a contiguous landscape. This requires a more sensitive approach rather than purely "hard core" policing measures.

The government could tap into well-established bodies like the organisations for Dimasa and Karbi women. In tribal societies, women have a major role to play in the overall decision making of the village. (Manipur and Nagaland are good examples of women's role in conflict resolution and management). The State as well as district administration could hold meetings with other active civil society groups in these areas to find realistic ways of dealing with the growing crisis. Basic facilities like roadways, hospitals, schools and water supply could be improved to bring about a steep drop in people's hardships and ease up a hard hill life. It is not true to say that resources at the districts' disposal for development activities are meagre.

A cursory glance at funds earmarked for these two hill districts in the Assam State treasury would reveal that they are more than sufficient to establish a "good enough" base for developmental purposes. For instance, under the Hill Areas Development Programme (HADP) of the Planning Commission, Assam was allocated ₹51.11 crores in 2003-04 and 2004-05 for the development of its two hill districts. Political parties do not help matters much either, with the Congress, the Asom Gana Parishad, and the Bharatiya Janata Party blaming each other for the volatile situation. These parties are clueless in finding a solution to the problem.

The primary fear expressed in policy and security circles is the growing prowess of the DHD (Gorlosa faction) and the rapid spread of its activities across the landscape of North Cachar Hills and Karbi Anglong. Given the fact that the cadres are mostly young men from the area, their understanding of the local terrain is intrinsic and therefore crucial in carrying out sudden surprise strikes. Perhaps, this local intelligence skill is equipping the DHD faction with the ability to outmanoeuvre the security forces. Growing nexus with larger insurgent groups like the National Socialist Council of Nagalim (IM) is also providing the DHD, especially the Gorlosa faction, with strategic and tactical guidelines, weapons and finance from across the border. New Delhi's lacklustre approach in rising up to the challenge of small insurgent groups is also becoming an obstacle in applying time-tested solutions to such crises.

The pro-talk DHD faction chief, Dilip Nunisa, is threatening to pick up the gun again as his security related proposals to the Home Ministry are yet to invoke any meaningful response. The group's deputy commander-in-chief, Nairing Daulagupu, was badly wounded in Haflong by the Gorlosa faction in April 2006. The last peace talks with the Nunisa group were held in January 2006 and the group's demand for more security cover has not been met yet. The dynamics of the situation is a struggle to gain dominance with the objective of establishing a totalitarian, ethnically slanted future political domain in the two hill districts. This has degenerated into a free for all pattern of deadly strikes and retaliation between the two dominant peoples, namely the Karbis and Dimasas, with the other smaller groups also being drawn into the conflict. The other major point of conflict is the bloody feud between the DHD factions. What is also frightening is the discernible NSCN-IM influence on the DHD's ideology of territorial claim in Karbi Anglong. Very much like the NSCN-IM's aspiration for a greater Nagalim, contested narratives of territory and tribal affiliation notwithstanding, the DHD Gorlosa faction is laying claim to typically Karbi dominated areas that have only a sprinkling of Dimasa villages. This is a deadly recipe for greater violence and ethnic discord.

As the law and order authority, the government has to contain the situation by clearly mapping the territories/peoples under consideration in any talks with these outfits. Dimasa land has to be clearly demarcated from Karbi land to discourage any extra-territorial claims. Out of area Dimasa villages could be integrated within a "Dimasa Tribal Council" very much on the lines of the indigenous peoples of the Americas, Australia and New Zealand. This arrangement would apply to Dimasas in both Karbi Anglong and Cachar districts. Overlapping/clashing jurisdictions have to be worked out parallel to successful models elsewhere. All claims/counter claims have to be ironed out through talks. The immediate ground measure would however be a strong military presence to discourage ethnic cleansing. This would also create conditions for enforcement of cease-fire ground rules especially in keeping the cadres of the UPDS and DHD in designated camps as agreed under the cease-fire agreements.

It would also be beneficial to the affected communities if the Assam government were to set up an institutional mechanism to monitor the cease-fire on a "round the clock" basis and keep a vigilant count on internally displaced persons. Intelligence gathering by a mountain trained and combat hardened military team is crucial for early warning and assessment of probable strike areas in an otherwise densely forested region. For this to happen in an effective and efficient manner, it is crucial to recruit local youths who inherently possess a deep understanding of the terrain. Also, the government would then have the doubly more important security task of protecting the villages and families from where these youths are recruited into the intelligence team, to avoid possible retaliation by rebel groups.

Though the task appears to be of a tall order, it is not impossible to achieve. There are many unemployed youths, who, if guided and trained well, would be an asset to the Indian military in these 'special' combat operations. Once security is ensured, more substantive measures of economic development and social harmony should be instilled by a well thought out and planned peace process. This must account for the complex ethnic dynamics. A sound rehabilitation package, which not only provides for reconstruction of destroyed houses, compensation for lost properties and food but also securing the affected areas must be set in place. The Indian state must be viewed by the local communities as a "welfare organism" motivated by a democratic ethos rather than one of a military nature, an image omnipresent in these hill areas on account of the frequent highly visible counter-insurgency operations.

These remote hill villages must come to look upon the 'idea of India' as one of their own, in which they have high stakes. Time is short. The government needs to act fast, with vision and fortitude and determination. If not, the danger of violent insurgencies spreading its network to even smaller tribes in Assam appears all but inevitable.

CONCLUSION

The month-long violence may have subsided in the hills of Assams Karbi Anglong district, but thousands of tribal people displaced in its wake would have to devote lot of time to rebuild their lives. Even if the situation stabilizes it will take months to instill confidence among the thousands of tribesmen staying in relief camps to return to their homes. Luckily for the state government, the feud has remained strictly between the Dimasa and the Karbi communities.

The violence in Karby Anglong has highlighted the problems of administering the district. It has also pointed out the inherent lacuna in the whole concept of the ceasefire because of which both the militant groups DHD and the UPDS could cause such violence. The dynamics of ethnic clash and of militancy in the Northeast have always been treated piecemeal. Probably, now its time to treat the problems of the region in a holistic manner.

5

Bodo Problem in Assam

WHAT IS BODOLAND

Bodoland is an area located in the north bank of Brahmaputra river in the state of Assam in north east region of India, by the foothills of Bhutan and Arunachal Pradesh; inhabited predominantly byBodo language speaking ethnic group. Currently the hypothetical map of Bodoland includes the Bodoland Territorial Areas District (BTAD) administered by the non-autonomous Bodoland Territorial Council (BTC). The map of Bodoland overlaps with the districts of Kokrajhar, Baksa,Chirang and Udalguri in the state of Assam. At present, Kokrajhar serves as the capital of Bodoland.

BODOLAND MOVEMENT

Demand for a Homeland, Called Bodoland

The early history of Bodos is largely unknown. By definition, Bodos do not display any tribal culture and they do not participate any tribal rituals, *i.e.* they do not live in caves or jungles or go hunting wild animals. For centuries majority Bodos remained as farmers, cultivators, and peace loving society. Like many cultures in the world today, Bodos are also ethnocentric or nationalist society.

Cultural assimilation withAssamese was not productive. In brief, before the British Raj, Bodo-kachari Kingdom may have included a vast area extending far and beyondAssam, a small province in the North-East India. History suggest that Dimapur was the capital of Bodo-Kachari kingdom (Dimasa Kachari kingdom and not Bodo Kachari Kingdom).

The British-India colonial rulers effectively adapted divide and rule policy for over 300 years. It is likely that Bodo-Kachari were lagging behind their fellow Indians in terms of education and employability. Since the time of British Raj, Assamis known to produce oil and natural gas, and Assam tea. Before independence (1947), North-East India was a remote place.

Compared to other parts of India, such as West Bengal and Maharastra, education came to North East India only after Indian independence (1947). Following Indian independence, the Bodos were given opportunity to take advantage of scheduled tribe (ST) status. This process lead to the creation of tribal belts and blocks, protected lands meant for farming and grazing, specifically for the Bodo people. However, the list of ST in Assam continues to grow. There are a sizable number of Assamese who are claim ST or SC status.

PLAINS TRIBALS COUNCIL OF ASSAM

In the early 1960's the Plains Tribals Council of Assam (PTCA), a political party representing Bodos and other plains tribals of Assam realised that tribal belts and blocks were gradually being acquired by rich landlords or new immigrants through illegal means.

Moreover, Bodos had little or no access to economic aid that were given by the central government. Without economic package to the Bodo dominated areas, education was a distant cry. In those days, there were hardly any roads that connected Bodo dominated area to the main cities ofAssam. These were several reasons for which, in 1967, PTCA demanded a Union Territory called Udayachal, to be carved out of Assam.

The proposed Udayachal map included mainly those areas that was known as tribal belts and blocks. The creation of tribal belts and blocks (for scheduled-tribes) was a mechanism to protect farming and grazing lands mainly from rich landlord and illegal immigrants.

The demand for Udayachal never materialized. Many government came and gone, players changed and so did the game. By the end of 70's it became clear that Bodos had a little or no influence in the Indian political process. Specifically, in

Assam Bodos areas were neglected. Neglects included diverting and misuse of tribal-plan funds. For similar reasons, Khasis and Garos, carved out Meghalaya from Assam.

In the late 80's, All Bodo Students' Union's (ABSU) became very concerned about decades of neglects. ABSU and Bodo political parties jointly moved and demanded a separate state, called Bodoland.

However their ultimate goal is to become an indistinguishable part of India. They equally want to contribute in the development of their nation.

ALL BODO STUDENTS' UNION (ABSU)

The official Bodoland Movement for an independent state of Bodoland started on March 2, 1987 under the leadership of Upendranath Brahma of the All Bodo Students' Union (ABSU). The ABSU created a political organization, the Bodo Peoples' Action Committee (BPAC), to spearhead the movement. The ABSU/BPAC movement began with the slogan "Divide Assam 50-50".The ABSU/BPAC leadership of the movement ended with the bipartite Bodo Accord of February 20, 1993 and the creation of the BAC. The accord soon collapsed amidst a vertical split in ABSU and other Bodo political parties brought about mainly by the split between S K Bwiswmuthiary and Premsingh Brahma, and violence erupted in Bodo areas leading to a displacement of over 70,000 people. GUWAHATI, APRIL 2: The Assam government today notified the Bodo Autonomous Council (BAC) area with the inclusion of a large number of tribal belts and blocks falling in the Bodo inhabited districts. A number of villages which have less than 50 per cent tribal population have been included in the BAC, accommodating the demands of the Bodo groups to the maximum possible extent.

Case pending in the High Court, whose interim order had prohibited inclusion of villages with less than 50 per cent tribal population in the BAC, had been withdrawn by the petitioner.

Subsequent to the withdrawal, the state government has notified the boundary with 2941 villages in the BAC area as against 2682 notified already.

BODO STUDENTS PLIGHTS

Even after independence, for several decades, higher education was out of reach for most Bodos. Universities and higher educational institutes are located in far away places such as Gauhati (now called Guwahati), Shillong, or Dibrugarh. Moreover, year after year majority Bodo students were not admitted to some of the best educational institutes in Assam like Cotton College, Assam Agricultural University,Assam Engineering College and Gauhati University. In addition, even after obtaining a college degree, Bodos had limited or no job opportunities. These reasons fueled disappointments among Bodo students. Although, Bodos were given ST quota, most of those jobs or opportunities went unfilled.

Every office in Assam were filled with Assamese speaking folks, from officers down to peons. Creating easier educational opportunities for Bodos became first goal for ABSU. When the All Assam Students Union's (AASU) agitation to drive out illegal immigrants (year 1979-85) was slowing down, the demand for a separate state called the Bodoland was gaining momentum. The demand solely depends on the so-called equal rights for everyone as described in constitution of India. Despite the Bodo accord, neglects remain, no economic parity is apparent. Lately, there are a few signs of efforts to improve these situations. However, there are thousands of people still languishing in refugee camps including Bodos and non-Bodos. Their lives have been disrupted several times in last two decades. Although, a few dozen single lane roads have been repaired in last few years, while hundreds of bridges remain in poor condition. Once in while, The Assam Tribune has been reporting those neglects. The national highway is in the process of expansion. Whether the BTC addressed the issues of Bodo self-determination is still an open question.

BODO ACCORD:A FAREWELL TO ARMS EMBRACING PEACE WITH DEVELOPMENT AND JUSTICE

On December 7, 2003, amid tumult, excitement and delight, a large gathering watched history being made at

Kokrajhar. On that crisp winter morning, as Bodo musicians played the flute and dhol and brightly as attired young women swayed to the rhythm of traditional dances, Deputy Prime Minister L.K. Advani watched the swearing in of the interim Executive Council of the Bodoland Territorial Council in Assam. Sri Advani has especially flown in for the occasion after Bodo Liberation Tiger (BLT) leaders baid a farewell to arms and cemented a negotiated settlement with the Government of India by committing themselves to a democratic way of life. Sri Advani called on other militant groups especially the United Liberation Front of Asom (ULFA) and the National Democratic Front of Bodoland (NDFB) to follow the example ste by the BLT, which had renounced violence and embraced peace with justice and development through a democratic process. The meeting was attended by Dr. C. P. Thakur, Minister, DoNER, Sri Tarun Gogoi, Chief Minister of Assam and Governor of Assam, LT. Gen (Rtd) Ajai Singh.

The Previous day, December 6, 2003 had witnessed another significant event when more than 2600 BLT militants bid farewell to arms and surrendered their weapons at a public function at Kokrajhar. The militants shed their camouflage uniforms and laid down their AK-47 rifles as they left the path of confrontation and violence, from an uncertain life in the jungles to a return home, where they can take up productive work without fear or favour. The Governor and Chief Minister of Assam as well as Sri Swami Chinmayanand, Minister of State for Home were present.

During his visit, the Deputy Prime Minister laid the foundation stone of a Central Institute of Technology (CIT) and emphasized the need to tackle the huge infrastructure needs in the area. Addressing the rally, Sri Advani assured the Bodos that the Centre was committed to the economic development of their areas as well as the entire North East, which lags behind other regions. In a step aimed at bridging infrastructure gaps, he announced the setting up of a 100 bedded hospital and nursing college for the Bodoland Territorial Autonomous District (BTAD). The Bodo Liberation tigers, formed on June 18, 1996—had earlier pledged to fight for a separate state out of Assam, but within the Indian Union, through an armed struggle. The demand for s separate state for Bodos was launched for the first time in 1986 by the All Bodo Students Union (ABSU) which culminated in the Bodo accord in 1993, after much social unrest, violence and disruption.

The 1993 accord led to the creation of the Bodoland Autonomous Council (BAC). However, BAC failed to fully meet the aspirations of Bodos and ABSU again lunched an agitation denouncing the accord and demanding creation of a separate state. The BLT also indulged in a few acts of violence during this period. But these difficulties did not deter the National Democratic Alliance government at the Centre from making fresh efforts to settle the Bodo issue. The Government of India kept all its channels of informal talks open with the BLT. After years of struggle, the BLT unilaterally decided to suspend its armed operations on July 14, 1999 and agreed to negotiate with the Government of India. This is an example to other underground groups in the region. Those seeking to improve the lives of their people through armed struggles should realise that this path cannot succeed. The conditions of people can be best improved in times of peace, leading to stability and development.

The BLT gave up its demand for a separate state and settled for the extension of the Sixth Schedule Status to the Bodo areas, which empowers them with rights over land, ensures protection of their traditions and ethnic identity and also enables them to govern themselves. The BTAD is an outcome of a growing understanding that political goals must be realistic and that peace and development must take precedence over emotions.

With their practical approach to a complex problem, the Bodos have shown the way forward to other militant groups in the North East, which are directionless and disruptive. But the road to the settlement was challenging and long. Representatives of the Government of India, Government of Assam and BLT held not less than 30 rounds of tripartite talks between March 2000 and February 2003 before finalizing an accord. The commitment from the Home Ministry was simple and clear: ensure the territorial integrity of the country and at the same time bring peace and development to a neglected region.

The Memorandum of Settlement signed between the Government of India, the Government of Assam and the BLT on February 10, 2003, was a path-breaking event, which seeks to assure all ethnic groups of development, equality, security and growth with stability. All major Bodo organizations including ABSU, Bodo Sahitya Sabha and All Bodo Women Welfare Federation extended their whole hearted support to the accord with the BLT. Perhaps not since 1986, when the Mizo Accord was signed between the Government of India and the Mizo National Front, has the troubled North East witnessed such a potential turning point. The Mizoram accord brought peace to Mizoram after decades of conflict and it remains one of the most peaceful states of the country.

The latest Bodo accord brings the promise of a lasting peace in the Bodo areas and to a larger extent across the Assam Valley. Its impact in other sttes should also not be ruled out for a major group h as shown that power flows from political wisdom and realism, not just from the barrel of a gun or through angry rhetoric.

SALIENT FEATURES OF MEMORANDUM OF SETTLEMENT AND PRIORITIES

The Memorandum of Settlement aims at fulfilling the economic, educational and linguistic aspirations of the Bodos, preservation of land rights, socio-cultural and ethnic identity of the Bodos and to speed up the infrastructure development in the areas under the BTC. In pursuance of MoS, an autonomous district known as the Bodoland Territorial Areas Disrict (BTAD) has been constituted under the Sixth Schedule of the Constitution of India. Its jurisdiction extends over 8,970 sq.kms covering the four district of Kokrajhar, Udalguri, Baska and Chirang.

The Bodoland Territorial Council will have legislative, administrative, executive and financial powers over 40 subjects. A major thrust has been given to the economic development of Bodoland to take forward the Central Government's agenda for peace and development in the region. Government of India is committed to provide additional assistance of Rs 500 crore over a period of five years, *i.e.* Rs 100 crore per annum, for developmental projects. One-time financial assistance to the BTAD is al envisaged for creation of infrastructure for the BTC secretariat and at the district, sub-division and block levels.

The centrally funded Central Institute OF technology, Which Was Inaugurated By The Deputy Prime Minister of 7th December, will provide diploma sources in the information technology, bio-technology, horticulture and food processing, computer programming and business management, enabling the development of better technical skills in the region. This is expected to help generate employment opportunities among the youth of BTAD in particular and Assam, in general. The Institute will functioning from 2004. The government is also committed to the inclusion of the Bodo language in the Eighth Schedule. The bill in the regard has already been introduced in the parliament.

The Government is equally committed to the empowerment of the Bodos as also the protection of the existing rights including land rights and privileges of the non-tribals in the BTAD. An amendment has already been carried out to article 332(6) of the Constitution to provide that the existing representation of scheduled tribes and non-scheduled tribes from the Bodoland territory in the state assembly will be maintained. Bodo leaders have also given assurance that the BTC will work and govern without bias or discrimination. The rehabilitation of surrendered BLT cadres is also being given high priority by the Government of India and the stage government. Eligible Bodo youth may be recruited into the police, army and paramilitary forces. They will also be provided with technical training through institutions like CIT to facilitate self-employment.

6

United Liberation Front of Assam

UNITED LIBERATION FRONT OF ASSAM

It is a separatist group from Assam, among many other such groups in North-East India. It seeks to establish a sovereign Assam via an armed struggle in the Assam Conflict. The Government of India banned the organization in 1990 and classifies it as a terrorist group, while the US State Department lists it under "Other groups of concern". ULFA claims to have been founded at the site of Rang Ghar on April 7, 1979, a historic structure from the Ahom kingdom. According to Sunil Nath, the ULFA established its relationships with Nationalist Socialist Council of Nagaland (NSCN) in 1983 and with KIA, operating in Burma, in 1987. It initiated major violent activities in 1990. Military operations against it by the Indian Army that began in 1990 continues till present. In the past two decades some 10,000 people have died in the clash between the rebels and the government. On December 5, 2009, the Chairman and the deputy commander-in-chief of ULFA fell into Indian custody.

There has recently been a large ULFA crackdown in Bangladesh, which has significantly assisted the government of India in bringing ULFA leaders to talks. In January 2010, ULFA softened its stand and dropped the demand for independence as a condition for talks with the Government of India.

The major leaders of the organisation are:

- Paresh Baruah (Commander-in-Chief)
- Arabinda Rajkhowa (Chairman) (released from

Government of Assam custody on January 1, 2011)
- Pradip Gogoi (Vice-Chairman) (released on bail from Government of Assam custody)
- Anup Chetia (General Secretary) (in Government of Bangladesh custody)
- Raju Barua (Deputy Commander-in-Chief) (Released on bail from Government of Assam custody)
- Sashadhar Coudhury (Foreign Secretary) (in Jail custody of Government of Assam)

HISTORY

The ULFA was started when the All Assam Students' Organization reached a high for its xenophobia of all foreigners in 1979. The founders included Paresh Baruah, Arabinda Rajkhowa, Anup Chetia, Pradip Gogoi and Bhadreshwar Gohain on 7 April 1979. It was formed at the Ahom King in Sibsagar to ensue upon an armed struggle to form a Socialist Assam. Recruiting for the front did not begin until 1983. Soon after it finished recruitment in 1984, it began to seek out training and arms procurement from other groups such as the Kachin Independence Army(KIA) and the Nationalist Socialist Council of Nagaland(NSCN). In 1986 it launched a fund raising "campaign" across India by way of extortion. It then began to set up camps in Tinsukia and Dibrugarh but was soon banned by New Delhi on November 7, under the Unlawful Activities (Prevention) Act of 1967.

Starting in the early 1990s, ULFA launched an aggressive campaign with victims such as security forces, political opponents, and blasting rail links. In July 1991 the front captured and held 14 people for ransom, included in the abductees was an engineer and a national of the Soviet Union. From the 1990s on the ULFA have continued to carry out terrorist attacks.

THE SECESSIONIST INSURGENCY

Though the Assamese speaking indigenous people of the State, known by the generic name of Assamese, are not the only ethnic constituency in India to have a secessionist group, it is the largest among ethnic groups in the country which have rebel elements practising armed activities for avowedly secessionist goals.

The Government of India (GOI) has shown remarkable flexibility in dealing with secessionist outfits elsewhere—the five-year old cease-fire with the National Socialist Council of Nagaland–Isak-Muivah (NSCN-IM), which is yet to renounce secessionism, being the most glaring and geographically proximate example in the context of Assam. By contrast, the proposal for so-called talks with the United Liberation Front of Asom (ULFA)—an organisation whose activities have kept the security forces engaged in the State since 1990—though much desired by the Assamese, has received only lukewarm response from the Union Ministry of Home Affairs (MHA).

Consequently, the popular perception, presently, is that the GOI is not really interested in solving the problems of Assam, echoing the old, though disputable, refrain of the Centre's 'step-motherly attitude' towards the State. While the MHA might have its own reasons for its apparent intransigence, the continuance of this perception is succeeding in deepening the feeling of alienation amongst the Assamese *vis-à-vis* Delhi. In this context, the old adage 'justice should also appear to be done' may be worth noting.

Contrary to the secessionist movements among some tribes and nationalities in the Northeast since the emergence of independent India, Assam is a late entrant to the arena of separatism. Despite appeals by the then leadership of the Naga secessionists, the Assamese, on the whole, with odd exceptions only proving the general rule, remained quite satisfied and optimistic about their Indian citizenship in the early decades of independence. In fact, Partition, conceived as a necessary evil in other parts of India, was seen as much-sought-after relief because, with the ceding of Sylhet to erstwhile East Pakistan, the Assamese gained a comfortable dominance over the affairs of the State by virtue of their newfound relative majority in the post-Partition demography of Assam.

Though the ULFA was founded on April 7, 1979, it came to be noticed as a nascent-armed organisation only in late 1983, when it commenced a series of political assassinations and audacious bank robberies, often abortive. Following the bulldozing through of elections to the State Legislative Assembly by the then Prime Minister, Indira Gandhi, in spring 1983, secessionist sentiments were rising amongst the normally timid Assamese.

Though quite a few secessionist insurgent outfits appeared on the scene in Assam at this stage, only ULFA survived the Assam Accord signed between the GOI and the Assamese nationalist leaders of the famous or notorious (as the perspective might be) Assam Agitation against unabated and unchecked illegal immigration from the erstwhile East Pakistan and present-day Bangladesh. Other linguistic ethnic groups in Assam have since sprouted their own secessionist-insurgent organisations like the National Democratic Front of Bodoland (NDFB) among the Bodos, United People's Democratic Solidarity (UPDS) among the Karbis and Dima Halim Daoga (DHD) among the Dimasas.

Nevertheless, for the Assamese—the single largest linguistic group in Assam—the ULFA remains the most serious issue. Irrespective of the level of activity of ULFA, not a single week goes by in Assam without the demand being made in one or the other widely circulated Assamese dailies for the GOI to negotiate a settlement with ULFA. It is also to be noticed that, though the ULFA has come up with some uncompromising pre-conditions for negotiations with the GOI, the basic thrust of most of the local commentators, including some leading Assamese intellectuals, is towards the GOI accepting the pre-conditions rather than of ULFA withdrawing them. Till a few years ago, criticising the ULFA was an assured means of earning unpopularity in Assam.

Statistically speaking, the ULFA does not possess the lethality that other insurgent groups in India have. Its armed activities are, in general, more in the nature of selective assassinations and acts of sabotage against State-owned economic assets like the oil pipeline, rather than aimless terror tactics. Of course, it is known that ULFA did carry out some typical terrorist attacks against the Hindi-speaking people of

Assam in year 2000. Though a hitherto unknown group calling itself the Assam Tiger Force claimed responsibility for the attacks, the State government and a large section of the people of Assam believe that the attacks were carried out by the ULFA, albeit clandestinely. The number of deaths resulting from attacks by the ULFA is quite low compared to some other insurgencies. The importance of ULFA lies, rather, in the sympathy it gets from the Assamese or, as M.S. Prabhakara expresses it, "ULFA is a state of mind in Assam."

Though the strength of ULFA lies more in the sympathy factor it gets among its home-population (despite lack of empathy for its declared goal) than in cadres and weapons, it is believed to have a cadre-strength of around 5,000 trained insurgents and, according to Indian intelligence agency reports, possesses thrice the number of weapons suitable for guerrilla activities. Continued operations against ULFA by the security forces (SFs) since December 1990 have contained the firepower of ULFA. According to government claims, till date, more than 8,000 ULFA cadres have surrendered. However, the recruitment of ULFA has also continued unabated. Furthermore, ULFA remains an influential factor in the electoral politics of Assam.

Following deliberated strategies, ULFA has extended selective and conditional support to different political parties alternately, or rather, has attacked selected political parties and candidates, thereby restricting the activities of the target party's workers during election campaigns to subvert its poll prospects, thus increasing the comparative advantage of its favoured political party or candidates.

Political parties have, more often than not, fallen prey to ULFA's tactics, unable to resist the temptation of securing the tacit support of the insurgents. ULFA has been able to regularly influence electoral outcomes since 1991. This has led to a periodical breakdown of morale amongst the State police, who are sometimes unsure of their political bosses' inclination towards curbing insurgency. The recurring phenomenon of newly elected State governments going soft on the insurgents has been quite visible in Assam. The invisible but strongly felt power of ULFA to further or hamper individual political careers has often made politicians hostage to ULFA. Similar pressures are also experienced among the local intelligentsia.

This unhealthy trend is destroying the democratic atmosphere of Assam and such destruction renders the ground more fertile for insurgency, with the resultant stultifying affect is gradually making important issues like large-scale corruption to be non-issues. ULFA's importance lies more in its all-pervasive effect on the Assamese society than in its immediate armed activities.

BYPASSING SEMANTICS

Before embarking on an attempt to analyse the insurgency related situation in Assam, one should be clear about what one means by these words. The semantics of non-state armed activity has remained a quagmire of conflicting and overlapping definitions. That is why the oft-repeated phrase that "one man's terrorist is another man's freedom-fighter" circulates. Xanana Gusmao, currently elected President of the newly formed state of East Timor, was a guerrilla commander.

He is not, quite justifiably, termed a terrorist by anybody now, but even while he was active in his earlier incarnation as commander of an armed secessionist-insurgent group, the sympathetic Western press did not use the term 'terrorist' for him. Yasser Arafat wears a military uniform and carries a pistol, but the anti-Israeli world does not term him a terrorist. For some, Ariel Sharon is the mad terrorist, while Yasser Arafat is a sinister terrorist leader for others. The subjectivity is starkly apparent. Moreover, the careless use of terminology by a section of the media and intelligentsia has created a veritable comedy of errors, which does not, however, lead to innocuous mirth. Rebels, militants, insurgents, terrorists are the words which have been used as freely interchangeable nomenclature for any arms wielding non-state group professing political goals.

The somewhat overlapping, generally accepted meanings of the words have also not been helpful. If the belief is upheld that proper analysis of a problem is a sure step towards its solution, then definitions should be unambiguously laid down beforehand.

As such, without going into pure semantics, it is useful to state what we understand by particular words in the present discussion:

- *Secessionism*: Desiring secession from a larger sovereign political entity, with the goal of creating a separate sovereign political entity for one's own people, as perceived. It should be noted that secessionism is not necessarily an armed activity. Examples include the ULFA, NSCN (both the factions), NDFB, Jammu and Kashmir Liberation Front (JKLF), Hizb-ul-Mujahideen (HM), etc. The left-wing extremist People's War Group (PWG) and Maoist Communist Centre (MCC), practising insurgency through armed struggle to install communism, would not fall under such a definition.
- *Insurgency*: Active rebellion against the state waged from the territory and population under the declared control of the particular State. Very often, but not necessarily, armed.
  Example: ULFA, NSCN, NDFB, JKLF, HM, PWG and MCC.
- *Armed struggle*: Using collective armed activity as means to an end, normally, but not necessarily, political.
  Example: All organisations in the above-mentioned examples.
- *Guerrilla activities*: Armed activity against enemy combatants and utilities. It should be noted that guerrillas generally hit selected targets only. Though the same armed insurgent individual guerrilla or guerrilla group may practice terrorist tactics simultaneously, guerrilla activities and terrorist activities differ in the matter of targets and methodology. State armed forces may also use guerrilla tactics and often do in counter-insurgency campaigns.
  Example: NSCN, to a certain extent ULFA and NDFB.

- *Terrorism*: Armed activity generally carried out against unexpected and unprepared non-combatants not directly involved with the conflict, instilling a sense of terror among a targeted population, to stimulate coercion. The intentions of spreading fear being given priority over the objective qualification of the targets as the enemy. Armed insurgents tend to adopt terrorist tactics, thereby becoming terrorists, when losing and on the run. The scrupulous guerrilla becoming a terrorist and using terror tactics is an oft-repeated phenomenon. So are the phenomena of state forces using terrorist tactics in counter-insurgency campaigns to subdue populations perceived to be sympathetic to the rebels.
  Example: HM, Lashkar-e-Toiba (LeT) are non-state examples. The killings of some relatives of ULFA members are examples of pro-state terrorism.17

HISTORICAL BACKGROUND

For those who are not acquainted with the history of Assam, a brief note on the relevant historical factors, which have contributed to the evolution of the present demographic scenario of the State, might be of use to follow the analysis and argument.

In 1826, the colonial East India Company annexed the erstwhile Ahom kingdom of 'upper' Assam, *i.e.* the eastern part of Assam, starting from Nagaon to the Naga foothills. 'Lower' Assam, from the western boundary of the Ahom kingdom to the north eastern frontier of the then British province of Bengal was already under British control following a transfer of power by the erstwhile Mughal rulers.

Initially, Robert Clive, the British officer responsible for this expansion of the colonial domain, faced disapproval by the Board of Directors of the Company, as the then famine stricken and sparsely populated Brahmaputra valley did not yield enough revenue to cover the administrative costs of retaining the expansion. Quite soon, however, the British stumbled on tea and oil in the Brahmaputra valley and realised the need for labour in order to exploit the natural bounty of the land. The local Assamese were an easy-going lot contented with the cultivated bounty of the fertile valley. The British entrepreneurs embarked on a policy of actively encouraging landless peasants of the neighbouring populous province of Bengal to migrate and settle in the Brahmaputra valley. Tribals from the Chotanagpur plateau and other parts of India were enticed and often forced to come to Assam to work as labourers in the newly grown tea gardens of Assam.

The flurry of economic activity led to the laying down of railway lines in far-off corners of the province. The arrival of the poor Bengali peasants and tribal labourers was of no concern to the rising Assamese middle-class deliberately patronised by the British to counter-act the influence of the erstwhile ruling feudal class of Ahom nobility. Bengali petty officers and clerks, disparagingly called 'Babus' by the British, were the immediate rivals for the residuary scraps of the colonial administration open to the 'natives' for grabs.

The British adopted cautious neutrality in the tussle between the Bengali Babus and the Assamese middle-class in pursuance of their notorious policy of 'divide and rule'. Christian missionaries, on the other hand, actively helped the Assamese nationalists in establishing the unique credentials of Assamese language, initially replaced by Bengali language in the courts and offices till 1872.

The fond hope of the missionaries of spreading Christianity amongst the Assamese were, however, belied due to the strong influence of the 15 century neo-Vaisnavism prevalent among the Assamese, and the missionaries gradually moved on to greener pastures among the tribes of adjacent hills, where success did not elude them.

The rivalry between the Assamese and Bengali middle class continues till date, but the bitter antagonism between the two neighbouring nations has not led to violent clashes since 1983, bringing to an end, it is hoped, the occurrence of violent clashes between the two linguistic communities.

While the immigrants, goaded on by the colonial British, continued to arrive in Assam, the indigenous people ignored this movement since the then-sparsely populated Brahmaputra valley could easily absorb the newcomers. However, the locals started taking adverse notice of the ubiquitous migrant settlements when availability of fallow land diminished noticeably. In their perception, the lack of easy availability of fallow land, crucial for the required expansion of agriculture and grazing of livestock, was related to the ever-increasing number of immigrants.

By the 1920s, the Provincial Council reverberated with heated debates on the issue between Assamese leaders (most of them Hindus) and Bengali leaders (predominantly Muslim). Nearly all the migrant peasants from Bengal were Muslims, naturally because Muslim peasants were the most destitute segment of the teeming population of land-starved Bengal.

The rise of the Muslim League in contemporary Indian politics galvanized the migrant Muslim peasants, who rallied around a charismatic, though rustic, leader called Maulana Bhasani. The decade preceding the advent of Indian Independence was an uninterrupted political battle between the Muslim League's Sir Saidullah (scion of an indigenous Muslim family), propped up by Maulana Bhasani, and Gopinath Bordoloi, leader of the Assam Pradesh Congress, heading the Assamese nationalist camp, dominated by upper caste Hindus.

When Independence and Partition came simultaneously, Assam escaped being clubbed with East Pakistan by a whisker. The ultimate losers were Maulana Bhasani and his followers. Though the pre-dominantly Muslim district of Sylhet opted for Pakistan in a referendum, the Muslims of Brahmaputra valley were left in the Indian State of Assam, where Gopinath Bordoloi and his camp were the unchallenged ruling class by virtue of the new-found majority of the Assamese, after the populous district of Sylhet separated from India.

In fact, the Assamese leadership discreetly rejoiced after the result of the Sylhet referendum was declared. At this point of time, Maulana Bhasani, the influential leader of the Brahmaputra valley's Muslim migrants, announced a directive to his followers, which had a far-reaching effect on the demographic politics of Assam, and which is followed to this day. The Maulana, bitter at the desertion by the central leadership of the All India Muslim League, directed his followers to accept Assamese as their mother tongue, and to assimilate into the indigenous population of Assam. The Assamese middle classes, who were more wary of Hindu Bengali Babus than of the lowly Muslim peasants, accepted this overture, much to the chagrin of the Hindu Bengalis.

This demographic equation continued till the late nineteen seventies when a sudden discovery of a substantial number of names of illegal immigrants from the newly created Bangladesh in the voters' list led to a mass agitation against the immigrants. This led to a souring of relations between the migrant community and the Assamese mainstream.

The Muslim migrant community who had sought shelter under the Congress umbrella during Indira Gandhi's leadership felt jilted when Rajiv Gandhi reached an accord with the leaders of the agitation and practically allowed them a 'walk-over' to the seat of the State government. They formed their own political party and contested the elections as a separate block.

With the gradual erosion in the popularity of the agitation leadership after it became the ruling party, however, their threat perception was significantly toned down. The disaffection among the migrant community, however, seriously affected the numerical majority of the Assamese *vis-à-vis* the Bengali, with many migrants declaring Bengali as their mother language before the census enumerators. Jolted by the 1991 census, the Assamese nationalist camp rediscovered the virtues of the migrants, and deliberate efforts by a changed leadership of the socio-cultural apex body, the Assam Sahitya Sabha, has resulted in a renewed spate of amity between the two socio-political groups. The Assamese-Bengali relation, a constant cause of worry to administrators earlier, is going through a period of unprecedented calm. In fact, from all appearances, one is emboldened to presume that violent clashes between these two formerly antagonistic ethno-linguistic communities are a closed chapter.

The mitigation of traditional antagonisms, however, has been replaced by newly aroused tensions running along perceived ethnic lines. The latest in this series is the mutually irreconcilable stand taken by the Bodos and the Koch-Rajbongshis, both indigenous local ethnic entities, hitherto abiding in non-antagonistic relationships, over the issue of the formation of the Bodo Territorial Council (BTC) under a revised 6 Schedule of the Indian Constitution. While the ULFA goes on waging a secessionist rebellion for an independent Assam, most of the indigenous ethnic groups of Assam are demanding a separate autonomous territory, if not a separate state. The ULFA rejects these differences of interests among the indigenous people, by conveniently, but unconvincingly, claiming that these problems would be amicably sorted out after the attainment of sovereignty.

RISE AND GROWTH OF ULFA

As already stated, the Assamese had neither empathy nor sympathy for the secessionist insurgency launched by the Naga leadership immediately after the advent of independent India. The Assamese never fancied themselves to be any different from the other Indian citizens and States. Gradually, however, the feeling that the Union government is neglecting Assam gained currency after Assam was deprived of major industrial projects being set up by the Indian state to fulfil the Nehruvian vision.

It is a fact that the general perception among the policy makers of India was that the Northeast was not a safe place for major industrial ventures, given its proximity to quite a few foreign countries. The feeling of alienation of the Assamese gained strength following a grossly misunderstood speech by Jawaharlal Nehru, the then Prime Minister, when the Indian Army and the administration evacuated the Assamese town of Tezpur, retreating after a debacle at the hands of the invading Chinese.

The consolidation of this ambiguous feeling of alienation into full-blown secessionism was achieved by Jawaharlal Nehru's daughter, Indira Gandhi, when, as Prime Minister, she imposed State Assembly elections on the unwilling Assamese in 1983. In the context of the ongoing agitation, the demand of the Assamese was that the issue of illegal immigrants should be solved before holding any election in Assam, since elections would have the effect of legitimising the presence of the names of the illegal immigrants in the voters' list, thereby entitling them to citizenship.

Indira Gandhi, however, unleashed brute state power to go through the motions of holding a sham election, with unbelievably low voter turnout, particularly in Assamese dominated areas. The lack of a provision in the Indian Constitution stipulating a required minimum number of votes to win led to a State government duly coming into being. For all practical purposes, this government had no legitimacy in the minds of the vast number of Assamese, the largest ethno-linguistic group in Assam.

The Assamese, for the first time since Independence, had no say in the State's governance. Consequently, while the mature segments of Assamese society became vehemently anti-Congress, the youth rejected Indianness altogether. Suddenly, there was a spurt of secessionism in Assam, and a number of separatist outfits announced their appearance through petty violence. The mainstream of the anti-immigrant agitation was avowedly non-violent, officially subscribing to the Gandhian methodology of political mobilisation and protest. Though over-enthusiastic young supporters of the agitation sometimes engaged in stray violence, the same young men would also dutifully participate in non-violent agitation programmes like hunger strikes.

The 1983 elections changed all this. A section of the youth completely rejected non-violent methods of protest and dedicated themselves to preparation for armed struggle. The newfound secessionism and attraction of arms was a heady cocktail and attracted many otherwise-sobre and intelligent young men to a dangerous path. The mushrooming of secessionist outfits dedicated to armed guerrilla methods gradually consolidated into two comparatively well-organised outfits, the ULFA and the Assam People's Liberation Army

(APLA). The APLA was larger and better organised at first, and it concentrated on cadre-formation. ULFA, utilising its geographical advantage, gained from having most of its founder members from areas adjacent to the inter-State border with Nagaland, and established contact with the NSCN (then a united entity, before the subsequent split in April 1988).

The last days of the year 1983 witnessed the first batch of Assamese youth crossing the international boundary with Burma (now Myanmar), to receive training at the NSCN Head Quarters. The NSCN and the People's Liberation Army (PLA) of Manipur, another secessionist insurgent organisation sharing the NSCN camp, received the new rebels warmly. The hosts were aware of the immense advantage of friends in the largest State of the Northeast.

Most of the APLA leaders gave up the path of armed secession following the Assam Accord and installation of the Asom Gana Parishad (AGP) government under Prafulla Kumar Mahanta. In fact, the general feeling among the Assamese after the perceived victory of the agitation, with the agitation leadership controlling government, was that everybody should return to their normal lives. APLA vanished with the majority of its member returning home and a few obstinate ones joining the ULFA, which had declared that the Accord and the AGP government were of no consequence to their goal of a separate and sovereign Assamese state.

The ULFA leadership painstakingly mobilised recruits from different parts of Assam and kept sending fresh batch of trainees to the NSCN camp. Before the completion of two years of the AGP regime, considerable disillusionment had set in among the Assamese, with the inevitable unfulfillment of the unrealistically high hopes reposed on the agitation leaders turned politicians of the ruling AGP.

With rising disenchantment against the AGP regime, ULFA was able to regain some amount of public support and sympathy for their 'cause'. The year 1988 saw a spectacular rise in the popularity and influence of the ULFA amongst the Assamese. There was competition—at times bitter—between district and local committees tc send more recruits for training.

In the spring of 1987, the first batch of 80 selected ULFA cadres went to the Kachin State of Burma for advanced training under the Kachin Independent Army (KIA). KIA was a battle-hardened fighting force, engaged in a secessionist war with the Burmese government, and was experienced in the art of guerrilla fighting since the Second World War. The Kachin connection helped ULFA create a cadre of well-trained guerrilla fighters.

The State police and the para-military forces could not match the zeal of these trained young men. The AGP government, failing on all fronts, sought to reach a tacit understanding with the rebels, so that their own interests would not be harmed by the ULFA. The ill-concealed understanding between their political masters and the insurgents led to the further evaporation of the already depleted morale of the police.

With the government firmly keeping its eyes shut, the ULFA commenced 'implementing social reforms', such as the ban on consumption of alcohol, which made them popular amongst women. It is often said that, in the late nineteen eighties, the ULFA ran a parallel government in Assam. It would, however, be more appropriate to say that ULFA *was* the government in those days. The state of affairs, however, abruptly changed after the Union government dismissed the AGP government in the State, imposed President's Rule and commenced counter-insurgency operations by the Army in the last days of the year 1990.

Though elections to the State Legislative Assembly were held within six months, and a Congress government was installed, the Army stayed on. To cut a long story short, by 1992, the ULFA was on the run, with many cadres, including scores of district level leaders and a few central committee members surrendering before the government. In the immediate aftermath of the 1992 surrenders, ULFA appeared to be a spent force. It regained strength, however, to become a force to reckon with after a downswing that lasted no more than a couple of years. It has been forced to abandon its previous high-profile 'social-reform' activities, but has continuously engaged the security forces, primarily through hit and run tactics. The Assamese, who have had to face the brunt of unabated counter-insurgency operations through over a decade, now increasingly wish to see a negotiated settlement between ULFA and the GOI.

The romantic fascination for secessionist insurgency has all but evaporated. The quelling of the secessionist tendency by security forces, at times with brute force, has resulted in a sullen silence. Gradually, the initial attraction of the armed 'boys' was replaced by consternation at their obstinacy regarding a negotiated settlement. Furthermore, terrorist actions by ULFA have led to a further erosion of its already emaciated support base. The discernible turning point was the ULFA leadership's posture during the Kargil war in 1999. ULFA declared the Pakistani intruders in Kargil to be Kashmiri 'freedom fighters' and issued a call to Assamese men serving in the Indian Army to desist from fighting against them.

The timing could not have been more inauspicious for ULFA. While its leaders were siding with the Pakistanis, the dead body of Captain Jintu Gogoi, an Indian Army officer, killed during action in Kargil, was brought to Assam. Huge crowds of people gathered to pay their last respect to the brave soldier, and ULFA was publicly denounced for advocating support for the Pakistanis.

CURRENT SITUATION

The last State government, led by Prafulla Kumar Mahanta, started off by being openly soft towards the ULFA. Quite a few top-ranking ULFA cadres, who had been captured earlier and incarcerated, were released.

The honeymoon, however, did not last long, and towards mid-1998, the State government was waging a vicious counter-insurgency (CI) campaign against the ULFA with the help of Army and surrendered ULFA militants (SULFA). Till the change in the State government in spring 2001, three years of lethal CI operations had made a mess of ULFA's organisational structure and confidence. The multiple terrorist attacks on targets in the US on September 11, 2001, and their aftermath have further aggravated its woes, since no regime in the world is now willing to be seen as being soft towards armed non-state actors in the current scenario. The ULFA has been maintaining an unprecedented and uncharacteristically low profile for some time now. From the outward appearances of the present situation, it may be construed that a GOI initiative to negotiate a solution with the ULFA could well prove fruitful.

Unfortunately, appearances are often deceptive. Like most other rebel entities, ULFA too has the phoenix-like habit of rising anew from its ashes. According to reports, fresh recruitment by the ULFA is going on unabated. All its important leaders, barring Anup Chetia, the General Secretary, who is under-going a jail sentence in Bangladesh, are active. It is quite probable, moreover, that Chetia might be allowed to walk away and 'disappear' after completing his sentence, which is nearing its end.

Although the Assamese do not support or empathise with ULFA at present, tacit sympathy for the local 'boys' has not vanished completely. Though very few support the use of terror tactics by ULFA, there is a general feeling that ULFA's demand for sovereignty is understandable, given the unacceptable attitude of the Union government towards Assam. And if the ULFA has lost popularity amongst the Assamese, this does not mean that the GOI has won wide acceptability either. The CI operations of the last three years, while succeeding in debilitating the ULFA, have also, unfortunately but inevitably, sharpened the feeling of alienation amongst the common people through the use of counter-terror through 'secret killings', a term used in Assam to describe 'mysterious' lethal attacks on supporters and relatives of ULFA leaders and members.

Nearly 200 young men have 'disappeared' after being picked up by unrecognised persons, reportedly security forces concealing their identity, aided by the SULFA. The total difference in approach of the GOI towards Naga insurgents and the secessionist agenda in Assam, too, have not gone unnoticed. Though the scale is currently tilted in favour of the GOI, there is no guarantee that the *status quo* will be permanent. The most worrying probability is that of the transformation of ULFA into a purely terrorist outfit. At first glance, it might seem that the detachment of ULFA from the public is good for peace, but the experience in many parts of the world is that a purely terrorist outfit is a more sinister problem than an ethnic insurgency.

The difference between a dictator and a democratically elected leader answerable to the public is quite similar to the difference between a terrorist and an insurgent guerrilla. Whereas an insurgency cannot survive without popular support, a terrorist outfit does not depend on such support.

A handful of terrorists are enough to create chaos. Terrorism undermines democratic processes and vitiates the political atmosphere, bringing society to a virtual standstill. The resultant stagnation leads to disruption of economic activity leading to a chronic lack of development. With foreign bases and foreign friends, ULFA is in a position to carry out terrorist activities against the Indian state for an indefinite period. If MHA entertains the fond belief that the ULFA leadership may lose steam with the aging of the top leadership, it should also keep in mind that, with continuous recruitment to the ULFA cadre, fresh and young insurgents are coming up, who would be only too willing to step into the positions of an ageing leadership. Though the actors would change, the morbid saga would continue.

ULFA ACCORDING TO ITSELF

The ULFA is a "revolutionary political organization" engaged in a "liberation struggle" against state terrorism and economic exploitation by India for the establishment of a sovereign, independent Assam. It does not consider itself a secessionist organization, as it claims that Assam was never a part of India and as a matter of fact the Treaty of Yandaboo was signed in 1826 by General Sir Archibald Campbell on the British side, and by Governor of Legaing Maha Min Hla Kyaw Htin from the Burmese side. With the British army at Yandabo village, only 50 miles from the capital Ava, the Burmese were forced to accept the British terms without discussion.

According to the treaty, the Burmese agreed to:

- Cede to the British Assam, Manipur, Rakhine (Arakan), and Taninthayi (Tenasserim) coast south of Salween river,
- Cease all interference in Cachar and Jaintia,
- Pay an indemnity of one million pounds sterling in four installments,
- Allow for an exchange of diplomatic representatives between Ava and Calcutta, and
- Sign a commercial treaty in due course.

It claims that among the various problems that the people of Assam are confronting, the problem of national identity is the most basic, and therefore it seeks to represent "independent minded struggling peoples" irrespective of race, tribe, caste, religion and nationality.

ULFA ACCORDING TO GOVERNMENT OF INDIA

The Government of India (GOI) has classified it as a terrorist organization and had banned it under the Unlawful Activities (Prevention) Act in1990. Concurrently, GOI started military offensives against it, named Operation Bajrang November 1990, Operation Rhino September 1991,Operation All Clear December 2003 and Operation Rhino 2 lead by the Indian Army. The anti insurgency operations still continues at present under the Unified Command Structure.

The Government of India accuses ULFA of maintaining links with the Inter-Services Intelligence (ISI) of Pakistan and the DGFI of Bangladesh, and waging a proxy war on their behalf against India.

The outlawed group was said to be looking to China for shelter following mounting pressure from both Burma and Bangladesh, in turn pressured by India.

The outfit's top commander, Paresh Baruah, was believed to be near the Sino-Burmese border looking for an alternative position for a hideout. Indian police and intelligence officials said there could be as many as 50 ULFA militants holed up in China's Yunnan Province led by the group's Lt. Partha Jyoti Gogoi.

ASSASSINATIONS BY ULFA

Some of the major assassinations by ULFA include that of Surendra Paul in May 1990, the brother of businessman Lord Swraj Paul, that precipitated a situation leading to the sacking of the Government of Assam under Prafulla Kumar Mahanta and the beginning of Operation Bajrang. On the ULFA's Army Day on March 16, 2003, an IED explosion under a bus on National Highway No. 7 killed six civilians and wounded approximately 55 others

In 1991 a Russian engineer, and national of the Soviet Union was kidnapped along with others and killed. In 1997, Sanjay Ghose, a social activist and a relative of a high ranking Indian diplomat, was kidnapped and killed. The highest government officer assassinated by the group was local AGP minister Nagen Sharma in 2000. An unsuccessful assassination attempt was made on AGP Chief Minister Prafulla Kumar Mahanta in 1997. A mass grave, discovered at a destroyed ULFA camp in Lakhipathar forest, showed evidence of executions committed by ULFA. ULFA continues to attempt ambushes and sporadic attacks on government security forces. In 2003, the ULFA was accused of killing labourers from Bihar in response to molestation and raping of many Assamese girls in a train in Bihar. This incident sparked off anti-Bihar sentiment in Assam, which withered away after some months though. On August 15, 2004, an explosion occurred in Assam in which 10-15 people died, including some school children. This explosion was reportedly carried out by ULFA. The ULFA has obliquely accepted responsibility for the blast. This appears to be the first instance of ULFA admitting to public killings with an incendiary device. In January 2007, the ULFA once again struck in Assam killing approximately 62 Hindi speaking migrant workers mostly from Bihar. On March 15, 2007, ULFA triggered a blast in Guwahati, injuring six persons as it celebrated its 'army day'.

ECONOMIC SUBVERSION

The ULFA has claimed responsibility for bombings of economic targets like crude oil pipelines, freight trains and government buildings, including the 7 August 2005 attack. ULFA carried out a bombing and destruction of a five million litre pretrol reservoir at Digboi refinery in Tinsukia with an estimated property loss of Rs 200million. On the same day they also damaged a gas pipeline in Tisukia

RECRUITMENT

There are regular media reports of ULFA recruitment drives, especially in the rural areas. Even though many times the estimated original membership have either been captured, killed or have surrendered to government agencies, the continuing presence of ULFA members suggest that these reports are true.

POLITICAL ACTIVITIES

After 1985 and before it was banned in 1990, ULFA was credited in the media with many public activities. It has continued a public discourse of sorts through the local media (newspapers), occasionally publishing its position on political issues centred around the nationality question. It has participated in public debates with public personalities from Assam. During the last two local elections the ULFA had called for boycotts, though media reports suggest that it had intimidated activists of the then ruling parties (Congressand AGP respectively).

EXTORTION

The ULFA is credited with some bank robberies during its initial stages. Now it is widely reported to extort businessmen, bureaucrats and politicians for collecting funds. In 1997, the Chief Minister of Assam accused Tata Tea of paying the medical bills of the ULFA cultural secretary Pranati Deka at a Mumbai hospital.

OTHER ACTIVITIES

The ULFA is reported to maintain a number of camps in Bangladesh, where members are trained and sheltered away from Indian security forces. Until recently, they had maintained camps in Bhutan, which were destroyed by the Royal Bhutan Army aided by the Special Frontier Force in December, 2003. These camps housed combatants and non-combatant families of ULFA members. The ULFA maintains close relationships with other separatist organisations like NDFB, KLO and NSCN(Khaplang). The Indian Army notes that Surrenders.

7

Violence by SULFA in Assam

Beginning in 1990, the Government of India has attempted to wean away members of the ULFA. This occurred due to the death of the ULFA's deputy Commander in chief Heerak Jyoti Mahanta on December 31, 1991. Mr. Mahanta strongly stood against any kind of surrendering, but after his death it nevertheless happened.

In 1992 a large section of second rung leaders and members surrendered to government authorities. These former members were allowed to retain their weapons to defend themselves against their former colleagues and were offered bank loans without any liabilities.

This loose group, now called SULFA, has become an important element in the armed politics and business ofAssam. However there have been cases of surrenderings being staged for political and economical reasons by local and national governments.

The total number of ULFA cadres to have laid down arms has gone up to 8,718. 4,993 cadres surrendered between 1991 and 1998. 3,435 surrendered between 1998 and 2005 when a new policy to deal with the ULFA was unveiled.

SECRET KILLINGS OF ULFA FAMILY MEMBERS

During the government of AGP leader Prafulla Kumar Mahanta, a number of family members of ULFA leaders were assassinated by unidentified gunmen. With the fall of this government following elections in 2001, the secret killings stopped. Investigations into the killings culminated in the report of the "Saika Commission", presented to the Assam

Assembly November 15, 2007. The report provides details about the killings, which were organized by Prafulla Mahanta in his role as the Assam Home Minister, and executed by the police, with cooperation from the Indian Army. The actual killers were surrendered elements of the ULFA, who would approach their targets at home, at night, knocking on the door and calling out in Assamese to allay suspicion. When the victims answered the door, they were shot or kidnapped to be shot elsewhere. Even the elder brother of Paresh barua,Dinesh Barua was picked up at night from his house by unidentified assamese boys along with army with weapons,and later his body was found lying near a cremation centre in Chabua.

NEGOTIATIONS/TALKS

The ULFA has put forward a set of three preconditions for talks and negotiations with the Indian government. The government has rejected these preconditions.

The preconditions are:

- The talks should be held in a third country.
- The talks should be held under United Nations supervision.
- The agenda of the talks should include the sovereignty of Assam.

In 2004, the ULFA dropped the first two preconditions and offered to talk with the government. The Government of India was not ready to negotiate on the issue of sovereignty. Still some progress was made when the ULFA formed a "People's Consultative Group" in September 2005 to prepare the grounds for an eventual negotiation between the government and ULFA, which the government has welcomed.

According to the India Times, talks were first held in December 2005 at the residence of the Prime Minister, Manmohan Singh. There were three rounds of peace talks with the 11-member People's Consultative Group (PCG), headed by noted Assamese writer Indira Goswami, leading to a temporary truce in August 2006. However the truce broke down by September 26 of the same year.

CEASEFIRE BY A PORTION OF 28 BATTALION OF ULFA

Some leaders and cadres of the A and C companies of ULFA declared unilateral ceasefire on 24 Jun'2008 at a press meet held at Amarpur in Tinsukia district. The declared the ceasefire in order to pressurise the top brass of ULFA to sit on negotiation table with the Government of India. But the top brass of ULFA expelled the leaders of 28 Battalion led by Mrinal Hazarika and Jiten Dutta. The group later renamed as ULFA (Pro-talk). Currently the 28th Battalion is under commandership of Lt Bijoy Chinese alias Bijoy Das.

THE 'NEO' COLONIAL EXPERIENCE

When we refer terms like "Colonial", and its subsequent "Neo-Colonial" phenomenon, we generally refer to the expoloits of the mighty British empire and the later exploits of the democratic mechanisms of the state. The Indian state has been no different. But here in this small article of mine I would like to bring forth the pscycology of "Colonising" that exists in all human minds.In pursuit of the best job, best food, best shelter humans have scorched the earth to its last dust.Our modern lives are based on the outcomes of these pursuits, which is almost natural to our existence.

When we bring these individual traits to a bigger, macro scale excersise, we witness the outward and inward migrations and prosperty and poverty (almost in the same breath). here I would like to bring in reference the case study of Assam; much because of the recent killings of 'non'-Assamesse people by the locals.I, myself being an assamese by birth,am deeply hurt by the killings that have erupted again, this time on a different note, claiming innocents. But the nation might see it as purely as a case of the rise of "Regionalism" and parochial tendencies of the Assamese, I would like throw some light on the causes of this present turmoil, which unfortunately, I do not see subsiding soon in the minds of the masses.

Assam has for centuries been a kind of a melting pot of peoples and culture. A true heteregenous state in terms of population composition.The Ahoms came from the Patkai's of

Burma, they brought in the Brahmanical clergy from North India, starting from the 12th Century, the Muslims made their entry, and at later stages the Britishers brought in the "coolies" or the tea plantation labourers from Bengal,Bihar and Orissa.

But the post-independence era saw the greatest inward migration-from Bengal(the middle class in search of govt jobs)the Marwaris(in pursuits of unexplored markets) and the Bihari labourers(in search of employment in infrastructure sector and under the Marwaris) and the (illegal) immigrants from Bangladesh(in search of food and shelter).But the societal reaction to this mass heterogenity has been quite a mixed one.The impact of Bengali culture has been quite a intense in the Hindu ritualistic festivities of the common man. Durga Puja (a relatively 'Bengali' symbolism is highy pronounced among the people).Diwali (a 'North Indian' identity is pompously celebrated in Assam), and lately "Chat Puja"(a Bihari festival attributed to the Sun God) have come to dot the official holidays schedule of the state administration. As a matter of fact, the months of Oct-Nov are ear-marked as time of festivities, even though the roots of these festivals are quite alien to the Assamese soil.

Assam, is the land of Sri Sankardeva, the great Vaishnavite reformer of the medieval century. He postulated a religion (akin to Sikhism) where idol worship is strictly forbidden, and the prayers are based on the Bhagawat Gita. This has been a unique cult (called as "Sankori") which have brought Bihu (Magh,Kati and Ronali Bihus in a year) as the first true identity and culture of Assam. But unfortunately, over the years the presence of this cult has dwindled steadily in the cultural life. This, owing to the gradual decline in the general economic standards of the Assamese middle class. It is nothing but an irony, to see that Bihus have now been restricted to the villages of Assam, at a time when Durga Puja, Laxmi Puja, Chat Puja and Diwali rule the roost in the urban centres.

These are nothing but some micro-level obsevations of the slowly changing dynamics of the society at large. The Assamese society now stands deeply polarised between the two opposing sides of the "indigenous" and the "alien". A divide that has been largely subjugated for the sake of running of the frail Assamese economy. The outsiders(Marwaris, Bengali,Biharis and the Bangladeshis) corner a huge bulk of the state's economy.This is the exposure of the "Colonising" behaviour that has come to the forefront. Assam has become a colony, a colony of Bengal, of Bihar, of Rajathan, and lately of Bangladesh! The core of this fact is the total disimiliation of these outsiders with the Assamese culture.The Punjabis also constitute a sizeable portion of the population, but they have never posed any threat because of their skillful absorption of Assamese language and cultural traits. The injury comes when festivals like Bihu are largely disregarded by the influential (outsider)class, who have seemed to make Assam their lodging, but not their abode.

A common joke among these outsiders relate to the "unenterprising", "lazy" and "dumb" characteristics of the Assamese people as "loathsome peoples" tuned and crazed only for white collar jobs. These ridicules are however not far from reality, and the common Assamese youth generally ascribes for careers in academics and administration. But sadly, they have fared poorly in this aspect. The administartive jobs (civil services) have been plagued by corruption and nepotism. Jobs in Central govt units like Railway and Bank services are capped by the Bengalis. The private sector jobs (although relatively few) have been occupied by the hardworking South Indians (notably Keralites).

Sadly, today very few options are left for youths of Assam to pursue any careers of their own in the State,the reigns of trade and commerce have been usurped by Marwaris (who run prosperous businesses in Garments, Hardwares, Grocery wholesale and lately of merchandsise and dealerships of the consumer goods industry), Bengalis(who have a monopoly over the Pharmaceutical industry and Marketing jobs) and Biharis (who have reigned in the informal sector). Joblessness, coupled with poor economic growth have been the fuel to the emergence of insurgency in the region. Extremism and insurgency have gradually brought under control, but it has beniffited only the trading and the Upper classes, leaving the vast middle class literally untouched.The middle class today, finds itself in a dilemma, caught between the 'devil and the deep sea'.

This frustrations have been aided and abbetted by political parties with with big promises and little deeds. The political scenario of Assam represents nothing more than a game of see-saw between AGP and the Congess.Issues of development have occupied backstage and vexed issues of infiltration,Central govt apathy have occupied the middle class mindscape. Needless to say that the political class have failed their electorates.In one of such, is the issue of the growing influence of non-Assamese in the running of the state's economy, which has been a relative and concious fact in everyones mindset. Such feelings cannot be drubbed as regionalism, Assam is an underdeveloped region(one among the bottom three poorest states of India).Its literacy is around 64%, density of only 340 compared to 880(Bihar), 904 (WestBengal) 819 (Kerala) and165(Rajasthan). It sees itself as a victim of population explosion of the other states. It sees itself being plundered and desecrated by outsiders for its resouces.It refuses to become anyone's colony. It refuses to carry the burden or meet the ambitions of the others.When silence is seen as meekness and cowardice, and hospitality is seen as weakness, mass violence perhaps, is then the final resort to clear some doubts.

The recent killings of hindi speaking peoples in various parts of Assam, is in my opinion is a resultant of the long brewing undercurrent of discontent against the mechanism of the state's economy, some sort of a economic class struggle (but in a regional colour).The legitimacy of which cannot be doubted if we do not want to betray the masses. And the solutions must be brought soon, otherwise it might just spill over the whole nation.

This is not only a political crisis but also a sociological and intellectual exigency. Because rationality often succumbs when pitted against forces of stealth and greed. A hurt and hungry stomach heeds no logic or reason of pluralism or heteroginity. It is unfortunate, but a bitter fact. Assam, is the latest sore of this "Neo-Colonising" tendency of we Indians. Afterall, the two hundred years of British rule was enough for us to teach that !!!

ISOLATES STATES

The Seven Sisters of India are the seven relatively unexplored and isolated Indian states—Assam, Nagaland, Tripura, Meghalaya, Manipur, Mizoram and Arunachal Pradesh—which for many years was closed to foreigners. This land, better known to the world as the North-Eastern region of India, borders China, Tibet, Bhutan, Bangladesh, and Myanmar. India's remote northeast, the area comprising the seven states stretching from Tibet in the north to Myanmar (Burma) in the south, among them Nagaland, Meghalaya, and Assam. In this area, rarely visited by foreigners, peoples scarcely known to the Western world continue a way of life steeped in ancient ritual.

Extensive, complex patterns of violence continues in the seven states of northeastern India. The main insurgent groups in the northeast include two factions of the National Socialist Council of Nagaland (NSCN) in Nagaland; Meitei extremists in Manipur; and the all Tripura Tiger Force (ATTF) and the National Liberation Front of Tripura (NLFT) in Tripura. The proclaimed object of many of these groups is to break out of the Indian union, creating new, independent nations. Their stated grievances against the Indian Government range from charges of neglect and indifference to the endemic poverty of the region, to allegations of active discrimination against the tribal and non-tribal peoples of the region by the centre. The oldest of these conflicts, involving the Nagas, started with India's independence in 1947. The insurgency was eventually quelled in the early 1980s through a mixture of repression and cooptation.

Only after Independence and re-organisation of the States was a semblance of real Government authority and administration brought into these far-flung areas. This was strongly resented by the newly educated elite of the tribal societies, who construed the efforts of the Government as an encroachment on their tribal way of life and freedom. Thus, on the basis of racial, cultural and religious differences from the majority stock of the plains, insurgency in the NE India came into being.

Issues of ideology were by and large irrelevant to the insurgency movements of the NE region. The single predominant factor that has withstood the test of time in this regard is either ethnic (such as in Assam and Tripura) or tribal as in Nagaland. It has also been seen that, within a particular State, insurgency by one set of tribals raises its head, finds roots and spreads and then dies with an agreement with the Government. Thereafter, in the same geographical area, another lesser tribe/sub tribe undergoes the same cycle.

Thus in Mizoram, once Lushai insurgency came to an end, the Hmars were up in arms. In the same manner, the Naga insurgency once spearheaded by the Semas passed into the hands of the Konyaks in Northern Nagaland and the Tangkhuls in Southern Nagaland and NE Manipur with the once dominant Semas and Angamis relegated largely to the side lines. Similar to the Bodos, the Karbi Anglongs of Assam are showing all the signs of the itch to raise yet another movement. Thus it is evident that even if, at the point of origin ideology had any role to play, in the long run it is the ethnic and tribal perceptions that truly matter.

The insurgency in the NE states first manifested itself in Nagaland and thereafter mushroomed to other areas. The insurgency in Nagaland has thus, in a sense, been an umbrella for all other insurgencies in the region. It is essential to know the historical context leading to these insurgencies. The map of the NE has been altered with new lines drawn to recognise new political and administrative realities. The names of these entities have changed; the Naga Hills has become Nagaland, the Lushai Hills has changed to Mizoram and the North Eastern Frontier Agency, still known to many simply as NEFA, has become Arunachal Pradesh.

The jungles of SE Asia sweep down from Bhutan and Arunachal Pradesh across seven other nations—Bangladesh, Myanmar, Thailand, Laos, Kampuchea, Malaysia and

Vietnam-spanning political boundaries regardless of physical frontiers. Ethnic coalitions, oral traditions and lifestyles based on respect for nature have mattered more in these regions than frontiers. Here men and women, with common origins but different nationalities, share a racial, historic, anthropological and linguistic kinship with each other that is more vital than their links with the mainstream political centres, especially at Delhi, Dhaka and Rangoon, or Yangon, as it is known today.

It is this affinity that has played a role in the unrest and insurgencies that have long troubled the NE of India. Affinity and Identity; these, more than any other factors, have represented the principal compulsions that triggered the Naga, Mizo, Meitei, Tripuri and Assamese affirmation of separateness from the non-Mongolian communities that dominate the India subcontinent.

India's NE is a misshapen strip of land, linked to the rest of the country by a narrow corridor just 20 kms wide at its slimmest, which is referred to as the "Siliguri Corridor". This region has been the battle ground for generations of sub-national identities. The anthropological composition of the inhabitants of North Eastern India presents a kaleidoscopic variety. Descendants of Aryan and Dravidian stocks co-mingle with the Indo-Burmese and Indo-Tibetan strains. Owing to its geographical isolation from the rest of India and the relative primitiveness of the tribal societies existing here, the region remained virtually cut off from the rest of India. From time immemorial till the near eclipse of the British Raj, and even to this day, this situation of isolation has continued in one form or the other.

To give a fair account of the feeling of non-"Indianness" of the tribal peoples, it is essential to understand that the phenomenon is more or less reciprocal with the rest of India being largely ignorant of the problems and privations of the peoples of NE India. One striking example of the psychological aloofness of the Indian people from this region is the massacre at Nellie in 1976. This incident in which over 3000 men, women and children were slaughtered in one go, could engage Indian media attention for barely two weeks.

There is now a perceptible change in attitudes. The sheer scale and intensity of the ongoing political violence in Assam and the resultant continuous media coverage has brought about a situation where the rest of India is now aware of the existence of the region. Similarly, the opening of roads and related means of communication in the region has served, in conjunction with the spread of education, to bring about an awareness of the rest of India. The veritable flood of Hindi movies and their popularity in the region have also assisted in no small measure in this slow but sure process of absorption in the Indian mainstream.

In October 2002 a dozen underground organizations of the North East India constituted a platform to carry forward their armed struggle together. The organizations had consolidated their bases in a common area of Burma—which they call "Liberated Burma"—with the help of Kachin Independence Army (KIA). An area of Burma bordering Nagaland of the North East India has been occupied by the militants, in which they have reportedly set up as many as 20 camps to provide training to their cadres. A stretch of Burma opposite of Mon District of Nagaland in the North East has been occupied by the militant groups, but the Burmese government cannot take action against them.

Bhutan on 15 December 2003 launched a military crackdown on three Indian separatist groups-the outlawed United Liberation Front of Asom (ULFA), the National Democratic Front of Bodoland (NDFB) and the Kamatapur Liberation Organization (KLO). The three groups, fighting for independent homelands, had set up well-entrenched bases inside the dense jungles in southern Bhutan. The ULFA and the NDFB are rebel groups from the border state of Assam, while the KLO is from West Bengal. Bhutan claimed it had smashed all the 30 rebel camps, but admitted the militants were still holed up inside the kingdom.

8

Insurgency on Economic Growth in Assam

The linkages between insurgency, or indeed any kind of civil unrest, and its adverse impact on economic development are generally taken for granted and have almost become a given. Such presumed linkages have become an axiom of political discourse in respect of the volatile situation, marked by legitimate protest, civil unrest and active insurgencies, that prevails in Assam and its environs in the northeastern region.

According to the Assam Human Development Report 2003, prepared by the Planning and Development Department, Government of Assam, which delineates some of the all-too-well-known social and economic indicators of poverty and underdevelopment in Assam, this situation has been further exacerbated by "two issues that have certainly been exceptional in the duration of their existence, the intensity of their occurrence and the extent of their impact". One of these, not particularly exceptional to Assam for the complaint is made routinely by most of the States, is the "severe fiscal stress... the mismatch between the resources needed to provide basic services, maintain assets, promote growth and development and create infrastructure and the resources available to the State...."

An even more important challenge, given a higher priority in the Report than the "severe fiscal stress", is posed by "decades of unrest, agitation, and at a later state, insurgency". Thus, the linkage between such "unrest, agitation and insurgency" and the lack of economic development, is boldly highlighted in the text of the Report: "Inequities, lack of development, perceived discrimination and lack of opportunities for employment have contributed to discord and strife. Such situations are rarely, if ever, conducive to development."

There is also a supposedly reverse kind of linkage between insurgency and economic development. This is that the absence of economic development is also a major factor that leads to disaffection that at some critical point takes the shape of insurgency.

This argument is not always convincing. There are obvious exceptions where so-called `ethnic factors', unrealised (and often imaginary) aspirations for national sovereignty and similar issues rather than economic underdevelopment have engineered discontent. In other words, these linkages between insurgency and development are canvassed at two levels. One, the reality of economic underdevelopment, the causes for which can be traced to factors deeply rooted in history as well as to the present political and economic policies of the State and Union governments. Two, the presence of an active insurgency inescapably frustrates and indeed hinders all initiatives, government and private, to encourage economic development.

Put simply, the people who live in areas affected by insurgency are doubly damned, suffering from both the causes and consequences of insurgency. In more personal and practical realms, they are constantly under pressure both from the insurgent groups, who simply could not exist without some support from the very people whose cause the insurgencies claim to espouse, and from the state and the government that too derive their legitimacy in the name of these very people.

Such circular reasoning is both persuasive and comfortable. It provides the rationale for official inertia and indeed inaction. It also puts the responsibility for the predicament of the victims on the victims themselves, almost as if they created the situation that is destroying them.

The State and Union governments too, not to speak of various organs of the so-called civil society, which are constantly `engaged' with this situation, find it convenient to go along with such a reading. Anti-insurgency operations by the security forces and initiatives by the government, or even by the insurgent groups, with the so-called facilitators from civil society (including the media) ever eager to highlight their own profiles, for a `political dialogue' with a view to resolving the issues raised by the disaffected groups, are now a matter of routine. Often, these go on simultaneously. Civil society, in particular the media and the powerful and resourceful non-governmental organisation (NGO) sector, is an important player in such processes. Its agenda is not always easy to decipher.

There is no gainsaying that the economic situation in Assam is dire. All socio-economic indicators of growth and development, almost without exception below the national levels, drive home this reality. Here are some of the facts paraphrased from the Report:

At Independence, Assam's per capita income was only marginally less than the national average. In 1988, the average per capita income for the country was over 1.8 times that of Assam.... The State's per capita income in 1950-51 was 4.1 per cent higher than the national average; by 1980-81 the State's per capita income was 27 per cent lower than the national average; and by1998-99, the gap had widened to 45.5 per cent.

The overall growth rate of Assam since the 1980s has been a little over 2 per cent. In absolute terms, the number of the poor has increased from 7.8 million in 1983 to 9.5 million in 1999-2000. As much as 36.09 per cent of the State's population continue to live below the poverty line, a figure appreciably above the national average of 26.10 per cent. The percentage of the poor in Assam is the highest among the seven States of northeastern India. Rural poverty is much higher (40.04 per cent of the population in 1999-2000) than urban poverty (7.47 per cent). The incidence of rural poverty is higher than the all-India figure of 27.09 per cent. The incidence of unemployment, measured as a percentage of the labour force, is higher than in the rest of the country. The unemployment rate in Assam in 1983 was 2.2 per cent as compared to 2.0 per cent for the country. By 1999-2000, the country's unemployment rate had increased marginally to 2.3 per cent while in Assam it had risen to 4.6 per cent.

Life expectancy at birth is below that for the rest of the country and is one of the lowest among the major States. The percentage of people who are not expected to live beyond 40 years (21.8 per cent in 1001) is higher than the national average.

About 12 lakh children were out of school in 1999. There is high incidence of child labour among the poor. Girls from poor families also have lower transition from the primary to the middle stage of schooling. Dropout rates at the high school and higher secondary levels continue to be high. For those who do not drop out, the chances of finishing school successfully are less than 40 per cent.

However, none of these depressing facts (the Report has many more) or their impact on the larger socio-economic situation can be attributed to or explained as the causes and effect of the volatility that characterises the situation in Assam. On the contrary, far from being an impediment to growth, one can argue that insurgency, even of the kind that has prevailed in Assam for over two decades, has been an engine of growth, though here again, of a kind. Even assuming that the State's economy was thriving in comparison to that of the rest of the country at the time of Independence-the point always made in much of the analysis of Assam's present backwardness relative to the rest of the country and is indeed the starting point of the Report-there were several other factors that contributed to that health.

The Assam at the dawn of Independence was very different from what it is today, in terms of its size and population, economic resources, the absence of strong separatist pulls Statewide, with Naga nationalism being an exception, whose stated objectives have ranged from greater autonomy within the State to separation from the State to outright independence from India and, above all, sharing a faith in the possibility of growth with equity and justice, all sustained by relatively stable democratic institutions within the State and nationally.

This is no more the case. Not merely is this the case in Assam where the fragmentation process that began in the 1960s is taking unexpected and ominous directions; increasingly, such forces are coming to the fore in the rest of the country, even in areas supposedly marked by stable democratic institutional structures and steady economic growth. Inasmuch as internal factors, also factors external to Assam have contributed to these changes.

ULFA'S ROLE

For instance, it is generally assumed that the forces released by the United Liberation Front of Asom (ULFA), the separatist and insurgent outfit that articulates the demand for restoration of Asom's lost sovereignty, have significantly impeded Assam's economic development, by scaring away potential investors by its acts of extortion and terrorism.

However, ULFA, which formally took its birth in April 1979, began to affirm its presence through its initial acts of 'armed propaganda' only after the bloodstained Assembly elections of February 1983; and secured some free space to operate after the first regional party government under the Asom Gana Parishad (AGP), a child of Assam's anti-illegal migrants agitation, assumed office in December 1985.

ULFA's transformation to an active insurgent outfit having links with international forces hostile to the Indian state, and prosecuting its stated objective of a 'sovereign Asom' with some vigour, is a post-1990 phenomenon. These international linkages, manifesting themselves in the consolidation of militant Muslim communalism countrywide (though still in pockets), were further facilitated by another development at the national level in which Assam had no role: the mobilisation of the forces of Hindutva terrorism culminating in the destruction of Babri Masjid in December 1992.

These developments coincided not merely with the dismissal of the AGP government and the launching of Operation Bajrang, but with important shifts in the direction of the economy nationally. A decade and a half later, in Assam itself one can see the impact of these changes wherever one's eye turns. Few now complain that Assam and the rest of the northeastern region suffer from the Centre's neglect. Assam and its neighbours now occupy a high profile in the national agenda precisely because issues of vital concern to the region have been thrust to the fore by the actions and potential of separatist organisations such as ULFA and its cousins in the other States.

Cumulatively, ULFA and the social forces from which it derives its support and with which it has symbiotic links have been both victims and beneficiaries of these developments. Notwithstanding its rhetoric about carrying on its struggle for a `sovereign Asom' until the end of time, ULFA has very nearly been destroyed by successive and ongoing military operations launched against it.

It is now reduced to making symbolic gestures of violence annually on Independence Day and Republic Day. Nothing else can explain its eagerness to seek a `negotiated settlement', though it continues the fiction that such talks as and when they are held will have to be on the issue of restoration of Assam's lost sovereignty.

And yet, the ideas and forces released by ULFA have not been defeated. They are bound to take new directions not easy to foresee. For instance, who could have foreseen at the height of the Assam agitation that there would come about within a decade a nexus between the extreme and exclusivist articulation of Assamese nationalism and its most visible victims at that point of time?

Finally, if ULFA has become a victim of the forces it has provoked (and released), the social forces that sustained the separatist and secessionist ideology have greatly benefited from these same initiatives taken by the Indian state to curb militant separatism in Assam. It is in this perspective that one sees that insurgency, even of the apparently self-destructive kind engaged in by ULFA, has become an engine of economic development, though of a kind, that has taken place in Assam in the last decade and a half, broadly coinciding with the high noon of ULFA and the beginning of its decline.

This correspondent, who has lived in Guwahati since the early 1960s, had been away from Assam for two long spells of eight years each, between 1975 and 1983, and again between 1994 and 2002. The re-entry in 1983 was seamless; four years since the last return, one still has to pinch oneself constantly to come to terms with the changes.

The world and the home have changed utterly. This again is in tune with the growth and development that has been taking place nationally, not merely in the urban metropolitan centres but in small towns and even in some rural areas. Perhaps these changes touch, very unequally at that, about 30 per cent of the population, perhaps less. This is certainly so about the development that has taken place in Assam in recent times.

However, as the Report notes, there is a causal link "between the process of liberalisation and the concomitant process of modifying the role of the Government" and the widening gap that the Report notes in almost every indicator of economic development, in Assam and nationally. The growth and development that has taken place is simply the obverse side of the denial and deprivation that sustain such growth even while destroying its victims. As was said in a different context, about another subject in another century, if you seek a monument for ULFA, just look around, the glamorous and tawdry glitz as well as the all-abounding squalour. (The writer is grateful to Dr. Jayanta Madhab, Economic Adviser to the Chief Minister of Assam, whose lecture, "Insurgency and Development", on the occasion of the Foundation Day of the OKD Institute of Social Change and Development, Guwahati, on March 30, 2006, helped him formulate this dissenting perspective.)

9

Terrorist Violence in Assam, 1990-2010

2010

- *November 8*: At least 19 persons, including 13 Hindi-speaking people, were killed and several others injured when militants of the anti-talks faction of the (NDFB), led by Ranjan Daimary went on a killing spree in four places in Northern-Assam.
- *October 3*: The Police shot dead four NDFB cadres during an encounter at a thickly forested area at Dekatan in Dhemaji District and rescued an abducted trader, Cotton Nandy.
- *July 30*: July 30: At least five CRPF troopers were killed and 33 others injured, when the ULFA triggered an IED blast by damaging a bus at Bhalukdubi under Goalpara District. Anu Buragohain, who introduced himself as the 'spokesperson' of ULFA, called up a local television channel claiming that the blast was carried out by the outfit. He said though ULFA had 'remained quiet' for some time, Security Forces continued to target its cadres and that is why it had retaliated. He warned of more such strikes. Intelligence sources, however, did not rule out the possibility of the anti-talks faction of the NDFB militants executing the blast at the behest of ULFA. "The precision of the execution certainly points to such a possibility," a source said.

- *July 26*: Four Sashastra Seema Bal (SSB) personnel, including an assistant commander, were killed and three others injured in an ambush by the Ranjan Daimary faction of the NDFB at Amlaiguri under Panbari Police Station in Chirang District along Bhutan border. A Police spokesperson said militants of the NDFB attacked a vehicle of the SSB's 15th Battalion. "The NDFB militants later decamped with two rifles and two pistols from the dead troopers," Inspector General of Police Bhaskar Jyoti Mahanta said.
- *March 1*: Four suspected militants of Bengali Tiger Force (BTF) were shot dead in an encounter with SFs at Chereng Chapori in Darrang District.
- *February 10*: Three militants belonging to anti-talks faction of the NDFB were shot dead by SFs during an encounter at Jaulia Centre near Jingabeel under Majbat Police Station in Udalguri District.
- *February 2*: Two suspected ULFA cadres were shot dead by troops of 65 Field Regiment of Red Horns Division during an encounter at Dakkhin Bhokelikanda under Kalaigaon Police Station in Udalguri District. A six year old boy was killed in crossfire of the encounter. A trooper was also injured in the encounter.
- *January 19*: Three militants of the anti-talks faction of NDFB were shot dead by SFs in two separate incidents of Kokrajhar District. Four militants, including three women, were also arrested by the SFs from the incident site.
- *January 4*: Unidentified militants opened fire on a Police convoy, killing a Constable and injuring two others, including a Sub-Inspector, near Impui Basti on the Haflong-Mahur road in the North Cachar Hills District. Two siblings, one of them a 10-year-old girl, also die in the ambush after they are caught in the cross-fire as the Security Forces (SFs) retaliate after the gunmen, hiding in the foliage on both sides of

the road, open fire on the two-vehicle Assam Police convoy.

- *January* 2: Unidentified militants shot dead three persons, including two pro-talks NDFB cadres, identified as Jwngsar Brahma alias B. Jwhwlao (28) and Losen Brahma (27) of Serfanguri designated camp, and one college student, Bilifang Basumatary (20), at Mukuldang under Gossaigaon Police Station in Kokrajhar District. A truck driver and two other students were also injured in the gun attack.

2009

- *November* 22: Suspected ULFA militants triggered two powerful bomb blasts barely 50 metres from the Sadar Police Station in Nalbari town, which killed eight people and injured 53 others at around 10 AM in the morning. The IEDs, planted on two bicycles, were kept in front of a tea stall and a saloon which were blown up. The deceased were identified as Paban Thakur, the owner of a nearby saloon, Sikandar Thakur, an employee of the saloon, Dipu Das, a driver, Ganesh Das, a businessman, Keshab Das, an employee of an insurance company and Mahabat Ali, a gaonburah (village head man) of Nalbari town. The Superintendent of Police of Nalbari District, Jitmal Doley, said that ULFA militants are suspected to be behind the blasts, which were meant to make its presence felt by creating panic among innocent people.
- *October* 4: At least 11 persons were killed in a attack carried out by suspected militants belonging to the anti-talks faction of the NDFB at Balichand area under Biswanath Chariali Police Station in Sonitpur District. At least ten others were injured in the attack. According to Police sources, a group of 10-12 heavily armed militants entered Bhimajuli village, inhabited mostly by the Nepali and Tea-tribe community, called out villagers from their houses, and opened

fire on them. On their way back, the same group opened also fire at two other places. Police sources said that attempts at extortion might be the reason for the attack.

- *October 3*: Three ULFA militants were shot dead by troops during an encounter near Kendubari village in the Nalbari District. "Based on specific intelligence about the presence of three ULFA militants in the area, an army column laid an ambush and there was a firefight in which the militants were shot dead," an Army official said. A carbine, pistols, grenades, detonators and gelatine sticks were recovered from the possession of the slain militants. "Probably the militants were planning to strike during the Durga Puja festival and hence carrying explosives," the official added.
- *August 16*: Two Army personnel and a NDFB militant were killed in an encounter at Garugaon on the Assam-Arunachal Pradesh border area under Dhekiajuli Police Station of Sonitpur District at about 4.45am (IST). Official sources said the Army personnel were conducting a search operation in the Garugaon area after getting intelligence inputs about the movement of militants. During the search operation, the Army came across a four-member group of the Ranjan Daimary faction of the NDFB and were engaged in an encounter with militants lasting for about an hour. Subsequently, dead bodies of two Army personnel and a NDFB militant were recovered. The slain NDFB militant was identified as B. Thungree. Meanwhile, three other militants managed to escape from the spot taking the advantage of darkness.
- *July 20*: SF personnel shot dead three militants of the NSCN-IM at Harmoti village near Nijlaluk in North Lakhimpur District, bordering Arunachal Pradesh. The slain militants were identified as 'sergeant' Nameng Kobin, 'sergeant' Babang Bake and Bhai.

Three 9-mm pistols, ammunition and SIM cards were also recovered from their possession. "These militants were operating from Arunachal Pradesh and frequently entering Assam on specific operations like recruitment of cadres and sabotage activities," Lakhimpur Superintendent of Police S.A. Karim said, adding that there were reports of the militants trying to carry out attacks in Assam prior to the Independence Day on August 15.

- *July 1*: Unidentified militants shot dead four children and a 25 year-old woman at Semkhor village under Maibong Police Station in the North Cachar Hills District. Three others were injured in the incident. A Police source said that all the victims were from the Dimasa tribe. The deceased were identified as Karong Thonglo, Lambo Langthasa, Warsi Thonglo, Depola Langthasa, and Senring Langthasa. With these killings, the death toll in the continuing ethnic strife in the North Cachar Hills District has gone up to 55 since March 19. Five unidentified militants were shot dead in an encounter between the SF personnel and a group of militants at Dehikata Reserve Forest under Mornai Police Station in Goalpara District. A revolver, two 7.65 pistols, a 9-mm pistol, a 12 bore gun (all factory made), a factory made hand grenade, 19 rounds of live ammunition and eight rounds of empty cases were recovered from the possession of the slain militants.
- *June 30*: NDFB militants shot dead four persons of a family at Naharani Grant village under Rangapara Police Station of Sonitpur District in the night. The OIC of Rangapara Police Station, Tapas Chakrabarty, said that four motorcycle-borne NDFB militants with AK series rifles entered the house of Munna Pal at about 11.30 pm (IST) and indiscriminately fired on the family. The deceased persons were identified as Munna Pal (30), his wife Subhapati Pal (35), younger brother Tunna Pal (30) and his three-year old son

Pankaj Pal. Munna Pal, a milkman by profession, was living in the area for the last many years.

- *June 22*: Five NDFB militants were shot dead and huge cache of arms and ammunition were recovered in two separate incidents in Assam. Three NDFB militants, including a self-styled 'area commander' B John Wan, were killed in an encounter with SFs at Majbat in Udalguri District. A 9 mm pistol along with several rounds of ammunition and some documents were recovered from the slain militants. In another incident, two NDFB militants were killed in an encounter with Police and Army in the same evening at Dhekiajuli in Sonitpur District. Two pistols, two bicycles and several documents were recovered from the possession of the slain militants.
- *June 17*: A joint team of Police and Army shot dead three NDFB militants during an encounter at Auguri village under Gogamukh Police Station of Dhemaji District. One of the militants was identified as Manu Basumatary (25) of Abhaypur village. The militants were taking shelter in the residence of one Niranjan Swargiary of Auguri village. One AK-56 rifle with 50 bullets, one 7.62 pistol, one loaded 9 mm pistol, one mobile phone and a money receipt book were recovered from their possession.
- *June 16*: Suspected BW militants shot dead 12 persons and set ablaze 20 houses in an attack at Michidui village under Haflong Police Station of North Cachar Hills District. Police sources said a group of armed militants attacked Michidui and opened indiscriminate fire killing 12 persons, including eight minors, on the spot. Two other persons were also injured in the attack. Police said the village, inhabited by Zeme Naga people, was abandoned following the recent incidents of ethnic clashes and the villagers had taken shelter near a camp of the Assam Rifles camp located around three kilometres away. But recently, the villagers had started going back to the

village during day time for cultivation and the militants reportedly took advantage of the situation to attack them.

- *June 4*: Four NDFB militants were shot dead by the Security Force personnel during encounters in the Sonitpur and Udalguri Districts. While two militants were killed by the Army at Khanamukh in Sonitpur District, two others were killed and arms recovered during another encounter at Jingebil in Udalguri District.
- *June 3*: Suspected BW militants shot dead five persons, including two children, and set ablaze 54 houses when they attacked Borchenam Basti, a Zeme Naga inhabited village under Haflong Police Station in the North Cachar Hills District. Police sources informed that BW militants entered the village at around 5am (IST) killing two minor girls, two old women and one teen-aged boy in the attack. Another child was seriously injured, the report added. Three militants, including a senior ULFA militant identified as Madhurjya Gogoi, were killed in an encounter with the Army at Chayabhata village in Karbi Anglong District around 1.30pm (IST). Gogoi was a self-styled 'lieutenant' of the banned outfit. Of the other two militants, one was Gogoi's bodyguard while another was a KLNLF cadre. An AK-series rifle, two 9mm pistols, a Chinese grenade, ammunition and cash-receipt book were recovered from the encounter site.
- *May 19*: 14 persons, including six NDFB militants, were killed in two separate incidents in the Karbi Anglong and North Cachar Hills Districts. SFs shot dead six NDFB militants in a jungle under Dokmoka outpost of Howraghat Police Station in the Karbi Anglong District in the early morning, which put the death toll in both the incidents at 10. Police sources said the militants taking shelter in a transit camp inside a deep jungle near Donghaf opened fire as the

SFs advanced towards the militant camp. The exchange of fire continued for more than three hours during which two militants managed to escape while the other six died on the spot. However, none of the slain militants were identified. Three 9-mm pistols, two 9-mm revolvers, two grenades and a hand-made carbine, a magazine, 23 live rounds of ammunition, 12 gelatine sticks, 150 metre fuse wire and 143 detonators were recovered from the encounter site. 10 unidentified militants shot dead four Dimasa tribals at Interim Bungalow, a secluded place on the highway about seven kilometres from Mahur town in North Cachar Hills District. Police sources said unidentified militants stalled the passenger jeep at Interim Bungalow and asked all the 14 passengers to get down from the jeep, lined them up and asked them to reveal their ethnic and racial identities. The militants then segregated four Dimasa tribals from the group and opened fire on them.

- *May 11*: Unidentified militants shot dead at least three persons, abducted another and set ablaze over 90 houses belonging to the Zemi Naga tribe at Gailung village in North Cachar Hills District. Police sources said militants attacked the village under Maibang Police Station with automatic weapons, killing at least three persons. An official source added that suspected militants attacked the Hindu Basti and Christain Basti at remote Guilung village and Jalwa village and set ablaze 90 houses. President of the Indigenous People's Forum, Josiaf Zemi, alleged lack of security in the area and stated that if such attacks continued, the tribal people would not be able to till their fields this season and that would lead to starvation later in the year.
- *May 9*: Three villagers were shot dead in an attack by unidentified militants in an interior village, 40 kilometres from Haflong in the North Cachar Hills District.

- *April 29*: Violence between the Zeliangrong community and Cacharis in North Cachar Hills District continued for the second day which had claimed 10 lives and 16 others sustained injuries. The clashes between the two communities of Zeme sub-tribe of Zeliangrong and the Cacharis (Dimasas) started after suspected BW militants killed nine persons of the Zemes sub-tribe of the Zeliangrong community on April 28. Later, suspected Zeliangrong militants retaliated and attacked a Dimasa village. The sources said that the Zeliangrong Chabuan have set ablaze 25 houses of Yekulua village between Boreneu and Guilong of Haflong in North Cachar Hills District. Before setting ablaze the 25 houses, the two communities exchanged gunfire and 10 Dimasas were killed and 16 others wounded. Meanwhile, Telegraph quoting Police sources said there the role of a third player, most probably of the NSCN-IM, was also being suspected.
- *April 28*: Three women were killed and more than seven villagers were injured when a group of unidentified militants, numbering 15 to 20, opened indiscriminate fire on a Dimasa village, Yeah, under Maibang Police Station in North Cachar Hills District.
- *April 20*: The BW militants shot dead six persons, including five SF personnel, in an ambush on the convoy of a private cement company's vehicles in the North Cachar Hills District. The militants ambushed the 20-truck convoy of Vinay Cement Company at Panimur Kalanala under Doyangmukh Police station, near the industrial town of Umrangsu and 170 kilometres from the Haflong, the District headquarters of North Cachar Hills District.
- *April 20*: The Army killed five militants, including an accused in the Dhekiajuli blast of April 15, during an encounter at Aka Basti in the Sonitpur District. Out of the five militants, Prabhat Basumatary, Krishna Basumatary and Deithang Basumatary

belonged to the NDFB while Babul Ali and Yunis Ali were of the MULTA. Defence spokesman Colonel Rajesh Kalia said the militants were planning to abduct a businessman, Paras Gurung, of Lokhra area in the same district. The army said Prabhat Basumatary was a known operative of Pakistan's ISI and a key perpetrator in the bomb blast at Dhekiajuli. The army recovered five 9-mm pistols, a Chinese hand grenade, five kilograms of explosives, 10 detonators and 107 rounds of AK-47 ammunition from the encounter site.

- *April 6*: Seven people were killed and 56 injured in a powerful blast in a crowded market in Guwahati's Maligaon area at around 2 pm (IST). The explosion sparked a fire that set ablaze two cars and 20 motorcycles and spread to a three-storey building housing the area police station. While six people were killed at the blast site, one died of injuries after jumping from an adjacent building which had caught fire. The bomb is suspected to have been hidden in a car or a motorcycle parked adjacent to the North-East Frontier Railway headquarters. "This is the handiwork of ULFA boys ahead of the outfit's Raising Day" said Director General of Police G M Srivastava.
- *January 29*: Two Police personnel and an ULFA militant were killed in an encounter in the Sivasagar District. According to Police sources, the encounter took place at Bengenabari area under Sonari Police station when a joint patrol party of the Police and Army was attacked by the ULFA militants. Assistant Sub-Inspector Bhim Prasad Upadhaya and Constable Debojit Borgohain were killed on the spot, while the slain ULFA militant is yet to be identified.
- *January 1*: The United Liberation Front of Asom (ULFA) militants triggered serial bomb blasts in three different areas of Guwahati city, killing five persons, including a minor, and injuring 50 others. The first

explosion took place around 2:25 PM (IST) in Birubari followed by high-intensity explosions in the Bhootnath area (5:25PM) and Bhangagarh area (5:40PM).

The blasts were triggered hours before the scheduled arrival of Union Home Minister P. Chidambaram. "From prima facie evidences collected from the spot, it appears to be the handiwork of suspected ULFA militants," said Additional Superintendent of Police of Guwahati City, Debojit Deori. "The Birubari bomb, which was planted in a GMC dustbin near the Assam Association of Deaf office, was a low-intensity one. However, the subsequent blasts were aimed to cause maximum damage as they were planted in crowded areas," added Deori. Another unnamed Police official claimed that the bomb in the Bhootnath area was planted in a bicycle.

2008

- *December 1*: At least three persons, including a child, were killed and 30 others injured in a bomb blast suspected to have been triggered by the KLNLF in a passenger train at Diphu railway station in the Karbi Anglong District.
- *November 3*: Three civilians belonging to non-Assamese community were killed by the KLNLF militants at Bamuni Sukanjuri village under Samaguri Police station in the Nagaon District.
- *October 30*: 87 persons were killed and about 200 injured in nine near-simultaneous blasts in Assam's capital Dispur and adjoining city Guwahati and three other Districts-Kokrajhar, Barpeta, and Bongaigaon. The first of the explosions was triggered at around 11.30 am near the Ganeshguri flyover near the high-security capital complex housing the Assembly building in capital Dispur, followed by explosions at Paltan Bazar and Fancy Bazar in Guwahati city within five minutes. Around the same time, bombs also exploded in crowded market places of Kokrajhar, Bongaigaon and Barpeta Districts of the lower Assam.

At least 51 persons were killed in three blasts in Guwahati. While at least 21 persons were killed in three serial blasts in Kokrajhar, 15 persons were killed in twin blasts in Barpeta Road town of Barpeta District. 10 persons were injured in the Bongaigaon blast.

- *October 30*: BW militants killed at least seven Police personnel at Langlai near Thujuari of North Cachar Hills District. Three militants were also killed in the retaliatory firing. Haflong Police sources said that the BW militants opened fire on the Police party who were carrying the body of a DHD leader, Naklai Dimasa, who was killed by the BW militants on October 29 from Haflong Civil Hospital to Diyongmukh after the post mortem.
- *October 25*: Five ULFA militants and a soldier were killed during an encounter between a joint team of the Army and CRPF personnel and militants at Mahina village in the Nalbari District. The slain militants, including one identified as Corporal Sanjit Sarania, belonged to the '709th battalion' of the ULFA. One kilogram of RDX, four pistols, two grenades, one radio set, 29 rounds of live ammunition, one K.G. of urea, two IEDs, nine detonators, five magazines of SLR and fuse wires were recovered from the encounter site.
- *September 30*: The dead bodies of four youths were recovered from a mass grave in the reserve forest at Kakopathar in the Tinsukia District, where makeshift camps of the '28th battalion' of the ULFA were located a few months ago. The mass grave was suspected to be the dumping ground of dead bodies of those who had been abducted and later killed by the ULFA militants.
- *September 26*: Seven suspected HuJI militants were killed in an encounter with the Army at Bashbari under Rupshi development block in the Dhubri District. Six revolvers, three grenades, two gelatin

sticks, six detonators, about two kilograms of explosives, some Bangladeshi currency notes, a Bangladeshi mobile SIM card and addresses of some hotels in Bangladeshi were recovered from the slain militants' possession.

- *September 10*: Unidentified militants opened indiscriminate fire in the market place at Bogajuli Belaisribazar in the Baksa District killing three civilians, identified as Suresh Basumatary, Sabu Basumatary and Dominique Basumatary.
- *July 23*: Three cadres of the ULFA's '709 battalion' were killed in an encounter with Army and police at Namati village under Ghograpar police station in the Nalbari district.
- *June 29*: Seven persons were killed and 35 others, including two policemen, were injured in an explosion at a weekly crowded marketplace in the Kumarikata village of Nalbari district.
- *June 15*: Four hardcore ULFA cadres of the 28th battalion were shot dead by the Army in an operation at Kanubari village of Charaideo subdivision of Sibsagar district. The slain militants have been identified as Badal Khargoria, Annie Bauri, Sumit Gohain and Ajit Gogoi.
- *June 10*: Three ULFA militants were shot dead in an encounter with the security forces at Borbam village under Tengakhat Police Station in the Dibrugarh district.
- *May 11*: A group of around 10 armed BW militants shot dead eight labourers engaged in the construction of a railway quarters at Thoibasti in the North Cachar Hills district.
- *May 10*: 12 Black Widow militants were killed and 18 others injured in a gun battle with the security forces in the North Cachar Hills district.
- *March 13*: Four persons were killed and nine others injured in a police firing on an irate mob which was protesting against the dismantling of a NDFB camp

at Bengtol in the Chirang district.

- *March 9*: Four Hindi-speaking people were shot dead by the ULFA militants near a brick kiln at Udalguri tea estate between Chabua and Tengakhat in the Dibrugarh district.
- *February 22*: Three KLNLF militants were shot dead by the security forces in an operation in the Kamalabhati village under Howraghat Police Station in the Karbi Anglong district. Two AK-56 rifles, four single barrel guns, 177 rounds of ammunition of assorted weapons were recovered at the site of the encounter.
- *February 19*: Five employees of a private cement factory, Vinay Cements, were killed while another was injured in an attack by the Black Widow militants at about four kilometres from Umrangshu in the North Cachar Hills district.
- *February 16*: Four ULFA militants were killed in a joint operation by the Army and police in the Sibsagar district.
- *February 11*: Four persons, including an Assam Police Battalion soldier, were killed and two more injured when Black Widow militants ambushed a convoy of the North Eastern Electric Power Corporation Ltd officials 20-km from Umrangsu in the North Cachar Hills district. Three Islamist militants with suspected links to the Inter-Services Intelligence (ISI), Pakistan's external intelligence agency, were killed in an encounter with security forces at Binajuli village under Agia police outpost in the Goalpara district.
- *January 14*: Two security force personnel and three civilians were killed by Black Widow militants near Umrangsu town in the North Cachar Hills district.

2007

- *December 31*: Three ULFA militants were killed by security forces in the Dibru Saikhowa National Park located across Dibrugarh and Tinsukia districts.
- *December 14*: At least four labourers were shot dead

by suspected BW militants at the Longpo area under Umrangshu police station in the North Cachar Hills district.

- *December 13*: Five people were killed and four others injured in a bomb blast carried out by suspected ANLA militants in a Delhi-bound Rajdhani Express train in Golaghat district. The explosion, which occurred between Naujan and Sugajan, destroyed the luggage van of the train and a small portion of the railway track as well.
- *November 27*: Suspected BW militants shot dead 10 unidentified saw mill workers and injured eight others in two separate attacks at Bithorgaon under Umrangsho police station in the North Cachar Hills district. The militants set ablaze two saw mills and attacked the migrant labourers working there.
- *November 2*: Seven CRPF personnel were killed in an ambush carried out by the BW militants at Theijuri in the North Cachar Hills district. The militants also took away arms and ammunition of the killed CRPF personnel and escaped.
- *September 30*: Four persons are killed and 21 others wounded in another blast triggered by the ULFA at Tinsukia town.
- *August 12*: Suspected KLNLF militants shot dead four civilians, Mahabir Swami, Nandalal Swami, Sila Gupta and Mohan Kanu, at Rongbonghat village under Bokajan police station in the Karbi Anglong district. Two other civilians, Kanhaiyala Swami and Ramesh Swami, sustained injuries in the attack.
- *August 10*: A group of 10-15 suspected ULFA and KLNLF militants attacked a village at Dolamara in the Karbi Anglong district and shot dead 11 Hindi-speaking migrant workers. The dead include four women and two children belonging to two families originally hailing from the State of Bihar.
- *August 8*: Nine civilians, including four women and three children, were killed and five others injured

when a group of ULFA and KLNLF militants opened indiscriminate fire targeting the Hindi-speaking people at Ampahar Basti village under Howraghat police station in the Karbi Anglong district.

- *August 7*: Suspected BW militants shot dead four civilians, Ashok Das, Santosh Mahato, Manna Dey and Bidhu Das, at Harinagar market under Joypur police station in the Dibrugarh district. Three civilians, Ajit Bora, Debo Bora and Pranjal Gogoi, were killed and eight others injured when ULFA militants triggered an explosion in front of the Jorhat police station in the Jorhat district.
- *July 24*: Three unidentified members of the BW group were killed in an internecine clash between rival groups of the DHD-Black Widow and the Nunisa faction, near a designated camp at Pathergaon under Diphu town in the Karbi Anglong district.
- *July 20*: Five civilians, including a four-year-old child, are killed and 18 others injured when suspected ULFA and KLO militants triggered a powerful bomb at Srirampur Chariali under Tamarhat police station in the Kokrajhar district.
- *July 5*: Three civilians, Sarabat Ali, Min Bahadur Chetri and Kamal Bahadur Chetri, were killed when hundreds of armed Naga people, reportedly backed by the NSCN (IM), attacked three villages-Sonapur, Borholla and Dhekiajuli-on the Assam-Nagaland border in Sivasagar district.
- *June 30*: Four persons were killed and at least 40 others injured in four bomb blasts—three in Tinsukia district and one in Karbi Anglong district. Three persons were killed in two successive bomb blasts at a fish market and a textile market in the Tinsukia town.
- *June 23*: Six persons, including three children, are killed and 14 others injured when suspected ULFA militants triggered an explosion in front of a mosque at Machkhowa in the Guwahati city.
- *June 3*: Four police personnel are killed and two

others sustained injuries when KLNLF militants ambushed a police patrolling party at Koilajan area under Bokajan police station in the Karbi Anglong district.

- *May 26*: Seven persons are killed and 18 others injured in an explosion triggered by suspected ULFA militants in the Athgaon area of Guwahati city.
- *May 16*: ULFA militants kill three civilians, Tankeswar Sahu, Dipak Agarwal and Srinath Agarwal, in the Golaghat district.
- *May 15*: The ULFA militants shot dead six unidentified Hindi-speaking people in various areas of the Dibrugarh and Sivsagar districts.
- *May 3*: Three ULFA militants are killed in an encounter with the Army personnel at Barkhajan village in the Nalbari District. Two of the them were identified as the 'second lieutenant 709th battalion' Chanakya Barman alias Khaplang and Pranab Kalita alias Jogesh Kalita alias Bastab.
- *April 23*: SFs killed three ULFA cadres, identified as Udhav Deka alias Sanjeeb Kalita, Parameswar Deka alias Mrigen Dutta and Ganesh Kalita alias Goutam Sarma, at Adingagiri Kalishola hillock along the Assam-Meghalaya border. They recovered one M-20 pistol, a grenade, five live cartridges, 500 grams of explosives, plastic jars and some incriminating documents from the incident site.
- *April 2*: In a counter-insurgency operation, security forces killed four ULFA cadres in the Udalguri district.
- *January 27*: The DHD leader, Dilip Nunisa, claimed responsibility for the killings of 13 of their cadres who had deserted their camp at Dhansiri to join the rival Black Widow in Karbi Anglong on January 14.
- *January 7*: Seven persons belonging to Bihar are killed and three others sustain injuries when ULFA militants called them out of their homes at Borali Bari near Mahmara in the Sibsagar district and opened

fire. Assam Police said that six Hindi-speaking persons were shot dead and one injured in an attack by the ULFA at Chokolia near Dimow in the Dibrugarh district

- *January 6*: KLNLF militants kill eight polling personnel and injure eight others during elections to the Karbi Anglong Autonomous Council. Militants exploded an improvised explosive device and fired on polling personnel when they were returning after the close of voting.
- *January 5*: At least 19 persons are killed and 25 others wounded, when explosions were triggered targeting migrant workers in six separate locations in the eastern districts of Dibrugarh and Tinsukia. Sibsagar district was also part of the area where explosion caused civilian casualty. Heavily armed ULFA militants attacked two brick kilns, fired indiscriminately on shops and business centres, besides triggering an explosion near a tea garden. Eight persons are killed and 11 others sustained injuries when ULFA militants opened fire at Bandarkhat and Langswal Tea Estates under Duliajan police station in the Tinsukia district.

2006

- *November 5*: At least 14 persons are killed and more than 52 others sustain injuries in two separate bomb blasts triggered by suspected ULFA militants at Fancy Bazaar and Noonmati area in Guwahati.
- *November 3*: Three ULFA militants are killed by SF personnel in a counter-insurgency operation at Kardoiguri under Moran police station in the Dibrugarh district. A huge cache of arms and explosives is recovered from the encounter site.
- *October27*: At least three civilians are killed and 22 persons, including one woman, a child and two Central Reserve Police Force personnel, sustain injuries when an improvised explosive device planted

on a bi-cycle parked in front of Paramount Restaurant is triggered at Dhekiajuli town in the Sonitpur district.

- *October 6*: At least 13 Railway Protection Force personnel are killed by in an ambush by the DHD militants belonging to the Black Widow faction in the North Cachar Hills district.
- *September 10*: The DHD cadres belonging to the anti-talks faction headed by Jewel Gorlosa set ablaze two labour camps at different construction sites of the Northeast Frontier Railway's broad gauge project in the North Cachar Hills, as the companies involved in the project fail to pay ransom to the militants. Additional Superintendent of Police Bidyut Buragohain confirmed that two labour sheds at Asong Haju and Saron Basti under Mahur police station were set ablaze by at least 12 cadres of the outfit.
- *August 14*: Three persons, including a woman and her son, are killed and seven others sustain injuries when suspected ULFA militants triggered a grenade explosion targeting security convoys near Lifecare Nursing Home at Duliajan town in the Dibrugarh district.
- *August 11*: At least six police personnel are killed after suspected ULFA militants ambush a police convoy at Ratanipathar under Pengeri police station in the Tinsukia district. While five personnel are killed at the incident site, another succumbs to injuries in the Assam Medical College Hospital.
- *August 1*: At least six police personnel are killed after suspected ULFA militants ambush a police convoy at Ratanipathar under Pengeri police station in the Tinsukia district. While five personnel are killed at the incident site, another succumbs to injuries in the Assam Medical College Hospital.
- *July 26*: An unidentified DHD cadre belonging to the Jewel Gorlossa faction triggers a grenade explosion,

targeting CRPF personnel, killing three civilians, including one female child, and injuring three others at a railway station in Maibong of North Cachar Hills district.

- *June 9*: At least five persons, including a 10-year-old boy and a woman, are killed and 16 persons wounded in a powerful explosion triggered by the ULFA at Machkowa vegetable market in the Guwahati city of Kamrup district.
- *June 8*: The ULFA triggers a series of grenade explosions, while targeting security force (SF) personnel, at various parts of the State leaving at least 25 persons wounded. While six persons are injured in a blast at Haiborgaon in the Nagaon district, another is injured when militants trigger a blast at Islampur Chowk in the Mangaldoi district.
- *February 10*: Eight civilians and one SF personnel are killed during clashes between the villagers and SFs following the alleged custodial death of a suspected United ULFA militant at Kakopathar in upper Assam's Tinsukia district. The ULFA cadre, whom the villagers described as a civilian, was detained by the army on February 6 and his dead body is subsequently recovered.

2005

- *December 3*: 379 houses are set ablaze by DHD militants in six villages of Mohendijua and Lunhnit areas in the Karbi Anglong district.
- *October 21*: Suspected DHD militants kill nine UPDS cadres at Tamulbari under Diphu police station in the Karbi Anglong district.
- *October 18*: Seven persons are killed in the continuing ethnic clashes in Karbi Anglong district. Six bodies are recovered from the Doyangmukh area while another was recovered from Borlangphar Tisso village under Diphu police station.
- *October 17*: Suspected DHD militants waylay two

passenger buses travelling from Zirikinding at Charchim under Kheroni police station in Karbi Anglong district and kill 23 persons, including nine women, belonging to the Karbi tribe. The same group of armed militants later kill seven persons in the nearby Sarsing village and five more persons in Prseck village.

- *October 10*: Six persons are killed during ethnic clashes in Karbi Anglong district. A group of 100 to 150 armed persons enter the Kheroni village, inhabited by the Dimasa tribe, and open indiscriminate fire killing six persons on the spot. Nearly 60 houses also set ablaze by the miscreants.
- *October 9*: Six persons from the Bura Fanchu and Longsing Engti villages are killed and hundreds of houses are set ablaze by unidentified terrorists in separate incidents under Diphu and Bokajan police stations in the Karbi Anglong district.
- *October 8*: Suspected militants enter the Karbi-dominated Borsing Bey village, seven km away from Diphu, and kill five Karbi villagers, including a two-year old child, and set ablaze more than 60 huts.
- *October 2*: Five members of a family are killed by unidentified militants at Hemari Terang village under Diphu police station in the Karbi Anglong district.
- *September 14*: Eight persons are killed and several others sustain injuries as suspected Kuki Revolutionary Army militants open indiscriminate fire at Thekerajan village in the Karbi Anglong district.
- *August 7*: Four persons are killed and 12 others sustain injuries in an explosion detonated by the ULFA at a bus stand at Boko in the Kamrup district.
- *June 19*: Four ULFA terrorists and one SF personnel are killed during two encounters in the Nalbari district.
- *June 16*: Four ULFA terrorists, including three woman cadres, are killed in an encounter with the police at

Doloni village under Khowang Police Station in the Dibrugarh district.

2004

- *October 29*: Five ULFA terrorists, members of the outfit's 'Action Group', are killed in an encounter at Kasojuli village under Laluk police station limits in the Lakhimpur district. A large quantity of arms and ammunition are recovered from their possession.
- *October 5*: Suspected NDFB terrorists shot dead at least ten civilians and wounded seven others in the Jalabila village of Dhubri district.
- *October 4*: Six civilians are shot dead and seven others sustain injuries when terrorists affiliated to the outlawed NDFB opened indiscriminate firing at Gelapukhuri village in Biswanath Chariali.
- *October 3*: Fourteen more persons are killed and at least 58 others sustain injuries in separate incidents of terrorist violence in Assam for the second consecutive day.
- *October 2*: Suspected NDFB and ULFA terrorists trigger a series of bomb blasts and open indiscriminate firing at various places in lower Assam killing at least 24 people and wounding over 40.
- *August 26*: ULFA triggers off a series of bomb blasts in different districts of Assam, killing six persons and injuring 80 others.
- *August 15*: 17 persons, including 16 school children, are killed as ULFA detonates explosives at the venue of Independence day celebrations in Dhemaji town.
- *June 24*: Seven bus passengers are killed and fifteen others sustain injuries as suspected ULFA terrorists detonate a bomb inside a passenger bus at Majgaon under Mathurapur police station limits in the Sibsagar district.
- *March 24*: Suspected KRA terrorists kill at least 33 Karbi villagers in three separate places in the Karbi Anglong district.

- *March 19*: Suspected terrorists of the anti-talks faction of UPDS kill six Kuki tribals and set ablaze seven houses at the remote Thengbong village in the Singhasan hills area of Karbi Anglong district.
- *March 3*: Four ULFA terrorists are killed in an encounter with troops of the Red Horns Division of the Army at Tepkilobana in the Kamrup district.
- *January 28*: Four ULFA terrorists trying to enter into Assam from Bhutan are killed in an encounter at Paharbasti under Tamulpur police station jurisdiction in the Nalbari district.
- *January 1*: Four NDFB terrorists are killed in an encounter with the Army along the India-Bhutan border at Paharpur under Darrangamela police station limits in Nalbari district.

2003

- *March 16*: Six civilians are killed and 55 others injured in an Improvised Explosive Device (IED) blast set-off by ULFA terrorists under a passenger bus on National Highway No. 7, Bamunghopha, Goalpara district.
- *March 8*: Suspected ULFA terrorists attack an oil storage depot and a gas pipeline in Tinsukia district, causing a loss of approximately Rupees 200 million to the Indian Oil Corporation.

2002

- *October 27*: NDFB terrorists massacre 22 civilians after dragging them out of their houses in Datgiri village, Kokrajhar district.
- *October 13*: Unidentified terrorists kill five persons in a grenade attack at a Hindu religious congregation in Bongaigaon district.
- *August 21*: NDFB terrorists kill four police personnel and a civilian in an Improvised Explosive Device (IED) blast at Maladhara, Lakhipur police station limits, Goalpara district.

- *July 30*: NDFB lays an ambush near Durgapur village, Kokrahar district, killing five security force personnel and two civilians.
- *July 18*: Seven security force personnel are killed and a civilian injured in an ambush, laid allegedly by DHD terrorists near Diyungmukh, a local market in the North Cachar Hills district.
- *July 14*: Suspected NDFB terrorists massacre nine tribals at the West Maligaon forest village relief camps, Kokrajhar district.
- *April 5*: NDFB terrorists kill five tribals at Hatiphuli relief camp in Kokrajhar and another at the relief camp in Tongsi, Dhubri district.
- *January 27*: Suspected ULFA terrorists kill Kamrup Deputy district police chief Devajit Pathak and his driver on the Boko-Nalapara road by triggering an Improvised Explosive Devise (IED) blast in Nalapara village.
- *January 23*: Unidentified terrorists kill 'vice-chairman' of the United People's Democratic Solidarity (UPDS) in Karbi Anglong district.
- *January 15*: Thirteen civilians are massacred by NDFB terrorists at Dailongjhar in Bongaigon district.

2001

- *December 3*: Eight persons, including six government officials on election duty, are killed in an IED explosion by suspected UPDS terrorists at Lamelangso in the Karbi Anglong district.
- *October 29*: Four persons, including two police personnel, are killed in an attack by suspected DHD terrorists at Dhanasiri in Karbi Anglong district.
- *October 19*: 10 NDFB cadres and three police personnel are killed as the NDFB attacks a police station at Labdanguri in Barpeta district.
- *August 25*: Suspected UPDS terrorists killed four persons by blowing up a truck at Bhuligaon, Karbi Anglong district.

- *August 5*: 10 persons, including eight security force personnel, are killed in an explosion caused by suspected NDFB terrorists at Silbari in Bongaigaon district.
- *July 31*: Six Bhutanese citizens are killed in an explosion at Dadgiri.
- *June 3*: 10 tribals are killed by suspected NDFB terrorists at the Lungsung Reserved forest area.
- *May 3*: Six Asom Gana Parishad (AGP) activists are killed by suspected ULFA terrorists in the Nalbari and Goalpara districts.
- *March 18*: Six persons, including two children, are killed by suspected NDFB terrorists at Ramgaon village in Kamrup district
- *March 6*: Six persons are killed in an ambush on a truck by suspected Adivasi terrorists at Fulkumari village in Kokrajhar district.
- *February 8*: Nine police personnel are killed and three others are injured in an ambush laid by unidentified terrorists near Dehangi in North Cachar hills district.
- *January 29*: 11 woodcutters are killed by suspected UPDS terrorists in the Thansa forest area of Karbi Anglong district.
- *January 13*: Four civilians are killed by suspected National Democratic Font of Bodoland terrorists in Nalbari district.
- *January 2*: Three Surrendered ULFA (SULFA) cadres, including former ULFA leader Abinash Bordoloi, are killed by suspected ULFA terrorists in Nalbari district.

2000

- December 31: Four Hind-speaking persons are killed by suspected UPDS terrorists at Disobai forest in Karbi Anglong district.
- December 28: Eight persons from the Hindi-speaking community are killed by suspected UPDS terrorists at Ranganagar village in Karbi Anglong district.

- December 7: 28 Hindi-speaking traders and farm workers from Bihar are killed by suspected ULFA terrorists near Sadiya.
- November 30: 22 persons—a majority of them non-Assamese, including eight Bihari truck drivers—are killed in three separate massacres in the Bongaigaon district.
- November 25: Eight woodcutters are killed by NDFB terrorists in the Lung Sung forest reserve.
- November 8: Eight civilians, including seven of a non-Assamese community, are killed by suspected NDFB terrorists in Barpeta district.
- October 23: 15 persons are killed by suspected ULFA terrorists in two separate incidents in the Tinsukia and Dibrugarh districts.
- September 14: NSCN-IM and UPDS terrorists kill eleven persons, including ten police personnel, in an ambush near Diphu.
- August 25: Bodo terrorists kill five persons in a landmine blast in Kokrajhar district.
- August 21: NDFB terrorists kill five civilians in Dhubri. At Garagaon, another group of NDFB terrorists kill Bodo legislator Mohini Basumatary.
- *April 19*: UPDS terrorists massacre 11 persons in two separate incidents in Karbi Anglong district.

1999

- *October 3*: Five police personnel are killed in an attack by ULFA terrorists near Rupasi in Barpeta district.
- *September 30*: Four persons are killed in an attack by ULFA terrorists on a election campaign party of the Asom Gana Parishad at Dholpur Chapori, Mangaldoi district.
- *August 23*: Unidentified terrorists launch a bomb attack on a vehicle of Central Reserve Police Force killing four persons at Maithang Bridge, Kakopathar police station limits, Tinsukia District.
- *June 29*: Seven police personnel are killed in an

explosion set-off by Bodo Liberation Tigers (BLT) terrorists in two separate villages near Rangiya, Kamrup district.

- *March 8*: Seven family members of ULFA terrorists are killed in a retaliatory attack by SULFA cadres in Guwahati.
- *January 23*: Seven civilians are killed by suspected NDFB terrorists in Darrang District.
- *January 1*: Three police personnel are killed in an attack by suspected NDFB terrorists on a camp of the 7 battalion of Assam police in Bhumka, Kokrajhar district

1998

- *December 20*: Six security force personnel and four civilians are killed in an ambush laid by ULFA terrorists in Dhubri district.
- *December 12*: Bodo terrorists kill 23 Muslim settlers in Kokrajhar district.
- *October 11*: BLTF terrorists kill 13 Assamese and Bengali-speaking people in Darrang district.
- *September 28*: Seven security force personnel are killed in an ambush laid by ULFA terrorists in Goalpara district.

1997

Incident Details 1997

- *January 13*: Bodo Security Force (BSF) militants kill nine cadres of the rival Bodo Liberation Tiger Force (BLTF) in a raid on their camp in Nalbari District.

1996

- *May 23*: Violent clashes between Bodo terrorists and Santhals leave more than 80 people dead in Kokrajhar and Bongaigaon districts.
- *April 25*: ULFA terrorists kill a local Congress (I) leader and four others near Margherita town, Tinsukia district.

1994

- *May 27-July 27*: Bodo terrorists carry out large-scale attacks on non-Bodos, leaving more than 100 people dead and over 60,000 homeless.

1990

- *May 9*: ULFA terrorists kill Surendra Paul, a leading tea planter, causing many tea estate managers to flee the State.

10

The "Tribal Unrest" in Assam

If the Northeast as a whole has been has long been neglected by the centre, so the hill tribes have also faced callous disregard by the state of Assam, and both these factors have given rise to separatist movements, from Nagas struggling for complete independence to Mizos wanting independence but settling for statehood, Bodos still fighting for their own state, and smaller groups simply demanding more local autonomy. All too often, it is the contempt with which these claims have been met that has turned them into violent uprisings"

INDIA: THE ROUGH GUIDE

"The...(argument is) that the 'tribal' situation in northeast India cannot be properly understood except by viewing it in its historical perspective...British policy with regard to the hill people was one of least interference, the impact of administration and its corollary, the church, significantly corroded their internal system of authority and exposed them to territorial power"-S.K. Chaube

The quotes above desperately seek to represents a political and social milieu where the subject is peculiarly silent. For those who are critical of such reductionism and socio-historical short hand, the issue of representation of regions, peoples and situations become a question that has to be engaged with and qualified over and over again. However, in the case of this particular representation of the Northeast (in general) and Assam (in particular), one senses an air of resignation, in the ability of both democratic logic and academic scholarship, to be able to qualify such representations.

It is true that secessionism and identity politics have defined political discourse in this region that was once the undivided (colonial) province of Assam. It is also true that disparities and differences have been at the core of this discourse. Chaube, suggests that the "tribal situation" is at an unfortunate position because its internal system was corroded by external actors. Similarly, the quote lifted from the Rough Guide, paints a chaotic political picture, where political positions are laced with violence.

In short, there is a general understanding that something is happening in the hills of the region, but academic (and leisure) pursuits stop short of asking questions that can adequately express the unrest, violence and assertions of ethnic identity. What this paper argues is that in the inability to tackle these questions, academic discourse on the tribal question has also been guilty, like the Rough Guide authors, of producing short-hand, easily accessible "knowledge" about the tribal question in the Northeast.

This paper tries to argue that the method of framing the tribal question within a particular political moment happened at a particular period when "frontiers" were being created. It was this process (of creation of frontiers") that the "tribal question" was silenced by conventional historiography of the region.

Since the middle of the twentieth century, the colonial province of Assam has had to engage with a multitude of ethnic assertions. There is an element of surprise in the commentaries that try to explain any of the ethnic assertions. To a large extent, this sense of sociological rootless-ness is blamed on the lack of any historiography of the tribal people.

In response, tribal/indigenous movements and assertions periodically raise their history, reaffirm their myths and legends and stake a claim for equality. What is striking about this phenomenon is that despite the passions they ignite in people, the contested symbols and iconography that they create, they are seldom subjected to a historical analysis that can explain the serious contests and revival of a community's sense of self.

There is no coherent historiography on the tribal question, in the erstwhile colonial province of Assam that is free from the overwhelming influence of an ethnological tradition steeped in romanticism and idealism. In fact, it is so common that even travel books do not hesitate to repeat what is appears as an unproblematic silence on the "tribal question" by historiographers.

It is as if the (tribal) question is irrelevant and by the same extension, the political realities of the Karbi, Tiwa, Boro and other indigenous peoples, being either a matter of journalistic political columns alone, or a rehashing of old ethnographic accounts in sociological research. The historiography of tribal people of the region is presented as not something that is necessarily fluid. It is presented in a form that fixes their history within a realm of myths and possibilities culled from secondary texts.

The historian dealing with the tribal question in Assam (and the Northeast) writes history in a form that will be accepted. In everyday life, people judge this act of writing history on criteria that may not quite correspond to the historian's. In the difference between how history is written and the manner in which it becomes relevant to political discourse lies the politics of categorisation of people to margins and partially explains the silence on the "tribal question".

"Frontiers, Landscapes and Peoples": Frameworks of Colonial Ethnography. It is almost the norm to begin a historical study of any of the tribal/ indigenous communities of Assam with a roll call of secondary sources that purport to be the "myth of origin" of the particular community in question. In Assam, usually it is some reference to nineteenth and twentieth century reconstruction of the chronicles of the Ahom period in eastern Assam.

In the modern reconstruction, the chronicles (bu'ranji) appear as the substitute for the truth, as though the historian by some twist in time is transported back to the day and age of the Ahom kings. Somehow, the tribes appear as extras in a grand production with the usual odd characters that shine briefly before disappearing again. Another way to begin would start with the physiognomy of the people in question which are then added to a liberal dose of possibilities from reconstructed Vedic texts.

For example: "...(The) Mishing tribe of Assam...a fragment of the great Mongoloid horde occupying the hills and dales of north-eastern India. Sir George Grierson has categorically divided these Mongoloids into (a) primitive long headed (b) less primitive short headed and (c) Tibeto-Mongoloids...and the Mishings form a fraction of this race"

This quote has been rather arbitrarily singled out from a multitude of similar texts. What is common to all of them is this (almost) naïve belief in secondary sources and their urge to rush headlong into finding a location and anthropological type for the subjects in question. Granted, that the lack of written sources play a huge in role in the manner in which they are defined. For scholars, this always remains a barrier in constructing a history of a people.

The reference to Grierson, a functionary of the colonial government and the director of the Linguistic Survey of India in the late nineteenth century, is quite significant. In a sense, it is difficult to circumvent colonial ethnography while working on any of the indigenous groups in the Northeast and in Assam in particular. However, the question bears repeating: just how useful are these sources in understanding the dynamics of the tribal question? Are they, in any way, so irrefutable that they must be reproduced in every subsequent text on any tribe/ indigenous population in Assam?

Obviously, colonial documents are good place to start for anyone who wants to construct a historiography of the Tiwa, Karbi or any of the other major/ minor indigenous groups in Assam. They tell a part of the story that can be used to build any historical edifice. In that case, what are the presuppositions and contingencies upon which the colonial ethnographic project came to be constructed? Some of the answers are captured in Pemberton's report to government in 1835"...(In the following report on) the eastern frontier of the British territories, it is proposed: ...In the first place to give a general description of the great chain of mountains...Secondly, to describe the nature and passes and countries by which the great mountain chain has been penetrated..."

The reference to frontier is quite obvious in this historical context. The nineteenth century was in fact the era of expansion of capital to hitherto untrammelled landscapes such as Assam. This "discovery" precipitated a move towards a fundamentally different type of economy, where the movement of populations became a condition for growth and colonisation.

The process of creating "frontiers" became a condition peculiar to the type of economy introduced. Pemberton was not directing his report to a prospective "pleasure traveller", but to policy makers keen on knowing the landscape they were entering. More: importantly, these were policy makers who saw the region as political frontier on the geographical northeast of their territories. This geographical location, would not only place the region in a hierarchical relationship with the metropolitan centres, but also remain rooted as a frontier, in the nationalist challenges that came later.

The politics of a descriptive generalisation of the political geography had one inherent problem. It was hardly the "uninhabited wasteland" that the descriptions made them out be. The presence of groups of people, locked in a political and economic relationship with one another, was underplayed in the initial colonial reports of the period.

Hence, a complicated process of mapping the region within notions of centre-periphery was being undertaken. With it, there was visible move towards what Rumley and Minghi call the "consideration of border landscapes as a set of cultural, economic and political interactions and processes occurring in space". Those inhabiting regions that were not immediately earmarked for expansion of capital and colonial administration were clearly subjected to a position of marginality precisely because they constituted a new periphery. It was only with the need to engage with policy making that Pemberton's exotic landscape became "populated" with people.

Not many years after Pemberton's geographical descriptions, the economy of the Luit (Brahmaputra) valley underwent changes where the colonial administration began an elaborate process of categorising the different regions, the people who lived there and their social and economic relations.

In his still popular "report", Moffatt-Mills, began the intellectually challenging work of mapping the region, along with its people. His work can be seen as the natural corollary to what Pemberton had done a decade or two earlier. Moffatt-Mills had the challenging task of rationalising the complex relations between the hills and plains, forest-dwellers, traders, agriculturists and others, and securing this knowledge to governance and administration.

It was imperative, for example, to have an adequate knowledge of the complex relations surrounding the haats (local marts) for the purpose of taxation and at times for retribution. The punitive expeditions against the Bhutiyas, Khasis and Nagas were all related to the need to secure land, by force as well as by law. This project is a fascinating dossier of manipulation of territory and people that is centrally linked to administering a frontier. Politics of the times dictated not only the fixing of people to territory, but also to "reopening" roads and trade routes.

In doing so, a particular intellectual space was created. A certain form of reading the histories of the indigenous peoples came to be accepted as the norm. The form and content of this reading followed a strict regimentation where the historical and anthropological location of the subject was made conditional to the linear passage of time and social formation. Hence, Gait's subsequent rendition of the history of Assam, now accepted as the standard text for history students, mixed an eclectic selection of Persian and Ahom texts and presented to the readers a view of history that was reassuring. This reassurance, however, should be read as a product of its time.

The weight of textual representations and archaeology meant that only selected formations appeared as actors in the ensemble of historiography. Thus, kings, texts and conquests formed the basis of recognition for the indigenous people. It is not surprising that Gait's book, in its published (and prescribed) form, appears with an introduction that first refers back to an older, idealistic notion of ethnography, wildly plotting the possible places of origin of the different peoples of the region. Having done that, the 'Introduction' meanders into a realm of myth and memory- the latter presented in medieval Persian texts. Hills and plains become mere textual markers and their inhabitants, the subjects of different disciplines. Those who were part of a semi-feudal state formation, with kings/ chiefs, and a cosmology that allowed social hierarchy, such as the Koch, Dimasa and Ahom are accorded a 'history', an identity that freezes them in time and politics.

MASSACRES, CONSPIRACIES AND POLITICAL CYNICISM

Two massacres have shattered the already fragile political situation in Assam, in the month of October alone. The timing of both massacres is important, as is the fact that in both instances the victims belonged to predominantly Hindi-speaking communities. In all, twenty-five people have been butchered and despite a cynical game of pinning the blame on the most convenient scapegoats, the administration has done nothing to determine the cause and effect of the cold-blooded murders.

This provisional report is an attempt to dissect the tragic events themselves, as well as analyse the response on the State and non-State actors. Our organisation reiterates that this report is more than circumstantial evidence, to try and pin the blame or absolve any one party in the massacres. It is the result of a long-drawn engagement with the ground realities and history of counter-insurgency tactics in Assam.

It is also an attempt to engage the State apparatus (yet again) in a process of democratic reconsideration of its militarisation policies. Due to certain restraints, we have had to rely mainly on media reports of the massacres. An independent fact-finding, by any civil rights organisation, seems impossible at this stage, given the deployment of armed personnel. Moreover, this report does not wish to contend the veracity of the reports in the press. Our intention is to relate disparate elements as they appeared in the local and national press, to the larger history of counter-insurgency and militarisation in Assam. As such, these massacres need some plausible explanations. The ones provided by the dominant political forces, one feels, are too simplistic and very misleading.

The Events: On October 22, 2000 a group of armed men dressed in jungle fatigues entered Kakojan village, fifteen kilometres from Doomdooma town, in Tinsukia district. They were all riding motorcycles. Once in the village, they went up to Keshab Kanu's (a local grocer) shop and ordered the assembled to line up there. They spoke in Hindi, all the while asking people to assemble there and wait for the 'sahib'.

Once the people were lined up, the armed assailants opened fire killing and injuring many of the people. Amongst the dead were- Keshab Kanu (35), Shankar Kanu (20), Binoy Kanu (17), Subhash Gupta (50), Raju Gupta (20), Parshuram Prasad (36), Sheikh Hazrat (56), Sheikh Mushtaq (35), Pawan Singh (20) and Manoj Singh (18). Three others, Ashraf Ali, Krishna Gupta and Rajen Prasad were injured and taken to a nearby hospital. As a result of the firing, a thatched house and cowshed caught fire. The assailants escaped from the spot soon after [As reported in *Assam Tribune;* October 24, 2000].

A few hours before the Kakojan incident, three armed youth barged into a shop in Naoholia market, under Jeypore Police Station in Dibrugarh district and opened fire. They shot dead the owner of the shop- Radheshyam Agarwal (39). As they were trying to make a getaway they also shot Talbi Mian (55), Harendra Shaha (30) and a child Jitendra Rai (3). Five people who were injured in the incident were identified as Sushil Rai, Sahadev Paswan, Sudama Thakur, Nathan Shah and Surji Devi [As reported in *The Telegraph;* October 24, 2000].

On October 27, 2000 a group of armed men *inside a Tata Sumo* vehicle, got off and began opening indiscriminate fire near the Hari Mandir area of Nalbari town, at around 6.30 p.m. Six persons were killed on the spot and three of the injured succumbed to their injuries later in hospital. In this case as well, the victims belonged to the Hindi-speaking community of the town.

The deceased were Biswanath Bajaj (55), Dharamchand Jain (51), Laxmi Narayan Bajaj (52) Godavari Bajaj (45), Sawarlal Sharma (50), Jaikumar Jain (52). The identity of the three other deceased were not immediately ascertained, though the names of the injured were- Inder Singh, Dinanath Rai, Umang Bajaj and Nandan Jain. The police recovered a lot of handbills bearing the name of 'Assam Tiger Force' from the area.

THE ROUND OF INEVITABLE ALLEGATIONS

In both instances, the local English and national press was quick to lay the blame for these killings squarely on the United Liberation Front of Assam. All the major English dailies carried headlines that were not exactly designed to leave room for doubt. A brief survey of a sample of headlines is in order to determine the knee-jerk reaction of the media and the authorities: '15 die in twin strikes as Ulfa ends lull' [*The Telegraph,* October 24, 2000]; 'Migrants bear brunt of ULFA terror' [*The Indian Express,* October 24, 2000]; 'ULFA strikes at Doomdooma' [*North East Times,* October 24, 2000]; 'Suspected ULFA ultras mow down 10 in Nalbari' [*The Sentinel,* October 28, 2000]; '10 butchered in Ulfa ethnic cleansing' [*The Telegraph,* October 28, 2000].

All the papers mentioned actually carried the news reports that were the police versions of who were responsible for this heinous crime. This of course was a fact that was understated and the brutality of the event made it so much easier to 'accept' the newspapers reportage. But the local Assamese dailies tried to investigate and convey to the reader the complexity of the events. Papers like *Aji,* also hinted at the possible complicity of Intelligence Agencies like Research and Analysis Wing (RAW) [*Aji,* October 28, 2000].

The sub-text in the narration of both these events leave a lot of loopholes that need to be plugged. However, the fact remains that civil society at large has been forced to uncritically accept the police version of the events, both in upper Assam and in Nalbari. Not once did any of the reports mention the basis upon which the police claimed to have 'solved the case'.

No investigation, either departmental or judicial was undertaken before the police issued its 'official' line.

In line with the official policy of pushing the dirt under the carpet, all the circumstantial evidence that could point to a larger, more complex web of violence, was downplayed. No details about the so-called 'Assam Tiger Force' were forthcoming. They were there merely to pull the triggers and leave behind pamphlets. It is not the first time that such an organisation has reared its head, claiming this dastardly deed on behalf of itself and whoever it represents.

There is a definite pattern to this. Six years ago, very few people had heard of the 'Bodo Liberation Tiger Force'. It wasn't until the Bodo-Santhal clashes and the ill-fated train bomb that people took notice. Today, they are a force that can claim some amount of dubious legitimacy as they bargain for scraps from the Central government. People have seemingly forgotten their violent acts or the fact that on many an instance, they were reported to have been backed by the Indian army and intelligence agencies, such as RAW. Even though the preliminary round of accusations by the State apparatus seeks to hold ULFA responsible, there is enough evidence to prove that this is not a 'cut-and-dry' case. Political organisations like Congress (I) have condemned the massacres and sought to distance themselves from it by demanding President's Rule in the state. CPI (M-L) have issued a statement saying that these massacres are an 'attempt by the ruling class' strategy to divide people along communal lines and to demolish the democratic movement surrounding the burning issues in the state [As reported in *Dainik Agradoot;* October 29, 2000].

The United Minority Front has claimed that 'massacres of such a scale cannot be carried out by an extremist group without the active support of a political party'; as such an event has never been carried out by any militant organisation before. The CPI (M) has said that this a political conspiracy that is designed to create clashes along communal lines, between different communities and the need of the hour is to identify the forces that endorse such trends [As reported in *Dainik Asom;* October 29, 2000].

It seems evident that most political groupings are falling all over themselves, to try and either distance themselves from this or pin it on someone else. The Chief Minister himself thinks that 'this is a conspiracy to dislodge him from power' [As reported in *North East Times;* October 29, 2000]. Instead of scouring the land for the killers, the police officials, like G.M Srivastava (the man responsible for implementing the counter-insurgency tactics of the police in Assam) have questioned the 'fact' that human rights organisations have not said anything against these encounters.

This is as far from the truth as possible. MASS' statements condemning the massacres were published, as was NECOHR's immediately after both the heinous incidents. What MASS and NECOHR failed to do however, was to accept the 'official view'. There is reason to be sceptical of any claim made by the administration on issues surrounding any form of violence in Assam, unless these claims are backed by infallible proof and endorsed by independent bodies.

In the meantime, the administration and a section of the media, have decided that there is only one set of possibilities in a tragedy of this scale. Find a scapegoat, paint it black and hope the persistent questions that remain will disappear.

WHY WE OUGHT TO BE SCEPTICAL

For one, the ULFA itself has claimed that it did not carry out these killings. Its commander-in-chief, Paresh Barua, issued a statement immediately when the events came to be known on October 24, 2000, saying that the proscribed organisation did not endorse such kind of violence. While it may be prudent not to accept any statement at face value, one needs to apply the same logic to statements of the police and other members of the administration.

However, if one goes by past experience, ULFA's stand on communal and ethnic conflicts has been rather consistent. In 1992, following the Babri Masjid demolition, there were strong indications that its effects would be felt in Assam too. The ruling Congress (I) and minority political leaders tried to ignite the flame of communal passion in Nagaon, the most sensitive area in terms of communal conflict. ULFA intervened in all the sensitive areas, cautioning people against sinister political designs. Their efforts averted a potential bloodbath in Nagaon in particular and the rest of the region in general.

Secondly, ULFA has suffered tremendous losses, according to the State's own admission. In upper Assam, the use of vehicles and the manner in which the details of the massacre were operationalised leaves room for serious inquiry into the police's version. In the Kakojan massacre, the assailants used seven motorcycles, which normally would also mean that they could be traced.

However, far from offering details about the bikes, the inexplicable is being sought to be passed off as 'truth'. In Nalbari, the assailants were aboard a Tata Sumo and in the middle of town. Such a conspicuous luxury, in times of great difficulty beats political and military logic of any group that is supposed to be 'on the run'. According to newspaper sources, the people of Nalbari are aggrieved with the authorities for a variety of reasons.

Firstly, Sanjay Bajaj, the son of late Biswanath Bajaj, informed newspaper sources that even though he had informed the police within five minutes of the incident, it took the police forty-five minutes to arrive at the spot, which is but a five minute drive from the police station [As reported in *North East Times;* October 29, 2000].

The police's claim that the attacks were part of a long drawn strategy of coercing people into paying money, by ULFA also seems to fall flat as Manoj Jain, son of the late Jaikumar Jain, said that no such demand was made on them by any organisation [*North East Times;* October 29, 2000]. According to another eyewitness, a small posse of CRPF personnel was present in the area minutes before the heinous event at Nalbari.

However, a police official came and asked them to leave the place [As reported in *The Telegraph;* October 29, 2000]. While such evidence may be attributed to coincidence by the cynical observer and die-hard believer in the administration's version, the lack of conclusive proof makes it impossible to rule out the existence of a larger conspiracy. The 'ULFA angle' is far too simplistic and repetitive.

Thirdly, the deployment of troops in the areas where the massacres took place is another disturbing factor that needs more explanation. In upper Assam there is hardly any scope for ULFA, or any proscribed group, to carry out an operation of such a scale without the knowledge and connivance of the police, paramilitary, army and SULFA renegades. To imagine that an organisation like ULFA would then negotiate with all the existing State forces is very far-fetched.

Equally implausible, is the theory that massacres of such a scale could be carried out and the perpetrators slip away like ghosts, given the tight security surveillance. Upper Assam, which is fertile ground for ULFA, an event like this would reduce the organisation's credibility and that itself defies political logic. In Nalbari, which was once an area where they were very active, subsequent military, paramilitary, police and SULFA deployment have made it almost impossible for any ULFA cadre to move around there. The joint activities of the former forces have created a wave of terror there. Even families and sympathisers of the proscribed organisation have been targeted and killed. Moreover, there were additional security forces deployed in Nalbari on that day, in preparation of the Chief Minister and Governor's visit that was scheduled for October 28, 2000 (*i.e.* the very next day of the massacre). In any event of this scope and brutality there are always telltale signs that point out to the bits that don't fit.

Fourthly, the history of the State's intervention in the ongoing low-intensity conflict has evolved in a manner that implicates it in events such as these tragic massacres. The conventional military strategy to combat ULFA head-on, which proved futile in the early 1990s, transformed itself into a kind of traditional counter-insurgency theatre. However, in this period the State also made use of underlying tensions within civil society in order to criminalise the struggles.

One needs only to refer back to the Bodo-Santhal clashes of 1995, which started with the discovery of three dead women, whom both communities claimed belonged to them. Instead of immediately assuaging their doubts, a situation was allowed to arise, whereby an obscure group, trained by Indian intelligence agencies and the army, called the BLTF was allowed to play upon communal tension and widen its own reach. Ironically, the three unfortunate women were neither Bodo or Santhal, but Nepali, as was 'discovered' earlier. By the middle of the decade the State had begun to utilise roving bands of surrendered ULFA (SULFA) renegades in its attempt to contain the armed movement for self-determination. This occurred with the parallel development of the police as a force that operated outside the framework of law. The militarisation process has been instrumental in the rise of the number of fake encounters and custodial deaths.

The use of renegades in counter-insurgency is standard tactic. It subverts the normal process of justice and given the fact that the legal structure is barely capable of dealing with normal rule of law, such a development renders it impotent. The number of crimes committed by SULFA renegades in connivance with the police/paramilitary/army, have never seen the light of day in a civilian court, despite all evidence of such a nexus being conclusive. In a sense, the new strategy of containing insurgency has given the State apparatus a literal monopoly to enact violence. Even the symbolic 'crackdown' on SULFA renegades seems empty in the light of the fact that those whose links with security personnel have been proved beyond reasonable doubt have been let off.

The capacity to terrorise civil society in Assam today, rests solely with the State apparatus. This is not a statement that can be repudiated outright, even by apologists of the administration. On the other hand, given the fact that ULFA is not considered a 'belligerent force' in an area where rule of International Humanitarian Law may be applicable, make it impossible for citizens to have access to their plans. What we get is what we receive from the authorities that treat the armed struggle as a law and order problem.

The ground reality however suggests that there is a definite low-intensity conflict that is being played out in Assam. The dual policy of the State, which on the one hand seeks to project this as an 'internal law and order problem' to the outside world, while on the other hand endorses extra-constitutional use of force, leaves us a little sick. The predictable response of the administration needs to be seen in light of this history.

WHAT IS TO BE DONE

In our haste to find the culprits of the dastardly acts of violence, one ought to be cautious in passing judgement.

If justice has to be done someone has to take responsibility for the following events in the history of violence in modern Assam:

- The process of systematic militarisation of the polity in Assam and the North East has to be questioned. The apportioning of guilt can happen only after the rule of International Humanitarian Law is made applicable and independent authorities allowed to independent the issue.
- The details of the use of renegades in counter-insurgency have to be made public by the authorities. The cases that for so long have been kept under wraps, as Assam's worst kept secrets, have to be tried by impartial bodies.
- Civil, Democratic and Human Rights organisations have to be allowed to work without fear of reprisal by the State.

While these steps may seem too huge a task, the absence of any will to realise them would be disastrous. With Assembly elections around the corner, this pattern of seemingly 'random' violence will only increase. Even as this happens, the administration will seek to fob the blame on non-State actors. In such a situation it becomes important for all democratic opinion to unite and unravel the sinister designs of the State apparatus in Assam. Their attempt is to discredit all voices of dissent, be it from proscribed organisations or from civil society organisations. The death of innocent civilians ought to shake us from our complacency and strongly articulate the need for realizing justice and applicability of rule of law for the people of the region.

11

An Assessment of Insurgencies in North East and Assam in 2009

INTRODUCTION

The North Eastern region of India is a rugged territory of 225,000 square kilometres of hill and plains located between four neighbouring countries of India, namely, Bangladesh, Bhutan, China and Myanmar. With an international border stretching up to 4,500 kms, the region has been plagued by instability, insurgency, and social unrest since independence. Leading the host of aggrieved and violent actors are the Nagas, whose movement can be traced back to 1918 with the formation of the Naga Club.

In 1946, the Naga National Council (NNC) was formed and it declared Naga independence on August 14, 1947, a day before India declared its own independence. The Naga movement turned violent in the 1950s and is active till date under the aegis of the National Socialist Council of *Nagalim*-Isak-Muivah [NSCN (IM)] and the National Socialist Council of Nagaland- S.S. Khaplang [NSCN (K)]. Manipur has also been greatly disturbed by armed violence with the formation of the United National Liberation Front of Manipur (UNLF) on November 24, 1964.

Another significant Manipuri armed separatist group known as the Revolutionary People's Front (RPF) and its armed wing, the People's Liberation Army (PLA), has been engaging in armed struggle since 1976. The RPF and the PLA were supposedly trained by the Chinese in the 1960s and 1970s in Maoist guerrilla warfare and both outfits aim at violent revolutionary change to bring about a classless society in Manipur.

Most feared in Manipur, however, is the *Kanglai Kana Yan Lup* (KYKL), which has taken up social afflictions such as fighting corruption, drug trafficking and sub-standard education practices. Another group known as the Peoples' Revolutionary Party of *Kangleipak* (PREPAK) was established in the 1970s with the objective of fighting for Manipur's independence from India. Neighbouring Assam, the most dominant state in the North East in terms of demography and resources, has also been plagued by insurgent violence since 1979 with the formation of the United Liberation Front of Asom (ULFA).

The hills districts of Assam, North Cachar Hills and Karbi Anglong, have also witnessed the rise of armed groups since the 1990s like the Dima Halam Daogah (DHD) and the United Peoples' Democratic Solidarity (UPDS). It is important to note that most of these insurgent groups have thrived primarily due to strong external connections. Countries like China in the 1960s and the 1970s as well as Pakistan and later on Bangladesh have supported most of these outfits in their fight against India by making available arms, training and most importantly base areas for underground camps. As recently as 2007, India accused Bangladesh of enabling insurgent groups like the UNLF, ULFA and NSCN (IM) with small arms through its Cox Bazaar area as well as with the establishment of underground camps in the Chittagong and Mymensingh areas. IDSA Issue Brief 3

2009: AN ASSESSMENT

While states like Arunachal Pradesh, Meghalaya, Mizoram and Tripura have been peaceful for some years now, 2009 witnessed significant developments towards peace in Assam and Nagaland, though Manipur continued to reel under multiple insurgencies. In Assam, the Dima Halam Daogah (Garlosa) faction [DHD (G)] surrendered and is now housed in designated camps; ULFA Chairman and founding member Arabinda Rajkhowa and Deputy Commander-in-Chief Raju Barua were arrested along the Meghalaya-Bangladesh

border by the Assam Police in December 2009. This is a critical development for Assam as most of the violence it has suffered over the years is suspected to be the handiwork of the ULFA operating from Bangladeshi soil. Nagaland witnessed further moves towards peaceful reconciliation between the insurgent factions in 2009 with the NSCN (IM) and NSCN (K) jointly signing a "reconciliation convention".

Violence levels remained high in Assam and Manipur in 2009 while Nagaland witnessed a steep drop in violence as compared to the previous year. Assam suffered 371 insurgency related deaths in 2009 as compared to 387 in 2008; Manipur, 369 in 2009 as compared to 499 in 2008, and Nagaland, 17 in 2009 as compared to 201 in 2008. While Assam and Manipur registered a drop in the numbers of people killed, the percentage of difference was not sharp; whereas in Nagaland, the decline in violence was in the margin of 80 to 85 per cent.

This is a good sign as it reflects the success of not only the cease-fires between the Government of India and the NSCN (IM) and the NSCN (K) in place since 1997 and 2001 respectively, but also the success of efforts for peaceful reconciliation between the two armed groups by Naga civil society actors like the Naga Hoho (Tribal Apex Council) and the Forum for Naga Reconciliation (FNR).

Let us now dwell on each individual state specifically with regard to the state of insurgency in 2009.

HIGHLIGHTS OF 2009

Assam witnessed the arrest of ULFA leaders and surrender of the DHD (G). Manipur witnessed 19 organizations of the Kuki National Organization agreeing to a Suspension of Operations (SoO) with the Government of India. Also, UNLF called for unified struggle with the Naxalites against the Indian state. Nagaland witnessed a steep fall in violence and progress towards peace amongst its various insurgent factions

ASSAM

2009 has been one of the most significant years for Assam.Amongst the armed insurgent groups, the DHD (G) is one of the most elusive and violent, operating in the North Cachar Hills and Karbi Anglong districts of Assam. The DHD was formed in 1995 after most of the cadres of the erstwhile imasa National Security Force (DNSF) surrendered with the exception of its commander Jewel Garlosa. It was under his leadership that the DHD was organized into a violent force.

The stated demand of the then unified DHD (it subsequently broke into two factions in 2003) was a unified *Dimaraji* state comprised of Dimasa-inhabited areas of North Cachar Hills district, Karbi Anglong district, Cachar district, parts of Nagaon district in Assam, and Dimapur and Dimasa inhabited areas in Dhansiripar in Nagaland.

In interviews with the Chairperson of the DHD (Nunisa) faction [DHD (N)], Dilip Nunisa, in February 2009 at Dhansiripar, Karbi Anglong district, Assam, the author came to understand that the armed outfit is a rational actor, which is under cease-fire with the Government of India since 2003 and will continue to do so in the future. In contrast, the Black Widow or the DHD (G) has been a rather reclusive group mostly based in the thickly forested areas of Langting, Darangibra, Mupa, Maibang subdivision, Mahur, Laisong, Harangajao, Boro-Haflong and Haflong area of Assam.

Its cadre strength is approximately 386 heavily armed youths mostly belonging to the above mentioned areas. Significantly, the leader of the DHD (G) group, Jewel Garlosa, was arrested in Bangalore in June 2009. Subsequently, the DHD (G) decided to surrender with its current 386 armed cadres in Haflong, North Cachar Hills, Assam.

Its Commander-in- Chief, Niranjan Hojai, declared at the surrender ceremony on October 2, 2009, which was attended by Assam Chief Minister Tarun Gogoi, that peace will reign from now onwards in North Cachar Hills and that both the East West Railway Corridor and broad gauge conversion projects will be successfully completed with their cooperation. This declaration is important since the construction of these two projects is critical for the overall IDSA Issue Brief 5 development of these remote areas of Assam; in the recent past, the DHD (G) had violently disrupted construction work either by killing construction workers or kidnapping site engineers. The DHD (G) cadres who came over ground in September 2009 are now housed in two designated camps in Jatinga and Kapucherra in North Cachar Hills of Assam. Peace negotiations are now scheduled to begin between the Centre and the DHD (G) in New Delhi.

The arrest of ULFA Chairman Arabinda Rajkhowa and Deputy Commander-in-Chief Raju Baruah is another significant development in Assam. The ULFA, which came into being in April 1979, had been behind most of the violent incidents in Assam in recent years. The ideology of the ULFA professed Marxism and advocated the Assamese right to dual citizenship and self-determination in the 1970s and 1980s. From 1992 onwards, the ULFA widened its support base to include all non-Assamese by stating that theirs was a movement for all Asombashis (people who resided in Assam). ULFA seeks to revert Assam's status to the Ahom ruled Assam, pre-1826 treaty of Yandaboo between the British and the Burmese, which ushered in British rule in Assam.

ULFA's Vice Chairman Pradip Gogoi states that his organization's political objectives are "Sovereign, Socialist Assam" in which "All indigenous people must stay, all others must leave".

While the ULFA enjoyed public support in the 1970s and the 1980s due to growing Assamese disenchantment with state structures, it is important to note that over the years its ideology and violent practices have made Assamese society wary of its end goals. This change occurred with the killing of noted social activist Sanjoy Ghosh. Ghosh, who headed the NGO AVARD-NE, was kidnapped by ULFA in July 1997 from Bongaon area of Majuli and was subsequently killed. Incidentally, on July 20, 2008, the man behind the killing of Ghosh, ULFA leader Amrit Dutta, was killed in an encounter with the CRPF and the police in Majuli. The spate of kidnappings by ULFA in the 1990s also added to societal discomfort. Added to this was the nexus between the ULFA and officials from the TATA Tea estates in Assam, including Executive Director S. K. Kidwai and General Manager S. Dogra. This nexus came to light after Pranati Deka, ULFA's Culture Secretary, was arrested in Mumbai on August 23, 1997. While ULFA's credibility started dwindling when these malpractices came to light, *Operation All Clear* launched by the Royal Bhutan Army (RBA) in December 2003 to weed out insurgent camps from Bhutan's territory further weakened ULFA's organization and leadership.

In this military offensive, 30 ULFA camps were burnt down, and ULFA ideologue, Bhimakanta Burhagohain, was arrested. In recent years, ULFA's claim of legitimate representation of Assamese aspirations for political sovereignty (if that is indeed the case) has also come under deep critical scrutiny since the outfit is non-transparent, run by a handful of men and women who are extremely dictatorial in behaviour. Also, the violent means adopted by the ULFA has increased apprehension in Assamese society about the effectiveness and cost to Assam's overall economic and political progress as a result of the existence of such a violent force in their midst, the issue of illegal Bangladeshi migration notwithstanding.

The ULFA has An Assessment of Insurgencies in Assam, Manipur and Nagaland in 2009 increasingly attacked Hindi speaking people especially from the year 2005 onwards. Hopefully, the arrest of the ULFA leaders in 2009 will bring about an end to the violence. The only caveat that remains as an obstacle to a peaceful settlement with the arrested ULFA leaders is that the ULFA Commander-in-Chief Paresh Barua is still at large and is now hiding somewhere in the Myanmar-China border from where he has been sending emails to the Assamese media about the continuation of the ULFA ideology under him. It is, however, hard to believe that without a proper political propaganda machine in place and the absence of popular Assamese support, Paresh Barua can singlehandedly revive the ULFA. It is perhaps the beginning of the end for the ULFA.

12

Amnesty International 2010 Report on India

Tighter anti-terror and security legislation in the wake of the 2008 Mumbai attacks was linked to reports of arbitrary detention and torture. Maoist violence in central India spread to West Bengal, with local communities being targeted and at least 300 civilians killed. Extrajudicial executions took place in a number of states and human rights defenders were threatened and detained arbitrarily. Judicial processes continued to fail to ensure justice for many victims of past human rights violations, violence against religious minorities and corporate abuses.

Adivasis (Indigenous communities), small farmers and city dwellers living in poverty across India whose livelihoods were threatened by fast-tracked development and mining projects continued to resist moves to acquire their lands and natural resources. At least 50 people were sentenced to death but, for the fifth successive year, there were no executions.

BACKGROUND

India-Pakistan peace initiatives languished, with the Indian authorities reiterating that the 2008 attacks in Mumbai had been carried out by people or groups based in Pakistan. The attacks lasted three days and killed 174 people. India-Pakistan initiatives on the Kashmir issue also failed to make progress, despite the Indian authorities resuming talks with Kashmiri leaders. Indian security forces launched co-ordinated paramilitary and police action against the spreading Maoist insurgency; there were protests over human rights abuses by both sides. About 200 people were killed in the political violence surrounding the April/ May general elections and in various bomb attacks throughout the country.

Economic growth remained confined largely to key urban sectors and was tempered by global recessionary trends, security concerns and ongoing human rights abuses by state and armed groups. Government estimates from 2005 indicate that around a quarter of India's population were living below the national poverty line.

COUNTER-TERROR AND SECURITY

Investigations into the 2008 terror attacks in Mumbai and elsewhere led to the detention under various security laws of more than 30 suspects without charge in several states, for periods ranging from one week to two months. Reports of unlawful killings, torture and other ill-treatment of suspects, and failure to hold independent inquiries into such incidents led to protests. In October, the Supreme Court rejected a plea to hold an independent inquiry into the September 2008 killings of two young men and a police officer in a shootout at Batla House, Delhi. The two men were allegedly involved in the serial bomb attacks in Delhi in September 2008.

VIOLENCE BETWEEN SECURITY FORCES, MILITIA AND MAOISTS

The conflict in Chhattisgarh, central India, between Maoist armed groups which are banned by the authorities and the police and paramilitary forces, spread to other states after months of political violence. Both sides abducted, tortured and killed people with impunity, often targeting civilians. The paramilitary forces include the Salwa Judum militia, widely believed to be sponsored by the state.

Around 40,000 Adivasis remained internally displaced by the ongoing conflict, with 20,000 living in camps and the rest scattered in the neighbouring state of Andhra Pradesh. Human rights defenders who exposed abuses by state forces continued to be harassed by the authorities. In May, Binayak Sen, a medical doctor working for the economic, social and cultural rights of Adivasis and contract labourers, and a critic of the Salwa Judum in Chhattisgarh, was released on bail after spending two years in prison. He continued to face charges of aiding Maoists.

On 17 September, police officers shot dead six villagers and burnt their houses in Gachanpalli, Dantewada district, Chhattisgarh. On 1 October, nine villagers, including four members of one family, were killed by police officers in Gompad in Dantewada district.

In December, Kopa Kunjam, a member of Vanvasi Chetna Ashram, a non governmental development organization working for the resettlement of Adivasi communities displaced by the conflict in Chhattisgarh, was arrested on politically motivated murder charges. The authorities had demolished the ashram premises in May. The conflict spread to Lalgarh in West Bengal. Around 8,000 Adivasis remained internally displaced there, some of them in makeshift camps.

In September, theWest Bengal authorities arrested 23 Adivasi women at Lalgarh and charged them with being Maoists, but later released 14 of themin exchange for a police official taken hostage by Maoist militants. In October, Maoist militants kidnapped and killed an intelligence official and dumped his mutilated body on a highway in the neighbouring state of Jharkhand.

UNLAWFUL KILLINGS

Unlawful killings continued to be reported from several north-eastern states, especially Manipur and Assam, where security forces and armed separatist organizations have waged low-intensity conflicts for decades. Despite ongoing protests in the north-east and Kashmir, the authorities refused to repeal the Armed Forces Special Powers Act, 1958.

The UN Special Rapporteur on extrajudicial, summary or arbitrary executions stated that the Act facilitated extrajudicial executions by allowing security forces to shoot to kill in circumstances where they were not necessarily at imminent risk. In March, Anil Mazumdar, editor of Aji daily newspaper, was shot dead by gunmen at Guwahati in Assam after he advocated peace talks between the banned United Liberation Front of Assam and the sate authorities.

In May, Satish Loitongbam and Pebam Gunendro Singh, both from Imphal, were detained by suspected Assam Rifles personnel stationed in Manipur. Gunendro Singh was released after three days. Satish Loitongbam was taken to an unknown location and shot dead. In July, Manipur police commandos shot dead Sanjit Chungkham and a pregnant woman, Rabina Devi, at Khwairamband Bazaar in Imphal. Video recordings of the event showed that Sanjit Chungkham was shot after he had been arrested.

ARBITRARY ARRESTS AND DETENTIONS

In August/September, Manipur authorities responded to protests by arresting more than 10 human rights defenders after raiding their offices. Among them was Jiten Yumnam, who remained in jail under preventive detention at year's end. About 90 other people were reported to be held in preventive detention in Manipur state.

CORPORATE ACCOUNTABILITY

Marginalized communities across the country bore the brunt of government failures to protect them from corporate abuses.

BHOPAL

Twenty-five years after the Bhopal gas leak tragedy of 1984—one of the world's worst industrial disasters—local communities continued to suffer its effects and maintained their campaign for justice. State action continued to be inadequate and compensation insufficient, the plant site remained contaminated and the authorities repeatedly failed to deliver on promises to the survivors and their families.

FORCED EVICTIONS

Marginalized communities, including landless farmers and Adivasis in several states, were threatened with forced evictions to accommodate industrial and other business projects. In some cases, Adivasis were threatened with eviction from lands defined a exclusively theirs by the Indian Constitution. Mandatory public hearings did not provide sufficient information on business or development projects, and government and business officials often excluded affected communities from decision-making processes. Dongria Kondh and other Adivasi communities at Niyamgiri in Orissa resumed protests after the authorities granted environmental clearance for a bauxite mine to be operated by a subsidiary of UK-based Vedanta Resources and the Orissa Mining Corporation.

EXCESSIVE USE OF FORCE

In several states, police used unnecessary or excessive force against protesters from marginalized communities. Human rights defenders campaigning for the land and environmental rights of rural communities were often detained, intimidated or harassed by the police. In November, police shot dead Adivasi leaders Singanna and Andrew Nachika of the Chasi Mulia Adivasi Sangh, an organization working for Adivasi land rights at Narayanpatna in Korapur district, Orissa. The two men took part in a demonstration highlighting alleged police brutality against Adivasi communities. The police described the demonstration as an attack. In October, Madhya Pradesh police used unnecessary force on peaceful protesters from the Save Narmada Movement, arresting 20 of its leaders. The protesters were demanding consultation and the implementation of judicial orders for the rehabilitation of Adivasi and other communities displaced by irrigation projects. In August, Orissa authorities released Abhay Sahoo of the Communist Party of India. He had been jailed for 10 months on 20 different charges after leading a protest against the threat of forced evictions spurred by the establishment of the South Korean POSCO steel plant.

IMPUNITY

The Indian government failed to ensure accountability for many past human rights abuses.

1984 MASSACRE

Twenty people have so far been convicted of the targeted massacre of about 3,000 Sikhs in northern India (including Delhi) after the assassination of the then Prime Minister Indira Gandhi in 1984. Public pressure forced the Central Bureau of Investigation to prosecute Jagdish Tytler and Sajjan Kumar, two Congress Party leaders accused of inciting their supporters to commit the Delhi massacres, after initially stating that there was no evidence against them. Protesters forced the ruling Congress Party to drop the two men from its list of candidates for general elections.

HUMAN RIGHTS VIOLATIONS

Perpetrators of human rights violations in Punjab between 1984 and 1994, and Assam between 1998 and 2001—including enforced disappearances and extrajudicial executions—continued to evade justice. Impunity persisted for past offences, including enforced disappearances of thousands of people during the armed conflict in Kashmir since 1989. The International People's Tribunal on Human Rights and Justice in Indian-administered Kashmir published a report documenting unmarked graves of more than 2,900 people who allegedly disappeared during the Kashmir conflict.

COMMUNAL VIOLENCE

Most of those responsible for the attacks on Muslim minorities in 2002 in Gujarat and other human rights violations, including extrajudicial executions in that state, were not brought to justice. Existing cases made little progress during the year.

A magisterial inquiry found the killing of Ishrat Jahan and three others by Gujarat police on 16 June 2004 to be "cold-blooded murders". However, this report was challenged by the Gujarat Government in the High Court which established a Special Investigation Team to look into the case. Acting on a petition filed by the family of Ishrat Jahan, the Supreme Court stayed the proceedings before the High Court while hearing the case. Some 15,000 people, mostly Christians, were displaced in 2008 in Orissa following violence by hundreds of supporters of Hindu nationalist organizations. By year's end, most had yet to return home. Judicial inquiries into the violence remained incomplete and the authorities failed to press charges against the majority of attackers.

An official commission indicted 68 leaders of the opposition Bharatiya Janata Party and other allied Hindu nationalist organizations for the 1992 destruction of the Babri mosque in Ayodhya. To date, no one has faced charges. Impunity continued for those who took part in the attendant violence and the ensuing massacres in some states.

In Kashmir, police and paramilitary forces killed one man and injured 150 people during a protest in June. Demonstrators were demanding an independent investigation into allegations of paramilitary forces' involvement in the sexual assault and murder of two women at Shopian, amidst reports of attempts to suppress evidence of sexual assault. An inquiry by the Central Bureau of Investigation concluded that no sexual assault took place and that the women had drowned, prompting calls for an independent investigation.

DISCRIMINATION

Members of Dalit communities in several states continued to face attacks, social boycotts and discrimination in accessing health, education and legal services. Special laws enacted to prosecute the perpetrators of such violence and discrimination remained ineffective. In August, four Dalits died of starvation in Nalanda and Jehanabad districts after members of the dominant landholding castes denied them access to food and other essential commodities. During the April/May general elections, Dalit communities in several states, especially Bihar, Gujarat and Andhra Pradesh, faced intimidation and violence. On 23 April, 74 houses belonging to Dalit communities in Madhubani district, Bihar, were torched, leaving 300 people homeless.

MINORITY GROUPS

In Karnataka, Hindu nationalist groups attacked several places of worship belonging to minority communities and targeted urban women and inter-religious couples.

On 25 January, activists from the Hindu nationalist group Sri Rama Sene attacked 10 people at a pub in Mangalore.

WORKERS' RIGHTS

Legislation guaranteeing rural people living in poverty a right to work for at least 100 days per year made headway in some states, but its implementation continued to rely on vigilant local communities. Human rights defenders involved in monitoring implementation faced violence and harassment.

On 10 February, Madhya Pradesh police arrested Shamim Modi on false charges after her organization, the Adivasi Labour Union, led a peaceful protest demanding the enforcement of laws guaranteeing labour and land rights. She spent 21 days in prison before being released. In July, the state police and forest department raided her office and arbitrarily detained 11 Adivasis. Shamim Modi, who had received threats to her life, sustained injuries during an attack in Mumbai by alleged mercenaries hired by forest contractors.

RIGHTS OF LESBIAN, GAY, BISEXUAL AND TRANSGENDER PEOPLE

In a historic decision in July, the Delhi High Court rejected section 377 of the Indian Penal Code in cases of consensual sexual acts. Section 377, which criminalizes homosexuality and was introduced under British colonial rule, was deemed discriminatory and "against constitutional morality". A formal repeal of the law remained pending.

DEATH PENALTY

No executions were known to have taken place during the year, but courts sentenced at least 50 people to death.

AMNESTY INTERNATIONAL VISITS/REPORTS

Amnesty International delegates visited India in February/March and August/September.

- *India*: Dodging responsibility—Corporations, governments and the Bhopal disaster (ASA 20/002/2009)
- *India*: Open Letter to authorities to withdraw the

clearance granted to Vedanta Orissa Mining Corporation for bauxite mining project which could threaten Dongria Kondh indigenous communities at Niyamgiri (ASA 20/004/2009)

- *India*: Authorities should avoid excessive use of force in West Bengal (ASA 20/006/2009)
- *India*: Revoke preventive detention of human rights defender in Manipur (ASA 20/019/2009)

ASSAM MOVEMENT

Assam Movement is a much maligned movement. Critiques have often tried to paint it as a chauvinist, communal, programme organised by an Asomiya speaking Hindu majority of Assam against a group of hapless immigrants who happened to be Bengali Muslims. Assam has a history of agitations led by students. In the post independence period the student agitations in Assam can be classified under the categories of struggles over economic issues and struggles launched for the protection of the linguistic and cultural identity of Assamese people. The Assam movement of 1979 to 1985, is regarded as one of the most vibrant democratic movements of independent India. The movement, led by All Assam Students Union and the 'All Assam Gana Sangram Parishad', set off an agitational programme to compel the government to identify and expel the land hungry illegal immigrants that poured in to Assam from Bangladesh, the erstwhile East Pakistan and prevention of free flow of a large number of people from Nepal. Though the movement seems more like a political movement, but it was considered as a social movement because of its strong social base and its effect on the society, particularly, among the people in the Brahmaputra Valley. It definitely had significant social implications in addition to the political, constitutional and economic impacts.

The main demands of this movement were to stop:

- The illegal immigration of foreign nationals to Assam from the neighbouring countries- Bangladesh and Nepal

- Prevention of their participation in the electoral process
- Deportation of all foreigners living illegally in Assam and
- Protection of the distinct identity people of Assam.

The issue of expulsion of foreign nationals was one of the sixteen-points of charter of demands made by All Assam Students Union (AASU) in July, 1979. In the meantime the two regional parties Purbanchalya Loka Parishad (PLP) and the Asom Jatiyatabadi Dal (AJD) were formed and they also took up the issue of the foreign nationals. At the official level, this problem was highlighted for the first time by the Chief Election Commissioner, Mr. S. L. Shakdhar on 24th October 1978 in a conference of the State electoral officers. He observed "the large scale inclusion of foreign nationals (in electoral rolls) in some states especially in the northeastern region was alarming and requires drastic action."

The then Janata party Chief Minister Golap Borbora spoke in the same strain and declared in the Assam Assembly on 16th March 1979 that influx of foreign nationals was assuming alarming proportions. The issue came to the fore in April 1979 when a by-election to the Loka Sabha in the Mangoldoi constituency was ordered. The death of Hiralal Patowari, the sitting member of Mongoldoi Parliamentary Constituency prepared the ground for a bye-election where it was found that an alarming figure of 45,000 foreigners infiltrated into the voter's list. Though large scale illegal immigration has been a problem that Assam faced after the independence and particularly after creation of Bangladesh yet it was not really perceived as a major threat to identity by a majority of Assamese till this detection of huge percentage of illegal immigrant voters in this constituency. We need to keep in mind that the pressure on land had increased enormously, and the employment market was cornered by non-Assamese in Assam by 70s of twentieth century.

As scholars like Gail Omvedt, Apurba K Baruah argued a sense of discrimination and deprivation emerging from an unequal competition for jobs, petty trade and land created conditions for an agitation. Assam Gana Sangram Parishad, was formed by a number of important socio-cultural and Students' organization of the Assamese.. Within a short span of time, AASU played a major part in bringing the support base of a large number of mass organizations. The movement involved various shades of people comprising the greater Asomiya nationality.

It became a movement that reflected the hurt and insecurity of the small nationalities, led by the Asomiya. Despite a campaign to project this movement at times as anti-utsider and at other times as anti- Bengali, anti-Muslim, agitation led by the Asomiya speaking Hindus, the movement received support from a large section of the Scheduled tribes like the Bodo, Karbi and Missing and also permanent residents of Assam irrespective of religion. Assam linguistic identity has remained a secular cause and found martyrs like Mozamil Haque who gave his life while defending the status of the Asomiya language. Except for aberrations when agent provocateurs succeeded in creating riots and when over enthusiastic young people could not be restrained it adopted Gandhian methods and remained non-violent and democratic. It is this character of the movement and the genuine cause that forced the Government of India to enter in to the Assam accord that brought an end to this historic movement.

13

North-East Insurgency: External Influences

Immediately after the independence of India, its northeastern part was gripped by insurgency. The banner of insurgency was first raised by Naga groups, who also supported other outfits by providing training and other logistics. Now, a number of insurgent and terrorist groups are active in northeast India, whose demands vary from in dependence to self-rule. Many external powers have tried to take advantage of this situation. This paper tries to examine the role played by various external powers in sustaining the insurgency in the Northeast. It argues that the situation in the Northeast would be vastly different once these external forces stop influencing the insurgency in this region. The external powers have been supporting insurgency to weaken the Indian state.

INTRODUCTION

Northeast India has been in turbulence since the independence of the country, making it a major trouble spot from the internal security point of view. A large number of groups are active in this region, with their demands varying from independence to self-rule. A plethora of ethnic groups are also clamouring for special rights and the protection of their distinct identity. To get some of these demands met, insurgent groups have indulged in armed violence against the state and security forces.

They have also resorted to the killing of other ethnic groups or even to fratricidal killings. This situation has often prompted the Indian state to undertake counterinsurgency operations. Under pressure from the Indian security forces, the insurgents in the Northeast have found it expedient to seek support from neighbouring countries. Forces inimical to India's interest have tried to take advantage of this situation.

The insurgent groups have also managed to get support from some countries as same ethnic groups reside on both sides of the border. In some other cases, a purely client-patron relationship has existed. This kind of relationship existed between the insurgents and the arms smugglers of Southeast Asia or the Mafiosi of Bangladesh.

This paper tries to examine the role played by various external powers in sustaining the insurgency in the Northeast. It argues that the situation in the Northeast would be vastly different once these external forces stop influencing the insurgency in this region. The external powers have been supporting insurgency to weaken the India state.

NORTHEAST: PROVIDING FAVOURABLE CONDITIONS FOR INSURGENCY

Northeast India has been facing insurgency since 1956 due to feelings of ethnic separatism among its inhabitants. Besides, this region has all other enabling conditions which a terrorist or insurgent outfit might need for continuing their activities. Ninety eight per cent of the Northeast is contiguous to the international border, which allows terror outfits to get sanctuaries in Bhutan, Myanmar, Bangladesh and even China.

In these countries, they also get facilities for training, and procure arms and ammunition from there. Ineffective administration in northern Myanmar, state-sponsorship from the intelligence agencies of Pakistan and Bangladesh and a regular flow of funds from the smugglers of narcotics from the Golden Triangle make their operation further easier.

BEGINNING OF INTERNATIONAL LINKAGES

The northeast insurgent groups started developing their international linkages immediately after the independence of India. The Nagas were the first to raise the banner of insurgency. The process started when the father of Naga insurgency, Angami Zapu Phizo, chief of the rebel Naga National Council (NNC), left the Naga Hills in 1956 to fight for an independent Naga homeland from London, after travelling through East Pakistan and Switzerland. He continued his activity from there till his death in 1990. His agenda is now being pursued by his daughter, Adinno Phizo, who has succeeded him as the NNC president and is also based in London.

The government of India outlawed the NNC in 1972 and started a major counterinsurgency operation, finally resulting into the controversial Shillong Accord on 11 November 1975. Under this agreement, the Nagas agreed to accept the Indian constitution, surrender arms and ammunition and join the Indian national mainstream. However, a splinter group of around 140 NNC cadres did not accept the Shillong Accord and formed a new insurgent group called the National Socialist Council of Nagaland (NSCN) under the leadership of Thuingaleng Muivah, Isak Chisi Swu and S. S. Khaplang. This new group was launched from bases inside Myanmar in 1980. In due course, the NSCN emerged as the most radical and powerful insurgent group fighting for the Naga cause.

The outfit split in 1988 because of the clannish divisions among the Nagas. The Naga insurgency in the Northeast is taken as the mother of all insurgencies in the Northeast. They were the first group to raise the banner of rebellion and also started providing arms training and other logistic support to outfits such as the United Liberation Front of Asom (ULFA), formed in April 1979 to fight for a "sovereign, socialist Assam." The ULFA started sending its cadres for advanced "military training" at the hands of the Kachin Independence Army (KIA), an anti-Yangon rebel group in Myanmar, from 1988 onwards. The ULFA set up its first camp in the Moulvi Bazaar district in Bangladesh in 1985. By 1990, the outfit had also established its Pakistani contact. Its top leaders, including Paresh Barua, travelled to Afghanistan through Pakistan's North West Frontier Province, where Pakistani Inter-Services Intelligence (ISI), assisted them in meeting Gulbuddin

Hekmatyar, a top Afghan Mujahideen leader of the time. By the end of 1990 and early 1991, the ULFA also set up wellentrenched bases inside southern Bhutan, mainly in the district of Samdrup Jhongkar, bordering western Assam's Nalbari district.

The ULFA moved to Bhutan after the Indian army launched Operation Bajrang in November 1990 and Operation Rhino on 14–15 September 1991. Though the information regarding Operation Bajrang had leaked, thereby allowing top ULFA leaders to escape to Bangladesh, Operation Rhino was extremely successful as tactical surprise was achieved this time.1 In Operation Rhino, 431 hard-core elements, including 46 top leaders, were arrested, along with 299 supporters and trainees, within a few weeks.

Sixteen ULFA camps were destroyed, and the material seized established ULFA's link with the KIA, the NSCN and the Liberation Tigers of Tamil Eelam (LTTE) and the existence of sanctuaries in Bangladesh. The ULFA chose southern Bhutan as a base as this area was not very well policed and thick jungles provided them suitable hiding places. Subsequently, Bhutan was also chosen by other insurgent groups like the National Democratic Front of Bodoland (NDFB) and the Kamtapur Liberation Organisation (KLO).

The terror groups also preferred Bhutan as it was easy for them to carry out attacks across the border in India and return back to their safe hideouts in southern Bhutan. Bhutan, with a small army, was hardly in a position to take any effective counterinsurgency operation. It took 12 years for Bhutan to launch operation against the insurgents.

BHUTAN'S WAR ON TERROR

The presence of Indian insurgents and terrorists in Bhutanese territory was causing damage to the Indo-Bhutan ties, which is excellent otherwise. India has been persuading Bhutan to takeaction against these groups since 1998. The virtual illegal occupation of southern Bhutan by the terrorists posed a serious challenge to its sovereignty. The state had actually started withdrawing from these areas by closing down various institutions and commercial places. The terrorists were also hampering economic activities in Bhutan, besides affecting its trade and commerce. Work in large industries such as the Dungsum Cement Project was suspended. Educational institutions in terrorist-infested areas were closed down. Trade, agriculture production and other commercial activities in several districts of the country were disrupted. Ordinary citizens were not feeling free to even travel across the country.

Many became victims of threats, coercion and extortion. Unprovoked attacks by the militants against Bhutanese nationals inside the country, as well as those travelling through the Indian state of Assam, resulted in loss of innocent lives. This situation forced Bhutan to take military action against Indian insurgent groups under the codename "Operation All Clear" on 15 December 2003 to oust them from its territory.

At the time of the operation, there were over 3,000 heavily armed Indian separatists belonging to three different groups, the ULFA, the NDFB and the KLO, based in Bhutan. They were operating from 30 camps inside the kingdom. Out of these 30 camps, 13 camps belonged to the ULFA, the NDFB had 12, and the remaining 5 camps were of the KLO. Before opting for this operation, Bhutan had tried to persuade insurgents to leave the kingdom peacefully. But, after several round of talks spanning over six years, it had become almost certain that the militants had no intention of leaving the soil of Bhutan. In all the meetings that were held between Bhutan and the insurgent groups, Bhutan sent its top officials.

On the other hand, insurgents were represented only at the middle level. Some ULFA leaders even said that the leaving of Bhutan was as good as bidding goodbye to their cause, for which they were not ready. Bhutan, however, wanted to remove a major irritant in its relationship with India, though it faced serious threats from the militants. The Bhutanese king was dithering before taking military action as he was not sure of the military power of Bhutan. Its forces had not been used for more than a century. Bhutan also knew that action against the insurgents would make them hostile against the Bhutanese citizens and even the Royal Bhutan Army. Most importantly,

Bhutanese had to travel through the Indian territory to reach southern Bhutan.

It has been suggested by some that the decision to take military action against the militants was also expedited by the formation of the Bhutan Communist Party (Marxist-Leninist-Maoist) on 22 April 2003. This party wanted to smash monarchy and establish a "true and new democracy" in Bhutan. It was also feared that one of the insurgent groups, the KLO—based in southern Bhutan—was in league with the Bhutanese and Nepalese Maoists.

Thus, the emerging Maoist threat could have forced the hand of the king, who was already under the pressure from India to act against these groups. Whatever may be the reason behind the Bhutanese military action, one thing is sure—that the Bhutanese action did set an example of cooperation in counter-terrorism in south Asia. The amount of risk taken by Bhutan to uproot the terrorists from its territory has only increased the importance of its action. Even countries like Bangladesh were prompted to say that they have sealed their borders with India to prevent Indian insurgents fleeing Bhutan or Myanmar from entering its territory.

It also took sporadic actions against insurgents operating from its territory. But, such actions were kept secret to buttress Dhaka's official stand that no Indian insurgents were operating from that country. There were indications that Myanmar was also tightening its noose on Indian insurgent groups like the NSCN-Khaplang (NSCN-K) and the ULFA, which have bases in the country.

INSURGENTS SEEKING HELP OF CHINA

During the course of the Bhutanese military operation, it became clear to insurgent leaders that they would have to vacate Bhutanese territory. This prompted the ULFA "chairman," Arabinda Rajkhowa, to appeal to the Chinese leadership on 25 December 2003 to provide safe passage to the insurgents from Bhutan for temporary shelter in China.

In his fax communication to the Chinese leadership, Rajkhowa said, "We have come under massive attack of Indo-

Bhutan joint forces and our combatants have been forced to retreat up to the Sino-Bhutan border due to all out air and artillery campaigns." Beijing, however, turned down the ULFA request and asked its frontier forces to remain vigilant against any effort by the insurgents to move into their territory.

This, however, does not mean that China has not been involved with insurgents in northeast India. These insurgents had not only visited China in the past for help, but had received assistance from sources within the country. The NSCN-Isak Muivah (NSCN-IM) "general secretary," Thuingaleng Muivah, admitted that Naga insurgents had, in the early days, obtained arms from China and Pakistan. Even the NSCN-K chief, S. S. Khaplang, has admitted that Nagas have taken help from China and Pakistan in the past.

The core leadership of the People's Liberation Army (PLA), an insurgent outfit active in Manipur, was trained in China. Though the ethnic rebel armies of the Naga and the Mizo hills had received military training in China before them, the Chinese only tried to politicise a few Naga leaders, such as Thuingaleng Muivah, the present general secretary of the NSCN. Muivah had some exposure to Marxist-Leninist ideology before he led the first batch of Naga rebels to China in 1966, at the beginning of the Cultural Revolution.

But there was no attempt to politicise the Mizos or most of the Nagas, who were devout Christians. China merely wanted to use them against India to counterbalance the continued Indian support to the Tibetans. But the PLA's core leadership—the first batch of eighteen "Ojhas" (pioneers)—went through heavy political training.

The Chinese had hopes they would coordinate their struggles with the Indian Maoist groups and strengthen the cause of the Indian revolution. China trained and armed several batches of Naga, Mizo and Meitei since 1966. But, this help stopped by the early 1980s. By then, however, Bangladesh's military rulers, who had come to power by the bloody coup that killed the country's founder, Sheikh Mujibur Rehman, had revived the Pakistani policy of sheltering, arming and training rebel groups from northeast India. Almost all the separatist groups in the Northeast—Nagas, Mizos, Meiteis, Tripuris and now even those from Meghalaya—have subsequently received shelter and support in Bangladesh.

Recent reports, however, indicate that insurgents from the Northeast are once again trying to take the help of China as the political environment in Bangladesh has become unfavourable to them with the return of Sheikh Hasina to power. Since October 2009, ULFA's commander-inchief,Paresh Barua, is believed to be somewhere close to the Myanmar-China border, scouting for help to relocate its bases.

China, in recent times, has also emerged as a major source of weapons for insurgents in the Northeast and the Maoists. Barua also visited China several time to procure weapons.9 He also sells them to terror outfits such as NDFB, the National Liberation Front of Tripura, the All Tripura Tiger Force and the Maoists.

BANGLADESH: A SAFE HAVEN FOR INSURGENTS IN THE NORTHEAST

Bangladesh has been a safe haven for insurgents in the Northeast since East Pakistan days. Though officially the Bangladesh government asserts that it has "never allowed or assisted insurgent groups of any country for acts against that country and this policy was being pursued by the Government consistently and rigorously," the actual policy of the Bangladesh government is completely different.

PROINSURGENT RECORD OF THE SUCCESSIVE BANGLADESHI GOVERNMENTS

Indian insurgents have received support under all regimes in Bangladesh. Under the Bangladesh Nationalist Party (BNP)-led governments, this support has been direct. However, when the Awami League is in power, insurgents get support of only a section of the Bangladeshi security establishment.

As a result, almost all northeastern groups engaged in insurgency in the Northeast have established their camps in Bangladesh. Begum Khaleda Zia in her last stint as leader of the opposition had hailed these insurgents as "brave freedom fighters" carrying out a "heroic battle against an oppressive regime." When Sheikh Hasina came to power for the first time, she disbanded most of the "overground" training camps of these insurgents but could do nothing to those going "underground" with the assistance of various government intelligence agencies.

It was during the Awami League's regime that the ULFA leader Anup Chetia was arrested, convicted and jailed, while there were up to four attempts on the life of the leader of the group's armed wing, Paresh Barua. This forced Paresh Barua to leave Dhaka for Karachi. He returned to Bangladesh again after the victory of the BNP in the elections.

Though Karachi was safe, it was too far off and it was difficult to run a rebellion in Assam from there. Besides, Barua also owns a number of businesses in Bangladesh that funded his once-powerful group. These insurgents and their leaders were jubilant when Khaleda Zia's BNP came to power after the parliamentary elections in October 2001. The BNP-led ruling coalition did not disappoint these groups either.

The insurgency in Manipur has also received support from Bangladesh. The United National Liberation Front (UNLF) was formed on 24 November 1964 under the leadership of Areambam Samarendra Singh to establish an independent socialist Manipur. This outfit shared a close "political relationship" with the then East Pakistani regime and, in 1969, underwent military training in that country.

The group is also said to have backed the Pakistani Army during the Bangladesh liberation war in 1971. In December 1968, a breakaway group of the UNLF, led by Oinam Sudhir Kumar, established a government-in-exile called Revolutionary Government of Manipur (RGM), with headquarters in Sylhet, in the then East Pakistan.

The RGM was backed by Pakistan. However, the Meitei secessionist movement received a serious jolt when most of its leaders were arrested during the Bangladesh liberation war in 1971. Subsequently, the UNLF also became close to China, with a team headed by N. Bisheswar Singh proceeding to Lhasa in 1975 to ask for Beijing's assistance. The UNLF is also close to the NSCN-K and has training camps in Myanmar and Bangladesh. In recent years, the insurgency has intensified in Manipur and the situation has become further complicated with the rise of Islamist groups like People's United Liberation Front (PULF).

Similarly, in Tripura, both the major outlawed rebel groups—the National Liberation Front of Tripura (NLFT) and the All Tripura Tiger Force (ATTF)—fighting for independent tribal homelands have operated from bases in adjoining Bangladesh. Tripura shares an 856-kilometre-long border with Bangladesh, with at least 70 per cent of the boundary unfenced and with concrete pillars separating the two countries. But Dhaka denies the presence of Indian rebel bases in their territory. The role played by Bangladesh has been an important factor behind the continuation of insurgency in Tripura.

ARMS SMUGGLING

Bangladesh has also been supporting insurgency in the Northeast by freely allowing smuggling of arms to take place from its territory. The Bangladesh police and coastguard stumbled across a huge consignment of sophisticated illegal arms and ammunition when they raided the government-controlled Chittagong Urea Fertilizer Limited (CUFL) jetty on 2 April 2004.

Reports indicated that, in this seizure, the smugglers were unloading the weapons with help from the local police. The Awami League after coming to power has restarted investigation into the Chittagong arms seizure. It has unmasked the government officials and agencies involved in arms trafficking.

The investigation has now also conclusively proved that the arms were meant for insurgents in the Northeast. The arrested smugglers have revealed that senior political leaders along with civil and military intelligence chiefs of the then Khaleda Zia government were involved in the botched arms shipment. The Sheikh Hasina government prosecuted two former Bangladesh army generals, Major General Rezakul Haider Chowdhury and Brigadier General Abdur Rahim, who headed the National Security Intelligence (NSI). They were prosecuted for facilitating the landing of Chinese arms meant for insurgents in India's northeast and for trying to smuggle these arms into India. It is also reported that Paresh Barua himself supervised the unloading of arms.

There were several seizures of this kind in 2003. Substantial caches of arms have been recovered from Chittagong and its three hill districts, Bogra in northwestern Bangladesh (this was the largest earlier seizure), and even from the capital, Dhaka.

Cox Bazar, in Bangladesh, has emerged as a major port for supply of illegal arms and ammunition to northeast insurgents.

FRATRICIDAL KILLINGS AMONG INSURGENT OUTFITS IN DHAKA

The insurgent groups using Bangladesh territory for terror operations against India have often indulged in fratricidal killings. This has further confirmed the presence of these groups in that country. Besides, there has also been action against these groups from the Bangladesh security agencies, often to keep the internal security situation under control. Dhaka has, however, denied all such incidents just to prove that insurgents are not using its territory.

In November 2009, the Sheikh Hasina government in Bangladesh took a significant step towards improving bilateral relations with India when it detained two top leaders of the ULFA— "foreign secretary" Sashadhar Choudhury and "finance secretary" Chitraban Hazarika—and handed them over to India. Subsequently, they have also handed over ULFA chairman, Arabinda Rajkhowa; his bodyguard, Raja Bora; and the deputy commander-in-chief of the ULFA, Raju Barua.

This has provided a much-needed impetus to counter terror cooperation in South Asia. But, there are other top insurgent leaders still residing in Bangladesh. They are Ranjan Daimary of the prosovereignty faction of the NDFB, Biswamohan Debbarma of the NLFT and Ranjit Debbarma of the ATTF. Paresh Barua has already managed to escape on

"Bangladeshi passport." However, the current cooperation of Bangladesh would pacify New Delhi to some extent.

WEAKENING SUPPORT BASE OF INSURGENTS IN THE NORTHEAST

Except for Manipur, insurgency in the whole of the Northeast is on a decline. Insurgent groups like the ULFA, the NLFT, the ATTF, and the NDFB have been considerably weakened. After 9/11, international opinion has decisively turned against terrorism. This has also resulted in the ULFA being branded a terrorist organisation by the U.S. The ULFA was considerably weakened when Bhutan launched its operation against the Indian insurgent groups (IIGs) in December 2003.

Along with the international situation, the domestic situation also turned against the outfit. There have been desertions in its rank. Sever al insurgent outfits of the northeast rank and file were disgusted with their leadership. While they were facing hardships, the leaders were enjoying opulent lifestyles in Bangladesh. Organisations have also faced stress on the grounds of ideology.

The discontent in the organisation even led to a split in the ULFA. The organization has now been divided into pro-talk and anti-talk factions. This decision has also prompted the most deadly 28 battalion to declare ceasefire and opt for talks. The constant operation of Indian security forces has also not made life of the cadres of insurgent outfits any easier.

The ULFA has tried to replenish its cadre base by reaching out to new sections. It attempted to recruit cadres from adivasis, or tea tribes. It also tried to indulge in terror acts in concert with other insurgent outfits. But, these tactics were not very helpful.

14

North-East India and Social Responsibility of Media

This paper examines the way media uphold truth, integrity and social responsibility. The focus of our attention is in particular, media in Northeast India and the way it responds to the challenges the region faces, and media's contribution to build peace and resolve conflicts. Are media helping or hindering the process of peace, development and well being of the region? The present paper attempts to propose how the media, while having to report on violence, conflict and bloodshed, should go beyond short-term goals, and tell stories that connect communities, foster unity and promotes development and peace.

Citizens as well as media professionals must strive to make media in the Northeast more truthful, dispassionate, objective and responsible. Truth, it is said, is the major casualty in war. For truth to be a casualty one need not wait for war. Truth is being put to test and sacrificed almost daily in the many media altars of the world. Speed and competition have reduced media's commitment to verify and counter check information. Accuracy has become a major victim in the age of instant communication. Today it is easy to plant a big lie or distortion along with truth and get some of the media audience to believe it.

The quantity of information the media as well as the audience handle on any given day has substantially increased. Today we hear of information glut or overload leading to attention blink. Quantitative increase in the information one needs to handle and process has considerably reduced the possibility of being critical, of verifying facts and checking veracity of sources. Often the audience lack the time and wherewithal necessary to check and verify what they read or watch. It is in this context that we underline the need for professional competence and social responsibility as essential requirements for media persons in order to report events objectively and accurately. Audience is left with the option of either accepting the lie as truth or suspend judgment and strives to look for other perspectives. It is not easy considering the fact that they do not often have the adequate tools to check the veracity of news and information concerning people and places which are far away from them.

Even if such tools did exist, they are not fool proof due to many subjective factors under which media might undertake to do the verification. Generally audience tend to trust the media, and therefore, media must ensure that the trust the audience place on it is not belied. That brings us to the question of the issue of prejudice or bias in media. When we look closely at the way the media function today it becomes obvious that media are bedeviled by prejudices of one kind or the other. Media are often used in order to cultivate and nourish, sustain and spread prejudices. Media can easily become a handmaid, a willing accomplice, a tool in stirring up sensation and prejudices that lie deep within individual media persons.

Besides helping to perpetuate stereotypes and prejudices, media can set agendas, criterion, and social norms and also become guilty of branding certain areas as 'trouble torn', 'militancy infested'. It could be anywhere in the world-Israel, Middle East, Pakistan, Africa, Sri Lanka. In India, formerly it used to be Punjab; now it is Kashmir and North East India.

People living outside these regions have a 'mediated' and largely distorted, picture of the places and people. Reporters admit that editors urge them to provide 'a militancy angle' to stories they file. Some media organisations have a cut off figure of people killed, if the story is to be carried. It is not that media always provide the bias; sometimes they just play up the prejudices that lie deep within people.

Sometimes we take comfort in our prejudices and do not care, or should I say, dare, to examine them and verify them, and set the record right. Prejudices are like the fog that prevents us from seeing the road ahead clearly as we drive along. They can affect our attitudes and conduct; they can colour our relationships, our private and public views and behaviour. Mutual trust and confidence in each other have been replaced by prejudices and suspicion of one another globally with the rise of terrorism and insurgency. The heightened security at airports, mounting travel restrictions which make international travel a nightmare for many, increased requirements of guarantees or sureties even in ordinary, day to day transactions, new security and surveillance systems are symptomatic of the lack of trust in each other in a globalised world.

Media, however, continue to enjoy great credibility. People often take information provided by media for granted and quote them freely with the presumption that they are accurate. That should make media all the more conscious of their responsibility. Media is a major force that shapes our opinions and affects our thoughts today. Hence it is important that we examine the way they influence our thoughts, our attitudes and our values, so that truth may shine forth and triumph, as the wisdom of our ancestors taught us in India: "Satyameva Jayade".

SOCIAL RESPONSIBILITY VERSUS COMMERCIAL INTEREST

But truth is also in competition with commercial interests. Proprietor-editors are often tempted to run a paper just like another business establishment. Financial interests might weigh heavily with such a tribe whereby public accountability of keeping society at large reasonably well informed dwindles (Nordenstreng-Topaz, 1989). Social responsibility demands that the media remain independent of the government, industry and business. The media's primary aim should be to be at the service of the public. If responsibility to the public is paramount, media need to be more comprehensive and deep in the way they report and publish events. Most often media cover 'events' without adequate in-depth analysis of issues. Social analysis calls for a breed of journalists who are schooled in understanding the social issues that concern the society.

'If media responsibility, in its ultimate analysis, is to the audience, then media institutions and persons ought to maintain a high degree of integrity and uphold the rights and hopes of all social segments (Nordenstreng-Topaz, 1989). This demands that greater attention and importance be given to adequate professional training and education for media persons.

There is the rising trend of competition among different kind of media. Newspapers and magazines face serious competition from the visual media, particularly television. Many newspapers are trying to be more visually attractive than focus on the quality of content. One can notice the all too increasing tendency of 'televisation' of the newspapers.

One of India's leading journalists, Kuldip Nayar (2005) says:"The media has been commercialized. Newspapers reflect more of industry's thinking than of people's afflictions. A wit says news is what is written on the back of the advertisement. A couple of leading English dailies have even begun to sell the editorial space to a hic provided he has the money to buy."

INFOTAINMENT AND TRIVIALISATION OF INFORMATION

Newspapers today seem to be trying to 'please the eye' than 'feed the mind'. The best and most attractive pages of a newspaper today are devoted to trivia featuring film stars, sports personalities and other celebrities. Even small town papers devote much space to Hollywood actresses and actors, models and celebrities and indulge in elaborate discussion on their private lives at the neglect of serious social and cultural issues that affect one's country or region.

There is serious erosion in the quality of content. Content is trivialized to create interest. 'Infotainment' is the new catchword, the mantra of the media. But unfortunately infotainment is neither information nor entertainment. It is simply trivia, pandering to the emotions and passions. It is cheap entertainment in sheep's skin, masquerading as information, pandering to emotions and feelings. There is a worrying trend in media today of converting information into entertainment. The value of news as entertainment is a serious threat to its value as information.

Another alarming trend in the Indian press according to K.E. Eapen, is the fact that "only five per cent of a newspaper's revenue, on the average, goes into gathering information." (Nordenstreng-Topaz, 1989). Many journalists depend heavily on official versions of the news, government press releases, dispatches, and hand outs from NGOs and other organisations.

Sometimes such news items are propagandist and not tested or verified for objectivity. Media sometimes fail to present independent reports gathered through its own sources as it entails time, costs and competence. The pressure to depend on official sources as against gathering independent reports is greater on small budget media organizations.

The celebrity obsession is a growing illness among the media. The news business builds people up and then acquires an interest in tearing them down (Schmuhl, 1989). Edwin Newman speaking as a media insider feels there is 'not nearly enough criticism of us, not nearly enough understanding of how we work, of why we do what we do, and of how powerful our habits and stereotypes are (Schmuhl, 1989).

The excessive pre-occupation of the press with politics at the cost of neglecting other socially relevant issues, and the confrontationist attitude to political forces are something that the Indian media have inherited from the colonial past. If one can notice some change in the press, unfortunately it is not always in favour of diversity of content, of qualitative improvement. The new trend, instead, is to cater to the needs and interests of the consumerist class, to provide instant gratification. Even the newly emerging media houses tend to uncritically follow the trend set by traditional media firms rather than fill the vacuum. People who control the media in the country think that media are like any other commodity. It should be nicely packaged. And their idea of "nice-packaging" is to fill the pages with semi-nude colour pictures of models and actresses and trash. The shallow, unthinking attitude gets reflected even in the news stories and articles that are printed.

COVERING CONFLICT

Coverage of crime, conflicts and controversies constitute a major component of the media. The way these are presented call for utmost caution and objectivity. How does a media person weigh conflicting ideologies in the context of communal riots, protest rallies, ethnic clashes, violence? It is on occasions of social turmoil and conflict that the society at large looks to the media for direction and light. The spotlights are turned on the media, and people expect them to be a saner voice, to inform accurately and truthfully, to clarify and interpret, to show the way.

The task of the media professionals are no doubt today enhanced by new technologies, but the speed with which information is gathered, presented and transmitted to the audience, make the task of being objective, accurate and responsible extremely challenging. The media coverage of some of the recent events in the Northeast raise worrying questions about objectivity and responsibility of the media.

In particular I wish to refer to alarmist newspaper reports which announced 'backlash' and 'retaliation' against the Adivasis after their demonstration in Assam's capital, in November 2007 turned violent. In the face of stiff competition to capture the time and grab the attention of the audience, a section of the media cry 'wolf', raise false alarms, exaggerate figures of death tolls. Television channels indulge in 'breaking' stories, by flashing the same images and visuals 24 hours. What we need is a responsible media, not an alarmist media.

According to Brucker (1973) most newspapers will suppress news if there are convincing reasons indicating that, under the particular circumstances obtaining, the value of suppression promise to outweigh those of publication. Things like the names of youngsters in trouble with the law, or of victims of rape, are frequently withheld. The news of a kidnapping, or of arrangements for ransom, may be left unpublished where there is compelling reason to believe a life may be saved by so doing.

AUDIENCE ARE BECOMING MORE CRITICAL

In the new media environment, watching the so-called watchdog has become essential. They raise ethical questions concerning such issues like the lack of fairness and balance, the disregard for privacy, the existence of bias, and the glorification of the sensational and trivia (Schmuhl, 1989). In the 'Global Village' in which we live today, information is available through several sources, and journalists do not have the monopoly as providers of news and information.

In addition, the readers, as well as viewers of media have become more sophisticated, more critical, discerning, conscious and discriminating than in the past. Hence they cannot be taken for granted. People inside the industry as well as social scientists and civil society have become more and more critical about the way media function.

They criticise the specific conduct and practices of media persons and institutions that are established to provide information. While a section of the media professionals are doing some soul-searching, the public is becoming more restive and less tolerant of aberrations by the media. Critical review of media has come from different quarters- public officials, individual citizens, from NGOs and citizen forums, courts and judiciary, media reviews, media critics, press councils and other bodies.

The way out of distortions and aberrations, is to fall back on to traditional ethical principles like social responsibility which guide the media profession. Media responsibility can be ensured when a reporter can answer questions like whether the report is accurate and complete, whether it is fair and balanced, whether the motives and methods used for covering the information are ethically sound, and whether he or she is aware of the legal and social consequences of publishing a particular report. The new developments and expressions that have come into media profession also need to be critically looked at. We have 'embedded journalists' and journalism.

Such a breed of journalists seem to have adopted bias and ideological positions already as a given. Another category, though less harmful, is Citizen Journalism.

Though citizen journalism has its own benefits and can play complimentary role to the overall media profession, the audience are not always in a position to distinguish between a media professional and a participant, a citizen, who may be deeply involved in the event and hence not necessarily as objective and accurate as a professional would be. A citizen journalist could easily tempted to become an embedded journalist, an agent of some vested interested party.

OBJECTIVITY, THE HALLMARK OF MEDIA

Media must tell what's going on as completely, accurately, honestly, and dispassionately as possible. And that is objective reporting. News is a competitive business and today with several channels airing round the clock news headlines, the press has a tough task on hand to be 'first and fast' with the latest news. Competition leads to some abuses too—hasty reporting, exaggeration or sheer sensationalism. Media often compete with one another. There are numerous examples every day in the press of what Edwin Newman has called 'flagrant examples of cheap scare journalism' (Schmuhl, 1989).

Journalism is often described as 'literature in a hurry.' Hasty reporting takes its toll on responsible and accurate reporting. Journalists should not be in a hurry to identify groups or individuals for bomb blasts, violent acts and crime. Adding words like ' allegedly' or 'suspected' do not justify unverified attribution of crime. If a journalist carries an accusation against somebody, or any group, he or she has the plain duty to ask that person or group for comment and reaction. So too a journalist should not edit what people say to make them look bad or look good. A journalist should not allow himself or herself to be used or manipulated. In Northeast India it is customary for media to jump to conclusion to blame one or the other of the militant groups for blasts or other violent acts. Quite often this is done without adequate data to substantiate and verify what is reported.

Competition exists within the organisations and among media persons who want to hit the front page, break a new story and make a name for themselves, and get ahead. But no institutional safeguards will protect media against bad reporting. What counts in the last analysis are the competence, wisdom and honesty of the people in the media profession.

But the hallmark of any media should be objectivity. But objectivity is something that needs to be constantly tested and proved. As Elmer Davis (1934) pointed out "the good newspaper, the good news broadcaster must walk a tightrope between two great gulfs- on one side the false objectivity that takes everything at face value and lets the public be imposed on by the charlatan with the most brazen front; on the other, the 'interpretive' reporting which fails to draw the line between objective and subjective, between a reasonably well-established fact and what the reporter or editor wishes were the fact. To say that is easy; to do it is hard."

The journalist's mission becomes that of telling us what's going on in as completely, accurately, honestly, and dispassionately as possible. And that is objective reporting.

MEDIA'S PRO-URBAN BIAS

Media managers and advertisers are today increasingly choosing to focus on the urban elite and neglect the rural poor as the former are among the most prized audience and it pays to inform or entertain them. The urban elite has greater purchasing power. Reporters are sometimes not so willing to go to rural areas to report on stories that concern the plights of the poor and the rural people as it entails a lot of hardships.

Even when such stories are brought to the editorial desk, they are relegated in favour of more urban, elite news by editors or proprietors. The media bias in favour of the urban elite at the neglect of the rural people is indeed a serious lapse as far as the media profession is concerned. Commercial considerations seem to take upper hand over ethical precepts. According to Newman 'news is also a matter of habit, of stereotype.' We are in the habit of looking for it where we have usually found it, and of reacting to it and judging it in the way that we usually have. What is news on television often depends on where your reporters and camerapersons are (Schmuhl, 1989).

This probably explains the reason why most of the news stories are urban centred and concerns the elite. Sometimes the cameras stagnate around one or the other event for a prolonged period of time at the neglect of other equally or more meritorious events. Often it is the poor and the rural people are those who get put aside in favour of the urban elites.

TRUST, INTEGRITY, EDITORIAL CONTROL AND SOCIAL RESPONSIBILITY

Media responsibility entails that media should help strengthen and support democratic and development processes. Although this is a concept, which is subjective and hard to define, arguments have been made for newspapers, television, radio, and perhaps types of internet communication to act as a government watchdog, as a gatekeeper and instrument to disseminate necessary information, and more popularly, as a reflection of cultural interests and trends.

On the universal plane, media persons should be aware of personal rights, like right to privacy that others are entitled to enjoy. Respect for these rights is the responsibility that should restrain journalists in the exercise of their freedom. The ideal of journalism is to be responsible to the truth. Whether individual journalists or publications meet that ideal is often debated, but they all, at a basic level, have a definitive responsibility to their audience (www.spj.org/ethics/-code.asp).

Media must not seek to lessen or to prevent some evil by withholding news of what has happened, or by playing it down or blowing it up. If they distort the truth, some evil worse than the one they seek to avoid may follow. The news is not a device to be turned on and off like a faucet, to achieve some end. It is an end in itself (Brucker, 1973).

While any form of government censorship is not healthy for media functioning, in the absence of any countervailing forces, the media must evolve internal, in-house systems to deal with issues that affect its responsible functioning. Media should create ways of dealing with coverage of issues like licentiousness, murder, violence, corruption, use of drug, alcohol, tobacco, immorality, 'objectification' of women, glorification of greed and force, and much more that is objectionable.

Media cannot overlook the fact that the environment of undesirable values, role models, and desensitizing experiences has important effects on every one-particularly the most vulnerable ones. Hence, media organisations need to think seriously before they add one more car chase or one more gratuitous bit of sex, rape or stripping story, violence or murder to the messages with which they are peppering us. Many media critics feel that right now, it looks like we have got far too much of creative freedom, and not enough creative responsibility.

The trust of its readers, viewers and listeners is crucial to the media. The public needs to trust the media, but trust is not given unless responsibility is demonstrated. Acting properly and responsibly is thus crucial. The public's notion of what is in good taste and bad taste cannot be ignored. Freedom of the press entails editorial independence.

The editorial work takes place in accordance with the legislation and ethical guidelines in each country. Some media houses have evolved internal regulations intended to ensure its editorial integrity, protect its sources and ensure that they maintain ethical standards. The editor-in-chief is personally and fully liable for the newspaper's contents as well as advertisements. In other media organisations there should be someone who assumes responsibility for the content they communicate to the audience. Writing about the responsibility of the media persons, Elmer Davis (1934) cautioned, "All of us in the news business ought to remember that our primary responsibility is to the man who buys the newspaper, expecting us to give him in so far as is humanly possible not only the truth and nothing but the truth, but the whole truth."

Many countries provide constitutional guarantees to ensure universal rights, freedom of speech, freedom of expression and freedom of the press. However they are not absolute in practice. These rights should be restrained by moral and legal responsibility as and when they may be in conflict with other rights similarly guaranteed. On the universal plane, journalists should be aware of personal rights, like right to privacy that others are entitled to enjoy. Respect for these rights is the responsibility that should guide journalists in the exercise of their freedom.

Joseph Pulitzer in a North American Review article in 1904 defended his proposal for a school of journalism with these words: "Nothing less than the highest ideals, the most scrupulous anxiety to do right, the most accurate knowledge of the problems it has to meet, and a sincere sense of moral responsibility will save media from a subservience to business interests, seeking selfish ends, antagonistic to public welfare" (Knott *et al.* 2002). Today many large media conglomerates have become so powerful that they "no longer feel compelled to consider the public interest as they pursue their goals of maximizing profits.

REPORTING VIOLENCE

Violence is one of the dominant contents of all media. How responsibly should media report violent incidents is a matter of debate. According to Herbert Brucker (1973) most press persons want to be responsible about reporting the news. Yet their first responsibility is to get the news.

The Eisenhower Commission on Violence, whose task it was to suggest ways of avoiding it, learned that for the press to soft-pedal reports of violence is a dereliction of duty: "Unless we propose to emulate the ostrich, we must expect—indeed the public has a right to demand—that the press will report the day's intelligence including that which is violent. As with other events, when there is violence, the public has a right to know it" (Brucker, 1973). Kerner Commission came to a similar conclusion: "...it would be imprudent and even dangerous to downplay coverage in the hope that censored reporting of inflammatory incidents somehow will diminish violence." The word will spread independently of television or newspaper reports, and it can diminish confidence in the media and increase the effectiveness of those who monger rumours and the fears of those who listen (Brucker, 1973).

Media, as the Kerner Commission observed, are not a cause of riots, "any more than they are the cause of other phenomena which they report" (Brucker, 1973). Rumours always fly when there is a vacuum of authentic, believable news. You can no more separate news coverage of a spectacular event from the event itself than you can get rid of a man's shadow. Therefore the wise course is neither to overplay violence nor to hide it. Sociologist Otto N. Larsen, author of *Violence and the Mass Media* said: "The basic issue is not the elimination of violence from the mass media. The matter rests more on *how* rather than on *whether* it is presented (Brucker, 1973).

Violence has always been good news as far as marketing media is concerned. A newspaper editor in the post Independent era in India is quoted to have confessed that he adopted a communal policy "because playing down riots and disturbances curbed his sales." "Even the newsboys", he said, "refuse to touch my paper if my rivals report a larger number of deaths than I do" (Parthasarathy, 1991).

Fascination with media violence is an expression of suppressed, aggressive impulses of frustrated people, who, unable to admit to themselves that these impulses exist, demand and expect that the crimes they enjoy be punished (Schmid-Graaf 1982). Reading and viewing about violence in media serve as a sort of catharsis. Some critics go as far as accusing media of being the handmaiden of those who indulge in violence and terrorism. They refer to a sort of symbiotic nexus between the two. Walter Laqueur called the media "the terrorist's best friend." Both have a common interest in reaching the audience, both want attention.

According to Frederick Hacker "because the terrorists offer very precious material to the mass media, the mass media generously and without costs conduct the terrorists' business with real enthusiasm and with eager professional competence" (Schmid-Graaf 1982). It would be futile to suppress violent events from being reported either through censorship or suppression. As mentioned already, rather than government action to have the media suppressed, it is better that the press and journalists practice restraint, moderation, caution and discretion. In the face of sensationalism, inaccuracies and distortions, media should strive to provide a balanced, factual and accurate report.

One way to address the issue responsibly is to ensure that reporting on violence include the causes, consequences of social disorders, the underlying problems that is responsible for the incident. But with the speed with which media operate, their penchant for breaking 'new' news stories, and their touch and go approach to issues do not help to effectively address the issue of responsible reporting on violence. Brucker (1973) calls media's penchant for manufacturing news and covering it as "making the news by covering it". Massed battalions of reporters actually change the news they cover by covering it. No longer are they neutral observers on the sidelines. Without intending any such thing, they have become a third force in human conflicts, a force that changes the outcome from what it might have been had they left it unreported.

Irresponsible media practices have at times aggravated riots and communal clashes. These include sensational headlines, identification of the communities involved in riots, exaggerated threats, unverified claims, suggestions of 'backlash', 'retaliation' and 'fallout'. Reporting tensions and conflicts requires utmost discipline, discretion and maturity on the part of the journalist.

Protesters have today learnt that they can manufacture news by planning a protest and then inviting TV and the press to cover it. As Brucker (1973) has said, it becomes common for demonstrators to stage a mass scene at noon and then to watch themselves on TV that night. Brucker (1973) quotes the Walker report on riot, which blamed the media because it found that on two occasions the camera crews did stage violence and did fake injuries for the benefit of media coverage.

Demonstrators did sometimes step up their activities for the benefit of TV cameras. Inevitably this raised the question whether journalism should deliberately reshape its reflexes, its normal news judgments, because of the effects its presence on the scene might have on what took place. ... "Downplay their stupidity," wrote Felix McKnight, Texas editor and a former president of the American Society of Newspaper Editors, to his fellow editors (Brucker 1973). Jenkin Llyod Jones of the Tulsa Tribune said: "The technique (of commanding press attention) is calculated, polished, and being used with increasing frequency" (Brucker 1973). 'The fact is inescapable: a moderate, says Brucker (1973), never gets the attention a firebrand does.'

ACCURACY: A MAJOR CASUALTY IN MEDIA

Accuracy has become a major casualty in the age of instant communication. Today it is easy to plant a big lie along with truth and get some of the media audience to believe it. The quantity of information has also affected the veracity and quality of the news. As mentioned already, the media audience does not always have the time, tenacity or tools to examine the veracity of what is reported. As media enjoy considerable credibility among the public, the onus is on the media to ensure that this trust is not belied. Reporters do not always crosscheck the information they get. They often give one-sided versions of events and people who do not matter- absolute non-entities. Often good stories are not followed up properly. Planted stores make the front page (Nayar, 2005).

The Associated Press in 1965 issued guidelines for its reporters. It begins with Joseph Pulitzer's three rules for reporting: 1 Accuracy 2 Accuracy 3 Accuracy.

It went on to provide the following guidelines for reporting:

- Be Precise. Tell exactly what happened without embellishment.... Choose your words carefully. If it's a minor disturbance, don't call it a riot. But if a full-scale riot develops, say so.
- Credibility. The source of your information is most important. We don't rush out with rumours of impending trouble. We don't rush out with a story about a disturbance on the basis of a single telephone

call. Agitators love to give false information. Well-intentioned persons let emotions sway their better judgment. Check and double-check. One should not be an alarmist reporting stories with such expressions as "tensions mounted steadily" unless they are verified.

- Damage. We report what qualified and responsible officials say, but we do not state it as fact.
- Perspective. We don't reach for headlines by throwing a story out of focus with an isolated cry, or an isolated shooting.
- Background. All disputes have a history and we should know enough about the town to say what it is...If the reporter finds that most of a crowd is angry, or troubled, he should say what it is angry at, or why it is troubled." Spell it out. Don't generalise. Get both sides of any grievance.
- Get people to the scene at the first hint of trouble. There is no substitute for the eyes, ears, and wits of our own staffers (Brucker, 1973).

The media must report situations and developments and conditions through the long months or years or even decades before anything overt happens. Because nothing spectacular was going on, media can be largely unaware of these long periods of incubation which set the stage for the seemingly spontaneous explosions that shock people when they erupt without apparent reason. A journalist must dig painstakingly for news where none seems to exist, by means of highly skilled, interpretive reporting.

The media need to be aware of and stress the ills and difficulties of sections of society, their sense of grievance, slights and indignities, the biases, paternalism and indifference to which they are subject to. As Brucker (1973) states: "If one backs off to see the whole forest of journalism's difficulty, one sees that the task of reporting becomes more subtle, more complex all the time.

It can be discouraging, as when a paper or a broadcaster takes the trouble and expense to dig into something that lies behind the excitement of the moment, only to find that most of its readers or viewers pass it by. But that's the way it is. ... Most of us seem to feel that, in this tumultuous world, we cannot even keep track of, let alone try to understand, all that happens. Yet journalism has no alternative but to try to make the individual see at least the things that matter.

Responding to editors who say that people do not read such stories, the Kerner Commission says, "find more ways of telling the story, for it is a story you, as journalist, must tell—honestly, realistically, and imaginatively. It is the responsibility of the news media to tell the story. According to Brucker (1973), with notable exceptions, the media have not yet turned to the task with the wisdom, sensitivity, and expertise it demands.

The challenge of reporting in depth and dimension is growing as society and social organisations get more and more complex. But if journalism learns that it has to anticipate the events it reports, and devotes its full resources to digging constantly under the surface for what may be going on there, it will be doing all we can ask of it (Brucker, 1973).

MEDIA IN THE NORTHEAST INDIA

Northeast India is a minefield for media persons. The region has sometimes been referred to as the "paradise in peril". With more than 100 tribes, over 240 languages and dialects, the region is a cultural and ethnic microcosm with conflicting ideologies and issues. With 98 per cent international boarders and only 2 per cent borders with the rest of India, the region has its own challenges to face. The terrain is a mix of hills and valleys. There are more than 30 militant organizations actively operating in the region and across the borders. Their demands range from autonomous districts to separate nation states.

Conflict is media's staple fare. As far as Northeast is concerned there is no dearth of conflicts for media to report. But one can discern different trends in the media in the region: the national mainstream media consider Northeast India to be too far from New Delhi and other major cities. Distance diminishes the importance of issues pertaining to the region. The proximity norm (news is what is closer home) seem to be taken seriously as far as northeast is concerned. Even when coverage about events in the region is given in the national press or electronic media, there is no serious, sustained and comprehensive reporting on the region and its issues. A vast majority of people outside the region knows little about the region and its people, politics, economy, culture, problems. Not only much of what they know is shallow and limited, but also biased and distorted.

Many militant groups feel the best way to get coverage is to indulge in violent acts like bomb blasts, killing of innocents, like the attack on unarmed labourers and Hindi speaking people in Assam. Militant groups kill innocent victims in bomb blasts, using them as scapegoats, as fodder to feed the flames of fear and hatred, to highlight grievances, to draw attention, to get publicity for particular causes, sometimes just to boost the sagging morale of their cadres, to send a message across to the administration that they are still alive and active.

They unleash terror and intimidation, strikes and protests. As Hazel Henderson (1969) pointed out minority opinion groups have discovered that whereas media ignore a traditional press release on their activities, they send reporters rushing to cover a picket line or any attention-getting "happening".... In psychological terms, the news media have been "rewarding" and therefore reinforcing destructive behaviour, by drawing attention to it and making national figures out of those who have learned what kind of behaviour keeps them in the camera's eye."

It is not surprising that the various militant groups also have well organised public relations set-ups with persons designated to get maximum mileage out of their heinous deeds. They maintain close contacts with media persons and institutions by fair or foul means. They get publicity for bandhs and other forms of protests through persuasion or intimidation of media. Readers will flock to a story that has shock value but ignore one that is routine. Terrorists, kidnappers and militants today include among their demands, publication in the media items like their manifesto, demands or other issues. There are also instances of media firms or individual reporters being sympathetic to militants and their causes. They speak and write patronizingly- sometimes even glorifying their deeds and motives. This is obvious from the way a section of the media present human rights violations by armed forces and get even international organizations to champion their cause. On the other hand they maintain a studied silence when militants violate human rights, kill and kidnap innocent people, intimidate and paralyse life and stifle economy.

Media, besides helping to perpetuate certain stereotypes and prejudices, also brand the region as 'trouble torn', 'militancy infested'. People living outside these regions have a totally distorted, 'mediated' picture of the region and its people.

Reporters admit that editors often urge them to provide and play up 'the militancy angle' in stories they file. With militancy and conflict dominating the media in the region, development communication does not seem to have received the kind of attention it deserves both in academic circles as well as journalistic praxis. All in all one can notice the shrinking space of social and development reports in our newspapers and electronic media.

The data pertaining to the quantity of reporting bias related to gender, religion and rural-urban as shown in a content analysis of two leading newspapers of the region, namely, *The Assam Tribune* and *The Shillong Times*, which I did over the last two years, show the serious rural-urban divide as far as news reporting is concerned.

The 22396 news stories and editorial items between 2004-2006, which was studied as part of a content analysis, showed a major urban-rural divide. There were only 1967 (8.78%) rural items as against 20392 (91.05) urban items. Among the 36 major categories into which I distributed the contents of the newspapers under study showed that the single biggest number of stories was related to crime and violence.

They number 3209. Militancy and terrorism was the second with a total number of 1261 items. If we were to add up all the stories (news plus editorial page items) pertaining to crime, violence, militancy, terrorism, kidnapping, bandhs, riots, agitation, ethnic clashes, the total would be more than one fourth of the total content.

An analysis of news items under positive, negative and other, showed that negative news items dominated the press coverage with 10,769 (48.08%) as against 7768 (34.69%) positive items. 3859 items (17.23%) was categorized as other.

The response to correct the imbalance would call for several steps that the media need to adopt: more coverage on development news, greater gender balance in news coverage, more representation to women in the media, a more comprehensive training for media persons on development communication and rural realities, promoting in-depth education for reporters on social and religious issues, a reduction in the space for urban coverage and allocation of more space or time for rural reports.

There are several issues in Northeast India that receive scanty attention or are totally ignored by the media. Among them I would list just a few: the role of women in improving the rural economy of the region through the efforts of women activist groups, NGOs, governmental organizations, banks, Self Help Groups.

The power and impact of women in entrepreneurship and economy, in peace building and conflict resolution are largely undermined by media. Today with economic liberalization and booming economy in the country, many companies are recruiting large number of young people from the region. The distinct edge of the youth of the region on account of greater proficiency in English language and communication skills on the one hand, the rising unemployment in the region, on the other, have favourably contributed to this phenomenon. This does not seem to be adequately reflected in the media.

The youth of the region are a force to reckon with and they enjoy considerable leadership in the community. But the media reports on the youth portray them mostly when they are in involved in anti-social or militant activities and agitations. The rich tourism potential of the region, its natural settings, wild life sanctuaries, biodiversity, ethnic and cultural diversity are largely ignored by the media. What is presented by and large is a picture of violence and hatred, unrest and conflict. Very little of the image of the region as inhabited by a people who are welcoming, hospitable, come through the media to the rest of the country. The dissatisfaction and discontent the people of the region feel about the way the media cover the Northeast and its people is voiced in meetings and conferences.

If media is to highlight the region in a more realistic and comprehensive way, it must go beyond blood-dripping stores of violence and crime. One is not asking to brush aside the ugly underbelly of the region and its woes, to do a plastic surgery and cover up the undesirable, but to adopt a more objective, realistic, balanced perspective.

Those who have the power to make the change are the editors, directors, and media managers. They need to ensure that there is space in the media for their reporters to file stories that build and connect communities and people. The remedy is not to shun media, but to help make it more responsible. What media critic William F. Fore (1993) said about television is applicable to all media.

According to him the ills of media can be countered not by shunning media or staying away from them but only by people moving into the media with greater vigour, to "tell stories that talk about community, connectedness, giving, sharing, helping and nurturing –rather than self, things, getting, keeping, forcing, using and conquering."

The issue of media induced or inspired violence is becoming a major issue globally. In the West where the issue is becoming more alarming, citizen groups are mounting pressure on media as well as authorities to curb increasingly graphic depiction of murder, mutilation and mayhem on television and other media.

Before the situation further aggravates, the media in Northeast India too must take adequate steps to reduce violence in its content. The authorities and the citizen groups can ensure that there are laws and policies to monitor the quantiy of violent content and the nature of their presntation. A 'violence rating system' could be established by which media content can be monitored. What Brucker (1973) said about the press is relevant for all media. The concept of news as something precious for its own sake, to be reported as accurately and honestly as can be, remains journalism's highest goal. To the extent that we have it, the media becomes a genuine Fourth Estate, serving impartially all the other estates that make up the body politic. Media organisations and the public need to assume responsibility for making media wholesome.

They need to ensure that the media persons are adequately trained in understanding the region in greater depth, enabling them to report more comprehensively on development issues, people's power, social and economic issues. Certainly all the ills that afflict society cannot be cured by media. It can be done only by long-time action by the appropriate agencies.

As noted, media do enjoy enormous power and it is the task of every concerned citizen to see that that power is not allowed to be misused in such a way as to become another problem along with the many problems we already encounter. Media instead, should become a beacon of light, a guiding force to understand and resolve the myriads of problems we already face.

15

A Report on Displacement in Assam and Manipur

While inter-ethnic conflicts have by no means been rare in India's Northeast, population displacement induced by such conflicts is sharply on the rise particularly since the 1980s. Conflicts and violence confined in the past mainly to the armed groups and the security forces of the state seldom triggered off population displacement of such scale and magnitude as one notices now. It is important that we take note of the changing dynamics of conflicts and violence in the region.

Conflicts today have acquired a truly mass character in the sense that they show an alarming propensity of engulfing an ever-greater number of people involved in them. In this situation, it is ironic that the two rights of home and homeland run at cross-purposes. This has its implications for the politics, ecology and topography of the region.

Mixed areas with historically practised exchanges and transactions between communities are at peril. And, thus for instance, never before in its history has Manipur been so much divided as it is now. Internal displacements sparked off by conflicts are a product of many a hidden partition in the society seldom officially acknowledged.

This study on fifty years of population displacement in Manipur tells us the story of a society that has hit almost a blind alley with little clue as to how to cross the divides and negotiate its rapidly changing ethnic landscape. We need to complement it with many other stories. As various stories marked by these divides unfold, they reveal a surprisingly similar structure—a structure that constantly reminds us of how violence once initiated eventually gathers its own momentum and takes its toll on each one of us—big or small, powerful or powerless.

The essay on Assam prods us to think in terms of formulating an agenda that takes us beyond the given fault lines. It underlines the need for dialogues as a means of addressing the issues of rights and justice. We cannot ignore the fact that the development-induced displacement against this backdrop of ethnic tensions has complicated the problem related to rights and justice in India's Northeast even more.

ON THE IDP SITUATION IN ASSAM

MONIRUL HUSSAIN

Internally displaced persons constitute one of the largest excluded groups in the society. Displacement from one's home and habitat is very pathetic because when the displacees move from their original habitats, they incur immense losses in life sustaining resources including social networks, neighbours and access to common property resources.

Although the problem of internal displacement is similar with the refugee problem, the plight or status of the internally displaced is even worse than the refugees as the former cannot cross international borders and has to seek help from that authority which is very often responsible for their displacement.

By and large, this group of people remain outside the public "consciousness" or "imagination", experiencing a high degree of alienation, marginalisation and exclusion from the larger society. Here emerges the question of human rights, care, protection and justice for the Internally Displaced Persons (henceforth IDPs). North East India has been a very distinct civilizational, geographical, socioeconomic, cultural and political entity in India. Of the 635 tribal groups listed by Anthropological Survey of India, 213 were found to be living in the Northeast India. This region is geographically isolated and connected with the rest of India through a narrow corridor. Besides, the region is also economically underdeveloped.

The migrations of different groups at different periods of history from the neighbouring areas have made the society in Assam rich and diverse in terms of race, religion, language and culture. Even the society in the hills of North East also reflects high degree of diversity though each community living therein has its distinct characteristics.

However, with its annexation into the British colonial India, Assam was exposed to a very high degree of in-migration as an inseparable part of the colonial transformation of society, polity and economy. Obviously, a large number of these migrants, were, in-fact the displaced people. Whether the tribal from the Jharkhand region who migrated to Assam's tea plantations, or the or the uprooted peasants of East Bengal who migrated to Assam in large number in search of land and livelihood, all of them were in fact the displaced people induced by the political economy of colonial India.

Briefly speaking, Assam remained the unofficial host to large number of displaced people throughout the colonial period. End of the British colonialism also forced Assam to become a host of a large number of East Pakistan refugees. Unlike, Panjab and Bengal the outflow of refugees from the North East was virtually insignificant. As Assam entered into the postcolonial phase it gradually transformed from a major host of displaced people to a major generator of displaced people in India. A large number of people are living in state sponsored relief camps for decades together without proper relief, care and protection. Their quest for return, resettlement and 6 rehabilitation has remained unfulfilled.

Most internally displaced persons in the North East are victims of environmental degradation, skewed development processes and political conflicts. Though they are technically citizens of the country, empirically they are refugees and their exact numbers are still to be estimated accurately.

CLASSIFICATION OF IDPS

One can find all the three kinds of IDPs in the North East India *i.e.*

1. Conflict induced IDPs

2. Development induced IDPs and
3. Natural disaster/environment induced IDPs (many preferred to call them Environmental Refugees).

Before presenting our report we must tell that North East is neither a homogeneous nor an even region as it is assumed to be in the rest of India. It is a highly heterogeneous and highly uneven region. Communication is still difficult, freedom of movement to a large part of the region has been restricted by the state and non-state actors.

In such a situation, it is an arduous task to prepare a status report on the IDP situation in the entire region. Perhaps the best way to present it would be to deal with each state individually with equal importance given to each of all the three categories of the IDPs and draw some broad conclusions about the region.

That too is difficult given the time and resources we have at our hand. Even then we are trying to present a broad view of the situation. It is difficult to collect data on IDP situation until and unless we have a day to day basis monitoring of the situation with an inbuilt mechanism for periodic verification.

DATA LIMITATION

Data on IDP is very scanty. Most difficult is to find data on natural disaster/environment induced displacement of population. Next in order of difficulty is to gather data on development induced displacement. North East has experienced a massive development induced displacement of population during the postcolonial period (Fernandes and Bharali 2006, awaiting publication, Hussain 2007, forthcoming). Compared to these two categories, it is relatively easier to collect data on conflict induced displacement of population. It is mainly because the media normally does not miss to report conflict because it is an important political event. Our media is largely obsessed with the political news and largely ignore the development and environment issues that displace people. Hence, in the process, we get some information about the conflict induced displacement but not much on development and environment induced displacement of population in North

East India. Besides, if not all, a significant number of media personnel accept the events of human displacement caused by environmental degradation as "natural" events.

Similar is the case with the displacement caused by development projects. Here too population displacement becomes natural!

CONFLICT INDUCED IDPS

Ethnic conflicts became endemic in postcolonial North East India. Here, ethnic conflict includes the conflict between the state and ethnic groups/insurgent groups, inter ethnic and intra ethnic conflicts. One particular situation of ethnic conflict may reflect one, two or all these three kinds of conflicts simultaneously.

Among the North Eastern states, internal displacement has been quite high in Assam. Conflict has been the main cause of major displacement of population in Assam. Although it is very difficult to give an exact data of IDPs caused by conflict in this region, we can give some estimates of government and some other agencies here. Tens of thousands of Bengalis, Hindus and Muslims, were displaced all over Assam in violence unleashed during the 1960s, 1970s and 1980s, particularly during six years of anti foreigner's agitation led by students and the dominant Asamiyas.

During the worst phase of violence in July-September 1960, almost 50,000 Bengalis, mostly Hindus crossed over to West Bengal seeking shelter there. Again, in 1972-73, 14000 Bengalis fled to West Bengal and elsewhere after the breakout of riots over language issue. However, the real figure of displacement is far more than mentioned here because government account includes only those people who took refuge in the camps of West Bengal. Thousands died in the riots during the agitation between 1979 and 1985-almost 2,000 in the village of Nellie alone. (*Bhaumik, 2005, Hussain, 2000*).

The inter-ethnic clashes in the Bodo heartland of Kokrajhar and Bongaigaon has displaced a large number of people. At one stage, the number of IDPs reached more than 3 lakhs. It should also be mentioned here that the Bodo-Muslim ethnic violence that occurred in October 1993 has displaced about 3568 families consisting of 18000 persons.

Again, a series of major incidents took place throughout the district in May 1996 when a section of Bodos attacked ethnic Santhals. This conflict has resulted in the displacement of a huge population. Almost 42,214 families consisting of about 2, 62682 persons were displaced by this conflict "at the peak of the Bodo Armed Movement, Assam accounted for nearly more than half of India's population of Internally Displaced Persons", says Sanjib Baruah of the Centre for Policy Research in Delhi (Bhaumik, 2005).

These victims were sheltered in 78-relief camps around Kokrajhar and its adjoining areas. After staying as inmates in the camps many of them return to their villages in 1997 with a small amount of returnees grant provided by government of India. However, in 1998 again conflict started between the two groups resulting in the displacement of 48,556 families consisting of 3, 14,342 villagers. Tiil April 2005, in Kokrajhar 1, 26,263 inmates were living in 38 state sponsored relief camps in the district.

Some of these conflict-induced IDPs are living in the relief camps for more than a decade now. The government is providing only rice to the inmates of some of the camps for 10 days a month. Even that supply too was erratic. Sometimes, the IDPs do not get their rations for months together. Assam government records, as informed by the BBC, indicates only 33,362 displaced people were left in the camps Kokrajhar district and 74,123 were left in the camps in Gossaigaon district.

Table 2 gives us the latest data on the IDP situation in Kokrajhar subdivision. It reveals the fact that in the Kokrajhar sub division number of inmates in the relief camps has decreased from 41,999 to 28,961 on August 2006. Little more than onethird are children and two thirds are adults. However, we could not verify the number of IDPs as given by the district administration. Still the number of IDPs is quite large despite settlement of the Bodo issue.

The leadership of the Bodoland movement now leading the Bodoland Autonomous Council as well as a part of the present Congress led coalition government of Assam. It seems they have given utmost priority to the rehabilitation of the ex-insurgents. And resettlement and rehabilitation of IDP is still a low priority issue in the political agenda of the state government as well as the Bodoland Autonomous Council.

If we combine the IDP population of the two sub-divisions, it becomes more than 54,000. The number is still quite high for the district. It needs o recollect that in the wake of Bodoland movement and its consequent inter ethnic conflict induced a large 10 number of IDPs from the early nineties of the twentieth century. Hence, a large number of people are living in these makeshift camps for more than one and half decade. The time period is good enough to asses the impact of IDP situation without proper care and protection. Community-wise break up of the inmates of IDP relief camps in Gossaigaon sub-division. Community-wise the Advasis have been the major victims of ethnic violence. Still, the largest number of the IDPs belong this category mainly composed of Santhals.

Though, the Kokrajhar district has been on focus for IDP camps, it would be wrong to ignore the IDP situation in the neighbouring Bongaigaon district. The following Table depicts the situation in Bongaigaon district. Although the government reports are claiming decrease in the number of the inmates of these camps but it is also found that these displacees are forced to leave the camps. Many tribal leaders allege that the administration was stopping rations to force these people out of the camps.

"We have been literally chased out of the camps by the officials. They said we have to go or else we will have to starve, "says Joachim Baxla, a Santhal tribal leader at Nabin Nagar, where only 103 families were left in the camps". (Bhaumik, 2005)

The Muslims of Bengali origin chased out by the Bodo rebels in 1994 are living in pathetic conditions in some places of Assam. Near Bijni on the National Highway, nearly 8,000 such Muslims live in huts on both sides of the National Highway 37. Another tribesmen Kartick Hembrom, in nearby Matiajuri said, "We are uncertain about our future. We may not get back our cultivale lands from the Bodos who occupied it after we fled the violence in 1996". (Bhaumik, 2005) "We cannot go and work in the fields because the Bodos threaten us, we cannot buy lands anywhere under the new autonomy arrangements, we cannot get back our lands," says Sabebur Rehman (Bhaumik, 2005).

The life of the IDPs living in the camps in Assam has been very difficult. Most of them do not get adequate food, nutrition and proper medical care. Children of these camps are deprived of formal education and health care services. Though, some receive food aid, but it often arrives sporadically and insufficient in quantity and nutrition. Thus these losing their possessions like land, home and livelihood live in a dehumanized condition. Mr Digambar Narzary, the head of Nedan Foundation, an NGO sponsored by UNDP is of the view that, because of poverty and conflict, there is widespread trafficking women and children in the North East. He further says that very often the trafficker carry out recruitment drives in the relief camps of Kokrajhar district.

They make false promises of jobs in the cities and bring the girls from the camps. According to the study made by this foundation, hundreds of girls of these camps have left their places in search of job. Interestingly, some of these girls are found in cities like Delhi, Chandigarh, Lucknow, Kashmir and Goa. Thus, it opens up huge possibilities for the spread of HIV/ AIDS. Therefore the study made by the foundation states that the inmates of the camps are contributing towards the enoromous rise of HIV positive in the state. (www.undp.org Amar Asom, 18th May, 2006)

According to the Home Minister of Meghalaya, approximately 350 Pnar people having close affinity with the Jaintia community of Meghalaya have fled the North Cachar Hills district following the Dimasa- Hmar conflicts in 2003. This has not only spread terror in and around the Cachar district, but resulted in thousands of Dimasas and Hmars being displaced from their gutted down villages, to take shelter in about 25 relief centres. "Almost a quarter of the population of NC Hills got displaced in this period. People belonging to both the communities fled to villages where their respective communities command the majority. These are not identified as refugee camps in the official 'situation reports' sent by the government agencies, which do not reflect the true magnitude of the tragedy." (Liberation, June 2003) Again, 4,000 Khasis and Pnars fled from Assam to Meghalaya after getting threat from Karbi militants in November 2003. The displaced were sheltered in camps.

However, after staying for a period of two months in the camps the displacees return back. However, in late 2005, the Karbi Anglong district witnessed one of the worst and longest spells of ethnic violence of Assam. Such violence continued unabated for over one month.

The two militant outfits of this district—United People's Democratic Solidarity (UPDS) and Dima Halam Daoga (DHD) faught with each other resulting in mass killing and violence in the district. The UPDS is the dominant Karbi militant group, while the DHD claims to represent the Dimasa tribe's aspiration for a separate homeland.

This conflict has also affected the Bodos living in the district. Not to speak about the Karbi and Dimasa villages, but the villages having the majority of other groups had to flee their places. At first, the conflict was concentrated mainly in Diphu sub-division, but later it spreads to Hamren subdivision also. Thousands of families have been rendered homeless with Karbis attacking the Dimasas in some places and the Dimasas retaliating in full measure in other areas The panic stricken people of villages though not directly affected, have also fled their houses to stay in the relief camps. All along the highway, scores of relief camps have sprung up.

However, people belonging to other ethnic groups are also taking shelter in the relief camps. Even when violence was abated to some extent, the people did not want to go back to what remains of their homes and hearths. Although, official sources asserted that there is no shortage of relief materials, many relief camps are facing shortage of food, medicine, clothing and kerosene. (*The Assam Tribune*, 23rd October, 2005). Another major problem is that the students of the districts are suffering as more than 40 schools have been transformed into relief camps. According to an estimate the ethnic violence of October 2005 has displaced more than 60,000 tribal people belonging to Karbi and Dimasa tribes. Hence, at the present moment it can be estimated that in Assam only, there are over two lakhs conflict induced IDPs in various relief camps both in the plains and the hills awaiting resettlement and rehabilitation.

It must be mentioned here that in many cases a number of displacees remain unnoticed and undocumented in the state. In November 2003, hundreds of Hindi-speaking people left Assam in the wake of the backlash that followed attacks on the train passengers of northeast India in various places of Bihar. Leaving aside the uncounted numbers of those internally displaced, about 20,000 persons, perhaps more, are believed to have fled the State." (*Frontline 6 December 2003)* Tension in the border areas also results in the displacement of the people.

Very recently, on August 10, 2006; the Bangladesh Rifles attacked two outposts of the Border Security force in Cachar and Karimganj districts killing two women. The BSF also retaliated and the firing between the two border guards continued for a long time. Anticipating further violence, nearly 3000 residents of Harinagar, Kinarkkal and Tukegram villages of Cachar and Karimganj fled their homes in panic. (*The*

The displaced people have been lodged in the relief camps opened at schools and club buildings at a safe distance from the international border. There are problems in the Indo-Bangladesh border over land in Cachar district, as it is believed that the Bangladeshi national try to cultivate in the land of Harinagar area of this district. This is stated to be the main reason behind such an incident.

However, later on Indian government has dismissed the report on land encroachment by the Bangladeshi National in the Indian side. (*Special correspondent, The Assam Tribune, 18th August 2006*). Again on 20th August there were exchanges of fire between India's BSF and Bangladesh's BDR in which a Bangladeshi woman died. People living in the border area, whether an international or inter-state in North East India always suffers from a deep sense of fear because of conflict between inter-state border and intra state border. Like Indo-Bangladesh border, the Assam and Nagaland border and the Assam and Arunachal Pradesh border have very often generate displacement of population. However, such displacements have not received adequate attention from the media.

Interestingly, anti-Bengali movement has displaced people not only from Assam earlier but also from Tripura and Meghalaya. In Meghalaya there was a largescale displacement of Bengali population, mainly from Shillong. Since the early 1980s, an estimated 25,000-35,000 Bengalis have left Meghalaya and settled down in some other states of India, mainly in Assam and West Bengal.

According to Meghalaya Census report, in 1981, there were 1,19,571 Bengalis in Meghalaya, constituting 8.13 per cent of the state's population. But in 1991, this stood at 144261, constituting only 5.97 per cent of the total population. (Bhaumik, 2005). There has been a steady decline of Bengali population in Shillong over last three decades.

In Tripura, attacks on Bengali has been more widespread. Here, the Bengalis constitute the majority and taken over land on a large scale from the indigenous communities. The violence started between the two communities with the riot of June-July 1980 in which about 1076 Bengalis and 278 tribals were killed. during this riot, 189,919 people, 80 per cent Bengalis and the remaining 20 per cent tribal were displaced and took shelter in the 186 camps that were set up for them.

After the return of normalcy, it was difficult for the Bengalis to return back to their villages as they were taken over by the tribal. Some of the tribal youths formed Tribal National Volunteers (TNV). Between March 1992 and March 2002, these rebels killed 823 Bengalis and 3312 were kidnapped. About 1/7th of those kidnapped did not return. Thus, after 1980 since the first major ethnic riot in Tripura, more than 100000 Bengalis have been displaced from the state. (Bhaumik, 2005). The Tripura State Revenue Minister, in a statement in the Legislative Assembly, on 24 September 2003, quoted IDP figures in the state; in what could be the first such attempt by any state government in the region to assess the scale of physical movement of people due to militancy. The minister said, "Between March

1998 to February 2003, 19,468 families have been displaced from their original places". If each family is estimated to have five members, the total number of people displaced would be around 98,000, roughly amounting to more than three per cent of the state's total population. (Routray, 2004). This is a very large displacement indeed. Similarly, Manipur has witnessed substantial internal displacement and ethnic relocation in the wake of the Naga-Kuki and the Kuki-Paite feuds in the 1990s that led to nearly 1700 deaths and destruction of property worth millions of Rupees.

At least 600 villages were burnt down during the Naga-Kuki feud, in which nearly 10000 houses were destroyed. The Nagas killed 898 Kukis during the eight-year-old feud while 312 Nagas were killed by the Kukis. On the other hand, the Paites killed 210 Kukis in clashes and lost 298 persons from their community. Almost 3000 houses in 47 villages were destroyed and 22000 Kukis and Paites were displaced. Again, during the riots between the meites and Pangals, more than 100 were killed in which 196 houses in 9 villages were destroyed. (Haokip, 2002).

On the other hand, the regrouping of Mizos by the Indian Army in the wake of Mizo rebellion had displaced a large number of Mizo population. During the first regrouping, 45000 and in the second regrouping 87000 Mizos were regrouped. This had forced the Mizo farmers away from his lands as they were forced to settle in roadside locations guarded by the army (Bhaumik, 2005). Mizoram has also witnessed a massive outflow of Burmese refugees in 2003.

The Chin refugees who had taken refuge in the state following persecution by the Burmese Junta in the post-1988 democracy uprising were forcibly repatriated to Myanmar during July-August 2003. It is reported that more than 4000 Burmese refugees went back to Myanmar after this violence.

More than 50,000 ethnic Chin, Kuki and Naga refugees from Myanmar have been left at the mercy of the state governments and the local populace. (Haokip, 2003) About 30,000 to 40,000 Brus/also called Reangs fled from Mizoram State of India to Tripura to escape from a campaign of violence and terror against them allegedly by members of the Mizo Zirlai Pawl (Mizo Students Union) and Young Mizo Association (YMA).

From 15 October 1997 onwards, Reangs from Tungbagin, Kawnmun, Pheileng, Laxmicheraa, Kwartha, Rangdil, Fileng and Tuipuibari areas of Aizwal district of Mizoram fled to neighbouring states to escape from persecution from the non-state actors. It is alleged that the state too remained as silent spectator.

According to an estimate of Tripura government, 30,690 Reangs belonging to 6859 families have fled into Tripura in last 3 years. Later on, at the initiative of the Mizoram government, almost 3000 refugees returned back to Mizoram but a majority has chosen to stay back in the IDP camps of Tripura. During the visit to the relief camps under Kanchanpur sub-division in North Tripura from 2-4 January 2006, Asian Centre for Human Rights found the conditions of over 34,000 displaced Brus in the camps in North Tripura as sub-human. Medical and sanitation facilities are almost non-existent in these camps. The inmates use the water from ponds and streams as a result of which water born disease spread out very easily. More than 5000 children in the camps are deprived of education. Even Sarva Shiksha Abhiyan has not been extended to these camps. (www.achrweb.org).

Another survey in these camps reveals the fact that the inmates are also becoming victims of AIDS. A survey at the refugee camps in Kanchanpur Subdivision of North-Tripura district conducted by the state health department has found that at least 6 Bru IDPs staying at these camps have been suffering from AIDS and 12 others are found to be HIV positive. Health department sources further say that a section of poverty stricken refugees were working as sex workers and a section of youth were drug addicts, who are contributing towards the spread of this disease. (*The Assam Tribune,* 28 May

2006). The Brus/Reang IDP issue is far from resolved. The Bru National Liberation Front (BNLF) laid down their arms in February 2005 following a peace accord with the state government of Mizoram. However, the Bru Liberation Front of Mizoram (BLFM) remained underground and according to the MIzoram Government, they are still involved in kidnapping and extortions. Besides, there exists some disagreement between the government of Mizoram and Tripura about the number of Bru IDPs living in relief camps in south Tripura adjoining Mizoram.

The Mizoram government identified five villages for the resettlement of 1,700 Bru families in the first phase of repatriation. Accordingly, Tuipuibari, Aampa, Tengpui, and Tuirum villages would resettle 500 Bru families each while the rest would be resettled in Thaidawr and Tumpuan Lui.

In the second phase, the Mizoram government instructed to prepared ground to resettle the remaining 1,300 Bru families in three villages *i.e.* Bunghmun, Rengdil and Zamung. However, quite a few influential Mizo NGOs opposed the move to resettle the BRu IDP families in the specific areas (Ibid) on the other hand, 16 point memorandum submitted by the Brus demanded that the Brus of resettled in group collectively and not in a divided manner (Ibid). All this has created a blockade for the return of Bru IDPs to Mizoram.

DEVELOPMENT–INDUCED DISPLACEMENT

Development projects are very often linked with the problem of displacement. The development projects of the North East region have directly affected the poor and powerless tribal both in the hills and plains. Absence of adequate resettlement and rehabilitation policy for the displaced has led to further pauperisation, marginalisation and helplessness among the oustees.

The South Asian Solidarity for Rivers and Peoples (SARP) maintained that from the 72 hydel projects proposed in the NE region only the contractors and dealers of cement, iron etc will be benefited, not the common people. It will also help the better off to lead a luxurious life, but at the same time the poor and the backward communities will be deprived of their livelihood. It is also interesting to see that Central Allocation for NE projects has increased substantially in 2005-06 financial year. Eighty new projects were sanctioned in this year for this region. By now it has become clear that mega damshave done more harms than good to the people.

But still the central government is proposing new plans having dangerous consequences ignoring the fragile ecology of this region. The common people have become conscious of the fact that such projects are not only going to displace them, but also discrete their timeless bond with the elements of nature. They will be alienated from their own place.

The people have now understood that Dams and other mega projects will imperil their sustainable modes of living making their life more difficult. Geological condition of this region is fragile. Instead of making any effort protect the rich flora and fauna, the central government is coming with new proposals for setting up different projects in this region, which will have serious consequences in the long run.

It is also interesting to see that are by some the development projects of the neighbouring states have also generated IDPs in this region, *e.g.*, the Kaptai Dam constructed on the river Karnaphuli across the international border in the Chittagong Hill Tracts has displaced a large number of Chakmas and Hajongs of the CHT. A large number of them settled down in Tripura and Arunachal Pradesh creating refugee problem.

The indigenous communities of Arunachal apprehend that the 65,000 strong Chakma-Hajong refugees could in future emerge as a dominant political force. Such an eventuality would seal any prospects of their deportation. They are also increasingly worried about the alleged gradual transfer of their land to the refugees. Besides, the refugees are also accused of encroaching on the reserved forestland. (Singh, 2005)

Among the northeastern states, development induced IDPs are more visible in Assam. The oil sector in Assam also contributed towards the problem of displacement. New oil townships are established in various places of upper and lower

Assam displacing the inhabitants of those areas. Two paper Mills of Assam at Jagiroad and Cachar have also forced people out of their homes besides destroying the greenery. The Jagiroad paper mill has mostly displaced the people belonging to Tiwa tribes. On the other hand, the Cachar Paper Mill in Barak Valley of Assam has reduced the bamboo forest in the neighbouring area.

Moreover, urban expansion of Guwahati city has displaced the tribal mostly belonging to Karbis and Bodos. Urban expansion is pushing these people out of the city to the periphery. In 1973, when Assam's capital was shifted from Shillong to Guwahati once again the tribals had to sacrifice. An estimated 1,00000 population were displaced at that time. Again educational institutions like Gauhati University and IIT, Guwahati have also displaced the original inhabitants of the outskirts of the city without proper rehabilitation.

The Pagladiya Dam Project is to be constructed in Nalbari District of Lower Assam. The project is going to irrigate 54,125 hectres of land, protect 40,000 hectres of land from flood and erosion, and generate only 3 MW of electricity. But it would displace almost 1,05000 population most of whom are tribal people.

The rehabilitation and resettlement package offered by the government is also not acceptable to the people of the area. Besides many of them do not posses proper ownership documents and therefore will not get any compensation. Hence, the people have started their movement under the banner called *Pagladia Bandh Prakalpar Ksatigrastha Alekar Sangram Samiti* against the implementation of the project. The Central government as well as the Brahmaputra Board, which is the implementing agency of the project, is making all efforts to construct the dam there. But till now the resistance of the people have been quite successful and the authority has failed to do even the ground survey because of the massive resistance of the people.

For the construction of the fourth bridge over the mighty Brahmaputra 'the Bogibeel Bridge', already more than 2000 bighas of land have been occupied. According to an estimate, almost 500 families having ownership documents of these lands are not compensated yet. It is to be mentioned that the land has been taken for keeping stones and other materials required for the construction of the bridge.

The 2000 MW Lower Subansiri project to be constructed on the border areas of Assam and Arunachal is already facing lot of opposition from the people as well as from the governments of both the sectors. The project was planned by National Hydro Electric Power Corporation (NHPC), a government run public sector unit and it is very keen to construct the dam as it has obtained environmental clearance for the projects.

The proposed height of the dam is 116 metres and it will submerge 3436 hectres of land. At the same time more than 1 Lakh tribals of Arunachal Pradesh will be adversely affected by the dam, out of which about 15000 faces the threat ofphysical displacement. Besides it will affect the rich bio diversity of the region as 42 hectres of land belonging to Tulley Valley reserve forest will also be submerged, where many rare animal species can be found.

The NHPC has already constructed their office on an elephant corridor. As a result of this the elephants have started attacking and destroying the neighbouring villages. The indigenous people of Arunachal are also worried over the threats posed by these projects to their habitats and unique cultural heritage. They further fear that the project would also lead to influx of outsiders creating social problems. Again, the project is going to submerge a vast tract of cultivable land in Arunachal Pradesh impoverishing a large number of indigenous people, while people of other states will get the benefit.

However in a significant development, the Ministry of Power has decided to drop plans for the construction of Upper Subansiri dam in Arunachal Pradesh following directions by the Ministry of Environment and Forest on the basis of Indian Board of Wildlife. (*The Assam Tribune*, 27 November 2005). The Dumbur Dam of the Gumti Hydel Project in South Tripura district, aims at generating 8.60 MW of power, has displaced a total of 5845 tribal families—between 35,000 to 40,000 people in all. The Gumti Hydel project has mainly displaced the people belonging to Reang community. Although a rehabilitation scheme was taken up for the permanent rehabilitation of the affected families and payment of compensation in terms of acquisition of their land was also undertaken by the state government but it is experienced that most of the affected population dispersed in different localities of Tripura States and they are not in a position to response during the course of rehabilitation activities. Another point to be mentioned here is that the affected Reang communities are mostly jhumias and they are having no land records even of their homestead land. Therefore it is virtually impossible for them to get resettlement without land document.

Likewise, the Tipaimukh Multi purpose project is also going to displace over 15,000 people. It would mainly attack two tribal communities- Zeliangrong Nagas and the Hmar. It is to be mentioned here that the tribal people have very close relationship with the nature. Moreover, they are attached to the mother earth and have a very well knit web of community life. The construction of such projects disturbs their community life and breaks their relationship with the nature. Besides, in the North East such displacement due to development creates the problem of space further creating ethnic conflicts among them. Tuli paper Mill of Nagaland has also displaced hundreds of tribal families and affected the rich bio diversity and environment. The Loktak Hydel project in Manipur displaced around 20,000 people as their villages went under water. In Arunachal Pradesh more than 20,000 would be displaced by the Siang project (Bhaumik, 2005).

DISPLACEMENT DUE TO ENVIRONMENTAL DEGRADATION

It is difficult to estimate the number of IDPs caused by environmental degradation, *i.e.* flood, riverbank erosion, and landslide etc. However, some reasonable conclusions can be drawn about the enormity of the problem. As a result of continuous environmental degradation; flood and riverbank erosion in the plains, and landslide in the hills have become endemic. This has caused innumerable deaths, destruction and population displacement.

The intensity of flood, riverbank erosion and landslide has increased substantially over the years in terms of area and victims. It would be pertinent to point out that the plight of the riverbank erosion induced IDPs are much more severe than that of the victims of flood. The victims of flood at least can go back to their original land once the flood water recedes.

However, the riverbank erosion induced ID peasants can not go back to their land. Because, their land has become a part of river's new/extended bed. It is not only the mighty river Brahmaputra but also the innumerable small and medium sized rivers are also causing havoc in the plains of Assam, *i.e.* the Brahmaputra Valley and the Barak Valley.

The flood of 2004 alone affected more than ten million people in Assam valley. Excepting two hill districts, all the districts of the plains of Assam experienced devastating flood and riverbank erosion. In an unprecedented flash flood in October of 2004, nearly one thousand people died in Goalpara district of Assam.

The government provided some relief to some of these flood-affected people, which was far from adequate. Besides flood, erosion has also created problem for the people of Assam. According an official report, the river Brahmaputra eroded 4, 29, 657 hectares of prime agricultural land. Roughly, 7% of the land in the plains has been eroded between 1951-2000. This has definitely displaced at least 3 million peasants. Today they constitute the most pauperised community in Assam's plains. In the absence of proper resettlement and rehabilitation policy, most of them haveexperienced multiple displacements.

UNITED NATIONS GUIDING PRINCIPLES RELATING TO IDPS: IMPLEMENTATION IN THE NORTH EAST INDIA

The United Nations Guiding Principles on internally displaced Persons has given a framework for taking care and providing adequate protection of the displaced. These 30 principles cover all three phases of internal displacement— the pre-displacement, situation during displacement and the post displacement *i.e.* the return and resettlement of the displacees. However, it is very unfortunate that these principles are not implemented in India in general and Assam in particular. It seems the state too totally oblivious to the UN guiding principles on IDPs.

Principle 1 says that IDPs shall enjoy in full equality the same rights and freedoms under international and domestic law. But the IDPs living in the camps as well as outside the camps in the North East never enjoy the freedom as enjoyed by other citizens.

Principle 2 states that these principles shall be observed by all authorities, groups and persons irrespective of their legal status and applied without any adverse distinction. So, all the non-state actors and different groups are under obligation to follow/obey it. However, these are not observed, rather violated very often in the North East India by different groups.

Principle 4 is very vital particularly to this region because it states that the IDPs should not face discrimination. It should be mentioned here that the displaced who mainly belong to the minority or backward groups often have to face iscrimination in various respects in this part of the country.

Principles 6 and 7 have been grossly violated in the Northeast India time and again. This principle states that every human being have the right to be protected against being arbitrarily displaced from his/her home or place of habitual residence.

Principle 7 states that it prohibits displacement unless the authority ensures the safety and security of the people to be displaced. Implementation of these principles will safeguard the people from development–induced displacement.

Observance of Principles 8 and 9 by the authority in the North East India would have led to the betterment of the condition of the displaced people. Principle 8 states that displacement shall not be carried out in a manner that violates the right to life, dignity, liberty and security of those affected, while principle 9 states that states are under obligation to protect against displacement of indigenous people, minorities, peasants etc. with a special dependency on and attachment to their lands. Contrary to this, in the North East India, most of the time, it is found that the displaced belong to the indigenous, minorities and peasant groups.

Again, principle 11 states that, the IDPs should be protected against rape, torture and other gender specific violence; slavery of any form and sexual exploitation. But the IDPs living in the camps are very often become the victims of these types of exploitation. Principle 14 of the UN Guiding Principles mentions about the right of the IDPs to move freely and to choose his or her own residence. But it is difficult for the IDPs of the North East to enjoy these rights in and out of the camp. Besides, it is nearly impossible for them to choose their own place of residence.

Principle 17 emphasises on the integrity of the family of the displaced and reunion of the members of the family. This is of great significance to the IDPs of the North East where a large number of people are displaced by conflicts and in case of such displacement it is likely thar the families will be disintegrated.

Principles 18-22 of the UN Guiding principle specifically deal with the basic needs of the IDPs, medical care and protection of the property. But the IDPs staying in the camps hardly receive all these facilities. Moreover, it is very difficult for them to get back their property.

Principle 23 speaks about right to education and states that special efforts should be made to ensure full and equal participation of women and girls in educational programmes. But the inmates of camps as well as those living outside hardly enjoy the right to education.

Principle 25 makes the national authority responsible for giving humanitarian assistance to the IDPs. Therefore, it has great significance as the displaced do not have to depend on the provincial authority for getting the assistance.

Principles 28, 29 and 30 specifically deal with the return, resettlement and reintegration of the displaced persons. It allows the internally displaced persons to return voluntarily, in safety and with dignity, to their homes or places of habitual residence or to other place. It also speaks about the full participation of the internally displaced persons in the planning and management of their own resettlement and rehabilitation.

Thus, the Guiding Principles emphasize on the individual's right to be protected against arbitrary displacement and providing basic facilities to the 21 displaced. Besides it also speaks about minimising the adverse affects of displacement. Implementation of these principles is the need of the hour to improve the conditions of the displaced, particularly in the North East.

Here it should be noted that in Assam, it is quite likely that one person may face different types of displacement during his lifetime. Fpr example, a person displaced by flood or riverbank erosion may cross the boundary experience conflictinduced displacement in his/her new place of residence.

Thus, displacement becomes a serialized and multipled experience. All these have made it very difficult to correctly estimate the number of IDPs in the North East. Usually, the method of head counting of those people who take shelter in the relief camps is used to make an estimate of it. However, such method excludes the population who choose to migrate to the urban centres of the state in search of livelihood.

POPULATION DISPLACEMENT IN MANIPUR IN THE LAST 100 YEARS

Any discussion on conflict-related displacements in Manipur will have to begin with a study of the larger political background that first of all introduced the conditions for these conflicts. The last 100 years have been particularly interesting in this regard. There have been other kinds of displacement of populations, especially related to development projects and in recent times, to economic factors, but the mandate of this paper is to focus on the conflict related category.

The physical scars of conflicts are starkly evident if one were to consider the present political map of the northeast region as such. It is not too rare to hear of the narrow 22 km or so "chicken neck" corridor between Bangladesh and Bhutan that connects mainland India with the northeast, being used as an apt image to describe the alienation of the northeast from the so-called national mainstream.

This 22 km of border is supposed to constitute only about two per cent of the total boundary of the northeast. All of the rest of 98 per cent are international borders, China and Bhutan in the north, Myanmar in the East, Bangladesh in the South and much of the West. The picture is unambiguous. It conveys an awesome sense of lack of contact, physical and spiritual, with sub-continental India.

Many have indeed argued powerfully how this physical condition portrays an inner psychological distance that is the destiny of the relationship of the northeast with the soul of India. From its lack of development to the numerous secessionist insurrections it is witnessing, have all been attributed in varying degrees to this distance.

The only shortcoming of this perspective is, the question as to how much this chicken neck is a political one and not physical, has seldom followed as a natural interrogation. This is serious because the omission results in the obscuring of a historical fact that the chicken neck is a residual fallout ofcolonial politics and administration, rather than a given, natural, physical feature.

To be precise, how responsible is the Radcliffe Line, the boundary drawn by the British colonial administration before they departed from India in 1947, the culprit behind the "distance" between the northeast and rest of India? Did this boundary commission have to have the northeast connected to India by a chicken neck? If the Radcliffe Line did not make this chicken neck a chicken neck, would the alienation of the northeast that has almost become a cliche today, have been the same? Of course the chicken neck does expose another general mindset of the Indian leadership at the time the Radcliffe Line was drawn, and perhaps even today.

They allowed the chicken neck to materialize, which it is doubtful they would have if any other part of the Indian heartland were to be thus isolated by an international political boundary. No war has been fought over the Radcliffe Line'schicken neck, but one was over another border demarcating the northeast—the McMahon Line.

Nothing as the northeast existed in pre-Independent India. It is, in every sense of the word a creation of the colonial politics and the confinement the region is subject to today is indeed a colonial confinement. Its map and regional identity are defined by colonial boundaries. In the south the Radcliffe Line, in the north by the McMahon Line and its eastern boundary was also very much a consequence of the Treaty of Yandabo in 1826, which too bears a colonial stamp. Then there was also the British policy of Partially Excluded and Excluded Areas with regard to their frontier policies in the northeast.

The logic behind these always had to do with protecting British commercial and strategic interests. Hence, it may be said that much of the British punitive expeditions into the Naga hills, most particularly the Angami territory, was to protect its tea gardens and Assam. No outsiders were allowed to enter the Excluded Areas, while outsiders could enter the Partially Excluded Areas with permits.

After India's independence, these policies have their inheritors in the existing inner line permit system, applicable in Nagaland, Mizoram and Arunachal Pradesh, by which all, including Indian citizens are required to have special permit to enter these states, and the Protected Area Permit, PAP, applicable to Nagaland, Manipur and Mizoram, whereby foreigners are restricted entry and have to pay a fee to enter these states.

These lines did much more to alter the face and psychology of the northeast. Ever since they came into existence, the sea suddenly became remote, the Barak Valley came to be undermined considerably politically and commercially, thriving border trades became stiflingly regulated or else condemned to slow strangulation etc. Without going into the rigmarole of the justness or otherwise of these lines, for indeed they are a reality today not to be undone, at least not easily, one simple question begs an answer. What was it like, or what must it have been like, before these lines were drawn, in the case of some of them, not much more than half a century ago?

The issue of migrations, and ethnic unrests must also take into consideration these factors for a fuller understanding. These questions are now beginning to be asked in so many other situations everywhere in the post-colonial world, and with astounding results. Economic and cultural zones that transcend but do not disturb national boundaries are emerging.

The Greater Mekong Sub-region, GMS, the Association of South East Asian Nations, ASEAN, the much heard of Track-II "Kunming Initiative" which envisages to create the BCIM, Bangladesh, China, India and Myanmar economic cooperation and connectivity, to name just a few. One way of attempting to answer the question as to what it must have been like before the national boundaries came up, could be to have a look at the unofficial relations that still exists despite the boundaries.

The popular unofficial trade routes, or smuggling and gun running channels if you like, is one such.

Would making these routes official make a difference to the scenario and bring what is underground, overground, as much as make what is illegal, legal? The other approach would be to refer to the abiding memories of the time that still lingers on. Just as Cox Bazar and Mandalay are familiar names to unofficial traders, so are Dhaka and Chittagong to many first, second and even third generation, Western educated literati in places like Manipur. Sylhet too is fond memory for many in Manipur who still have distant relatives living there.

The legacies of these political developments are still very much visible in the northeast. Boundaries coming up in haste, where earlier there were none and at best were frontiers. This however does not mean there were no organized polities in the region and that these took birth as a consequence of colonial influence. I make this qualification for very often the "indigenous other" has been viewed by the colonial eyes as basically unaccountable or un-assessable in terms of modern values and understandings of political organizations. The vision determined by a mimicked "coloniality" persists even today, and the northeast often falls under this cloud. Hence many, even academics have tended to see the northeast as constitutive of places and peoples without history: A region whose dominant characteristics are ones of lawlessness, atavism, mindless and violent tribalism, etc. Things however are not so simple.

DEFINING THE OTHER WORLD

How do we imagine or define Manipur? The question is posed sometimes provocatively and at other times honestly, during seminars and symposiums outside the state of Manipur, as to what the nature of the presumably ancient Manipur is all about.

How could it ever qualify to be a "nation" or even a polity before the modern times? Where are the proofs that the Kabaw Valley ever belonged to Manipur etc? We sense a similar flawed presumption of historical progression in these questions. Who says a nation has always to have hard boundaries with boundary pillars, fenced off by barbed wires, guarded zealously by professional soldiers etc.

The pre-colonial world outside of Europe did not understand nations and territory this way. Rather than national boundaries, there would have been frontiers only. In the Hindu epic *Ramayana* there was a particular ceremony Rama performed to demarcate the domain of his kingdom, whereby he released a white stallion and let it run free.

If anybody stood in the way of the free run of the horse, he would have to face the might of the king and if he managed to stop the king, that would be where the former's kingdom was deemed to have ended. Such understandings would be more applicable to say, the contested ownership of the uninhabited Kabaw Valley of the time between the kingdoms of Ava and Manipur. For that matter the very frontiers of Ava or Manipur or other Southeast Asian kingdoms, and indeed the rest of the non-European world would have been determined by such principles. If a king stuck his flag on the bank of a certain river and nobody dared oppose him, that point would become the extent of his kingdom. These understandings cannot simply be forced into the nineteenth century European

The point is, not everything outside the so-called "civilized" world is "uncivilized." This acknowledgement is absolutely essential in all our efforts to understand the northeast. The place is not ruled by inexplicable tribal feuds, mutually hostile bands of wild people, with customs and traditions beyond comprehensible and not worth attempting to understand.

There is nothing so mysterious, wild or inaccessible about the ways of the northeast. It does not need to be tamed, but understood. If there are tensions between the Nagas and the Kukis, or between the Nagas and the Meiteis, it is not out of any instinctive tribal xenophobia or any basic bloodlust. There are objective reasons for all these frictions. Understanding these is the challenge before any peace arbitration effort.

CASE STUDIES

Manipur is today an ethnic cauldron but one in which the different ethnic groups have not been able to evolve a common identity. Tensions between them have traditionally been determined by competition for the control of resources and land, but in recent times, it has been politics-which has given these tensions a new and dangerous dimension, altogether. Manipur's geography was always embedded in the potential for a divided population, a condition-which is a reality today.

This Northeastern state of 22,327 sq km constitutes 20,089 sq km mountainous terrain surrounding an oval shaped valley of 2,238 sq km in area located almost accurately in the middle of the state. It is only to be expected that the first major psychological division that the state is stymied by today, coincide with this topographical feature.

There is a paucity of scientific studies on the migration patterns in prehistorical as well as the proto-historical periods of this region, but it is generally believed that the hills were first populated, the valley being initially largely waterlogged and marshy. Evidences of a water-logged past of the valley and the gradual drying process are to be seen even today in the continued shrinking and disappearances of many lakes and other forms of wetlands that dot it. The 200 sq km freshwater Loktak Lake is itself, according to experts, in danger of dying up, largely because of heavy silting caused by many rivers that empty into it from the surrounding mountains.

The Loktak serves as the reservoir of the waters from these rivers and the excess that it cannot hold is drained out of the state to flow into two major transnational river systems. One of them is the Chindwin which joins the Irrawaddy at Kalewa in Myanmar. The other waterway is an artificial tunnel dug through the hills that flank the Imphal valley in the west, to power a hydro electric power generation project, which ultimately flows into the Barak River which meanders through the Barak valley in Assam onto the adjacent Surma valley in Bangladesh and meets the sea at the Bay of Bengal.

Mythologies of the various ethnic groups living both in the hills as well as the valley somewhat coincide on the belief of migration of population from the hills to settle in the valley. The most popular and touching of these tells of two brothers in their mountain home parting ways. The elder decides to remain in the security of their established home, while the younger and more adventurous opts to look for his fortune in the valley below. The younger valley dweller later came to be the Meiteis and elder who stayed behind are the hill tribes, in later years the Nagas, and Kukis (Naga and Kuki are recent nomenclatures, each tribe was then known by its individual tribe names only).

It is not difficult to imagine that the Meiteis discovered what a blessing the fertile, well-irrigated, alluvial river valley proved to be for a farming community. They would have progressively grown more prosperous, opening up an economic gap with their brothers in the hills, thus setting the roots of all the complicated problems of disparity and inequity.

This divide was to continually widen in the years ahead, and indeed one of the most daunting challenges before the Manipur administration today is to bridge this hill-valley chasm, and since the hills and valley dwellers have come to acquire different ethnic identities, an ethnic problem as well along this divide. (Pradip Phanjoubam, 'Fractured Land' in Geeti Sen (ed.), *Where the Sun Shines and the Shadows Fall*, New Delhi: OUP 2006). Manipur has seen four major ethnic feuds in the recent decades.

- 1990s: Kuki-Naga clashes:
- 1993: Meitei-Pangal clashes:
- 1997: Kuki-Paite clashes:
- 2001: NSCN(IM) ceasefire extension troubles
- 2006: Hmar displacement because of underground clashes and harassment

"THE MOTHER OF ALL INSURGENCIES"

It is amazing how an iconic image can influence decisions not just at the individual level, but at community and governmental levels. The advertising world will know better of this power, and indeed they recommend pumping in billions of dollars to the effort of creating such images for the products they sponsor.

The makers of these products too willingly spend these astronomical sums, obviously realizing the wonders that these images can do their businesses. Indeed much of the world of advertising is about promoting an illusory world of these iconic images to whet the worldly appetites of consumers and make them simply continue buying compulsively. And it succeeds, that is why the phenomenon has not only remained but also grown.

But the iconic image business is not always a success especially when it strays out of the confines of the consumer market. In politics especially it has proven to be a flop far too often. We have a very immediate example in the northeast to demonstrate this. The current philosophy of the counter insurgency policy of the Government of India for instance is built on a single, widely circulated

Iconic idea: "The Mother of All Insurgencies". Anybody who has been following the affairs of the region close enough will understand who this supposed "mother" is, although many of the numerous insurgencies will disagree if at all they consider this so called "mother" as their "mother". It is uncertain where the idea may have had its genesis, but probably it was a phrase coined by some journalist struck by a flash of bright idea to colour up his copy of the day. The image however has struck a chord in popular imagination and has been somewhat immortalized. As we have said, without doubt, it has also influenced profoundly, government policies on insurgency.

The understandable approach has been to tackle the mother in the hope all its supposed offspring will come under control. We also know today how badly this approach has misfired. At this moment, it is practically impossible to say which is the mother and which the child in the complex matrix of northeast insurgencies. Considering the endless complications the approach has led to, all concern would have also realised by now that tackling the "mother" is hardly the key to a final answer to insurgency in the region.

The decade of 1990s in Manipur was very interesting in this regard. The chain reaction in the multiplication of insurgencies amongst the Kukis, to say the least, was phenomenal. It began with the Naga-Kuki clashes that left over a thousand dead and many more destituted and homeless.

Unlike the Nagas, who had 50 years of militancy behind them, insurgency amongst the Kukis at the time was nascent and marginal, and if it did have a cognizable presence, it was the Kuki National Army (KNA) in the Moreh area but mostly along the Burmese side of the international border. But the clashes, in which the Kukis bore the major brunt, exposed the Kuki community's vulnerability and it was this insecurity that became the fertile ground for the spawning of various armed militias amongst the community.

This process was catalysed by the virtual absence of any effective state intervention, or its impotence in instilling any sense of confidence amongst the victimized community. If this was the reason for the sudden growth of Kuki militancy in the mid-1990s, this phenomenon in turn left other smaller kin communities of the Kukis insecure. To resist Kuki hegemony, they began making friends with the adversaries of the Kukis, angering the latter. The bloody fratricidal Kuki-Paite clashes in Churachandpur district even as the Kuki-Naga feuds subsided will have to be explained as a part of this vicious chain. Each link of this chain has also now become a separate reality not to be taken for granted at all. But this is just one chain to demonstrate how such a chain works. There are plenty more.

The interesting thing is, once formed, no part of a chain is the "mother" to the other partsanymore and they become all the same. There is also no other way than to treat the whole chain as one entity. In the insurgency scenario in Manipur today for instance, it would be unrealistic to have cessation of hostility with one group and expect peace to set in, just as it would be equally unrealistic to ask only one group to disarm while the rest remain armed.

KUKI NAGA CONFLICT

One of the major ethnic clashes in recent times has been undoubtedly the one between the Nagas and Kukis that turned the hills of Manipur red during much of he early and middle parts of the 1990s. In the early 1990s, tension between the Nagas and Kukis reached a flashpoint with the United Naga Council serving a quit notice to the Kukis settled in "Naga areas" in 1992. Manipur has nine districts, four in the valley, dominated by the Meiteis and five in the hills, four of which are dominated by the Nagas. The Kukis and other kin tribes dominate in one. The Nagas consider much of the Manipur hills as their traditional homeland and that the Kukis living in these districts were in a way their tenants, hence the UNC quit notice. Persecution of the Kukis began thereafter but it was only in 1993 that the feud broke out in the open.

The Kukis being largely migratory, were scattered and were hence much more vulnerable. Moreover the Kukis at the time did not have any well organized militia of their own whereas the Nagas did, having run an insurgency for over 50 years then. The results were predictable but the Kukis were the main victims, although in the years to follow, the Kukis too became more organized, and did hit back-causing casualties amongst Naga villagers too. The Kuki-Naga feud has now concluded, but the bitterness remains. There has been a multiplication of militant organizations amongst the Kukis since. Amongst these are the Kuki National Front (KNF) and its factions, Kuki National Army (KNA), kuki Liberation Army (KLA), kuki Revolutionary Army (KRA) etc.

It also caused the largest single displacement of population in recent times. Constituency profiles have virtually altered in many cases because of the ethnic cleansing. While some villages have disappeared new ones have come up. The ethnic divide between the two groups of tribal population have also become virtually water-tight with even government servants from either communities remaining away from areas dominated by the rival tribes. Without doubt again, this is the conflict that resulted in the most of displacements.

In the other conflicts, if there have been displacements, they were temporary. After the condition of feuding concluded, most of the displaced returned back to their original homes. In the case of the aftermath of the Kuki-Naga feud however, there were huge population shifts. Many villages were uprooted for good while new ones came up in different districts. A good many of them too joined the (urban migration basically to Imphal) to eke out a living, often not in legally permitted ways.

POLICE ANNUAL REPORT 1997-98

Ethnic clashes between the Nagas and the Kukis "The clashes between the kuki and Naga tribes which started in June 1992 when a Kuki youth was kidnapped at Moreh Bazar by suspected Naga extremists and was later found dead in a nearby jungle, continued unabated in 1993 1994 and 1995.

Since then there has been a downward trend although sporadic incidents take place every now and then. "The Naga kuki clash was (sic) first started in the hill areas of state in the middle of the 1992. The starting point being form the brother town of Moreh. In Manipur mass scale forced displacement and migration of small villages to their safer and nearer to the larger groups of major community which they claimed to belong to started in thes years."

SADAR HILLS LITMUS

The little news item some days ago about a certain organisation demanding that the creation of the Sadar Hills administrative district must precede any move to implement the Sixth Schedule provisions in the state is a matter that must not be taken lightly. The first time the Sixth Schedule came very close to being implemented, if we remember correctly, during Prof. Meijinlung Kamei's stint as a Union minister of state for home affairs in the mid 1990s, among the foremost stumbling blocks the move encountered was the Sadar Hills lobby.

The issue continued to be a virtual nemesis of the Sixth Schedule in the days that have followed since. As many commentators have pointed out, we too tend to agree that the opposition to the Sixth Schedule in the hills from the valley would not have been as vehement as it is now, 5 years ago, and perhaps it will not be so again 5 years or less hence.

The picture of a possible vivisection of Manipur thrown up by the developments that culminated in the June 18, 2001, explosion of public sentiment, has come to be the dividing line. Rightly or wrongly, there is a strong apprehension that the schedule is a first step, and an indirect route to breaking up of Manipur.

We are not so much concerned about the veracity of this logic, but the important thing is, the apprehension this has created is very real and strong, and as long as the perceived threat to the territorial integrity of Manipur remains, it is also unlikely to go away at anybody's wish or curse.

We are not interested in campaigning for any side of the argument, but we are definitely interested in a settlement of the issue, and for that matter all other issues of public importance, amicably. This can happen only if all concerned parties try to understand each other's aspirations as well as apprehensions honestly.

It is here that we feel that the Sadar Hills issue can be the litmus test for the honesty of purpose of those demanding the implementation of the schedule, as well as those opposing it. When Prof. Meijinlung made the proposal for creating

Autonomous District Councils, ADC, under the Sixth Schedule in the state, for reasons that proved quite controversial and also fuel for suspicion, he advocated the creation of either two, three or five ADCs.

In the two ADC option, there would be the traditional Naga districts in one and the non-Naga district, namely Churachandpur in another. In the three ADC combinations, Ukhrul and Chandel would form one ADC, Senapati and Tamenlong another and Churachandpur the third. In the five ADC combinations, the existing five hill districts would each be an ADC. Sadar Hills was never in the picture as a separate entity, and the boundaries of these ADCs always had an ethnic colour, separating the Nagas from the Kukis. It may very well be that there was very neutral and motive-free logic behind these proposals, but the fact is they fed not so innocent speculations, not just among those in the valley, but also amongst other non-Naga population, being as it was in the wake of the bitter Kuki-Naga riots in the hill districts.

Assuming that there were no motives behind these proposals, let us test the same waters again by making a different set of proposals. What if we have six ADCs, with Sadar Hills included over and above the five existing hill districts. Or what if we have seven or eight or 10 ADCs, with the ADC boundaries drawn purely on considerations of administrative convenience, such as general accessibility, population, resources etc, as is generally the case in the case of Panchayati Raj institutions in the valley districts. It will be interesting to note who protests against such a proposal and for what.

If the valley still protests to such a proposal, our conclusion would most likely be that the hill public were always correct—the valley population do not want the fruits of development and administration to reach their brethrens in the hills. If on the other hand the hill public, more particularly the Naga population protest, then we would most likely conclude that the wide apprehension in the valley that the Sixth Schedule demand is rife with less apparent agendas, was not altogether baseless after all.

NATIONS WITHIN NATIONS

Observers from outside the northeast, including journalists who are not too familiar with the northeast, are often awestruck by the complexity of the nationality question in Manipur. Often, the reason they had been given northeast assignments, in the first place, is that they have had the experience of covering Kashmir and hence presumed that it would not be difficult for them to get at the roots of the conflicts in the northeast.

To their utter dismay, they discover that although the conflict in Kashmir is much more intense, they need only to understand certain direct equations between state and non-state power players. Not so in the northeast. The vogue has always been to talk of a dominant national current so that it is relatively easy to identify the undercurrents that run counter to it. Hence, the "mainstream" and the "sub-stream" become distinct and non-confusing. The northeast ethnic cauldron defies such simple equations. There is the Indian "mainstreams" and there are not just "substreams" that run counter to it, but also "sub-streams" of the "sub-streams" and so on and so forth, in a progression that can extend right down to the village community.

Often they come to Imphal in the hope of studying what they believed was Manipur's problem with the Indian Union. In Imphal they do get the impression of such an antagonism, hearing of complaints against Central acts such as the Armed Forces Special Powers Act, AFSPA. They gathered information about Manorama and Sharmila, of the two Nupi Lals against the colonial state etc. Soon enough they get the feel of the hill-valley divide, after all, local newspapers screamed daily of the verbal duels in the regard.

In 2005 July there were two simultaneous bandhs, one by the All Naga Students' Association Manipur, ANSAM, and the other by the Sadar Hills District Demand Committee, SHDDC, both along the National Highway-39. Journalists who had come to Manipur at the time thought the two added up to the same hill-valley divide equation and decided that a trip to Senapati, the hub of the ANSAM's activities, would further clear up their understanding of the issues involved. Sure enough, at Senapati they heard angry voices against how the Nagas had been suppressed by the Meiteis of the valley; how the latter had forced their language and script to them; how developmental funds meant for the hill districts were being routinely diverted to the valley; how the Meiteis were standing in the way of the Naga aspiration for a unified, sovereign Nagalim etc.

All this would have been well, but for what the journalists heard from the agitators along their way to Senapati from Imphal. They discovered all too soon that the ANSAM blockade and the SHDDC bandh were about similar issues but not the same.

If Senapati district wanted to break away from Manipur on the plea of unfair deals to them by the Manipur government, Sadar Hills wanted to be separated from Senapati on the charge that the district was doing to them what Imphal is deemed to be doing to Senapati. On a larger plane, Manipur is pointing similar accusative fingers at the Union Government.

1993 MEITEI-PANGAL CLASHES

On May 3, 1993, an aberration in the history of ethnic relations between the Meiteis and the Meitei Pangals (Manipuri Muslims) happened, surprising everybody. In all 97 Muslims were killed and several of their settlements burnt down. Only two Meiteis were casualties. Fortunately the trouble did not last long, nor the bitterness remained. Displacement was virtually nil and a commission is today looking into the matter of resettlement. The riots lasted basically for two days and were completely controlled in a week's time. One of the consequences of the clash however was the emergence of two militant organisations amongst the Muslim population the NEMF and the more dominant PULF.

The feud, provoked by a hitherto unheard of militant group called People's Revolutionary Army, PRA, left 102 Muslims dead and 3 Meiteis killed. It also left many Muslim villages burned down. All of these villages have since been resurrected and returned to their original inhabitants.

ETHNIC CLASHES BETWEEN THE KUKIS AND THE PAITES

The Kukis and Paites are kin tribes. In fact, till about a decade ago, they were all known collectively by a generic nomenclature of Khongsais by the valley dwelling Meiteis. (Yambem Laba, "Cant See Guitars for Guns", mimeo): Small tribes, like the Paite, Vaiphei, Simte, etc. had been remaining aloof from all armed movements but with the rise of Kuki militancy after the Kuki-Naga clashes, started feeling insecure and unprotected.

They also feared surrender of their identity to the dominant Kukis and decided to form their own armed organization called Zomi Reunification Organisation (ZRO) with its armed military wing Zomi Revolution Army (ZRA) on May 7, 1993 under the leadership of one Khaizang Guite at Phapjan Chin state, Myanmar. Later on 2-9-95, the leaders of Paite, Simte, Vaiphei and Tadim Chin along with the ZRO/ZRA leaders took a formal customary oath affirming their unity and solidarity. (Police report)

As a direct consequence between the Kukis and Nagas, militant organisations of both the tribal groups began wooing the Zomis and because of their perceived threat of losing their identity to the Kukis, the latter began showing inclination to align with the National Socialist Council of Nagaland (NSCN-IM). The Kukis too startedsuspecting the Zomis of having nexus with the Nagas and charged them for giving shelter to the Naga militants with the alleged intention to wipe out all the Kukis from Churachandpur district, the territory traditionally shared by the Kukis and the Paites.

With the intention to check this alleged activities of the ZRO/ZRA, KNF activitist attacked the Saikul Paite village under Churachandpur district on June 24, 1997 in which six villagers were killed and 6 other villagers injured, One more succumbed to his injuries at the District hospital the next day. A series of clashes between the Kuki and the Paites at different villages in Churachandpur district resulted. "Besides it, above figures, many Government quarters, Schools, Churches, Community Halls were also set ablaze and many houses damaged during the period in the ethnic clashes." (source Manipur Police) Interestingly however, it was the accord that ended the feud on October 1, 1998, which spoke eloquently of the causes of the feud between the kin tribes, speaking virtually the same language, following virtually the same customs, and celebrating virtually the same festivals.

THE THREE MAIN CLAUSES OF THE ACCORD

1. The nomenclatures of both Kuki and Zomi shall be mutually respected.
2. Surrender all forcibly occupied houses of either of the former warring groups
3. Militant groups of either side would indulge in collection of taxes from members of the other communities, be they government officials, contractors or businessmen

2001 NSCN (IM) CEASEFIRE EXTENSION TROUBLES: LAND, HOMELAND, INSURGENCY ETC.

In 2001 June 14, the Government of India and the Naga militant group NSCN (IM) reached an understanding whereby the ceasefire agreement the two parties had agreed upon in 1997 would be extended "without territorial limits". This implied the ceasefire between the NSCN (IM) and the GOI would come into effect in Manipur territory. A huge agitation erupted in the state, particularly in the Imphal valley climaxing on June 18 when agitators burned down the Manipur State Legislative Assembly and many official quarters of legislators protesting against the decision.

The contention was that the agreement implied an acknowledgement of Greater Nagaland and thus the disintegration of the historical state of Manipur. In the agitation 18 people lost their lives to bullets of security personnel in charge of the VIPs, and even after this, when there were no signs of the agitation subsiding, the GOI withdrew the clause of the ceasefire extension that said "without territorial limits". The agitation cooled gradually after that. The pitch of the agitation was such that many Naga residents in Imphal Valley fled to the hills although in a phenomenon that surprised even the die-hard pessimists, not a single Naga resident or their properties were harmed during the agitation. The number of people who fled contrasts greatly between what Naga NGOs projected (close to 40,000) and the government's figure which put it at about 3000 during the heat of the agitation. The government also claims that all but a few have returned.

2006 HMAR DISPLACEMENT

Meitei militants have been using the remote Tipaimukh subdivision as a stronghold for a long time, but especially after they were flushed out of the Sajik Tampak area of Chandel district, close to the Myanmar border. They were then allies of the Hmar militant group Hmar People's Convention or HPC. But towards the middle of 1995 they fell out and as did many other Kuki militant groups at the time, entered into a clandestine accord with the Army.

The Army crackdown began on the Meitei insurgent groups thereafter and the bitterness between these militants and the HPC grew. Harassment of Hmar villagers which were considered sympathetic to the HPC by the former intensified until it overflowed on January 16, 2006, when a group of 18 militants, six belonging to the United National Liberation Front or UNLF and 12 to the Kangleipak Communist Party (KCP) arrived in the dead of the night at Lungthulien, and after calling out and beating up brutally more than 400 villagers, allegedly raped 21 girls.

The allegation of rape was however denied by the accused although they admitted to beating up villagers who they thought were sympathetic to the HPC. The matter is now being probed by a Judicial Commission. More than 800 Hmar villagers fled their villages and took shelter in neighbouring Mizoram in makeshift refugee camps. 685 of the Hmar villagers have since returned to their homes as on October 24, 2006 (IFP report quoting official sources) from the Sakawrdai refugee camp in neighbouring Mizoram. These are from 155 families. Each of the families was given Rs.5000 to reestablish itself. Of the 685, 459 were adults and 226 minors. They belonged to Lungthulien, Tuilbung, Parbung, Phulpi, Moulien, Damdei, Taiithu and Rovkot.

SECOND WORLD WAR: INDIANS TURNED OUT OF BURMA: M. K. BINODINI'S ACCOUNT

Another cataclysmic event in the iast century that visited Manipur and Nagaland was the World War II. The Japanese after virtually taking over Burma from the British began their push towards Delhi along with the Indian National Army, INA of Netaji Subhas Chandra Bose. The battles fought in the two states were some of the most bitter, according to Field Marshal Sir William Slim in his book *Defeat Into Victory*, but were not given their due because of the North Africa campaigns at about the same time which were thought to be more immediately threatening to Europe. There were 65,000 soldiers who died in these battles, 45,000 of them Japanese.

But Japan's initial victory in Burma had another consequence. The Burmese took the opportunity of the administrative chaos to launch xenophobic campaigns against its citizens of Indian origin who left their homes in hordes and walked with the retreating British forces towards India. They arrived in Imphal and went on to Dimapur railhead. Many of them settled in the two states. The conditions in which they arrived in Manipur is described in the account of a lady whose husband was a doctor at the time, as told to noted writer M. K. Binodini and translated from Manipur by the author:

- "We came to learn of the imminence of the war reaching Manipur months before it actually broke out. There were plenty of rumours, some plausible, others wild. One of them said if the Japanese took Singapore, they would arrive in Manipur before your day's laundries dried.
- "Prophesies from the purans (Meitei ancient books of prophesies) began floating freely, with nobody actually knowing how they originated. The one that caught the people's paranoid imagination most was that the flight of 18 white egrets across the Manipur

sky would signal the beginning of the war. When the phenomenon was sighted the advice was to flee and take shelter at places with names beginning with the consonant 'K'. Everybody watched the skies day after day for the white birds with anxious expectation and apprehension. My son Jotin, the eldest of 11 siblings was 11 years old at the time.

- "The Allied troops began arriving into Manipur in endless convoys. Soldiers of different colours and built that we have never seen before, huge armoured military vehicles, tanks and anti-aircraft battery began filling up our roads. It all made up for a very awesome and intimidating picture.
- "The war time administration then began bombarding the place with pamphlets, instructing the civil population of the dos and don'ts during the war. One of the many advices was to dig trenches to hide during bombing raids. Trainings were also imparted on these precautionary measures. Amidst the growing nervous tension, we continued to watch the skies for the 18 egrets in flight.
- "My husband was then posted at Thoubal. He left me and the children in the relative safety of Lilong but he became so busy those days that he was unable to visit us for extended periods. It was a time when refugees of Indian origin began pouring into Manipur from Burma. Many of them, especially women and children, were sick and on the verge of death from starvation and fatigue. He was busy attending them.
- "One day he showed up at our residence at Lilong briefly. He seemed depressed. He told us the story of a refugee then on his last leg, brought to him for treatment. The unfortunate man had been suffering from cholera for some time during the trek to India. My husband treated him but was too late to rescue the dying man. On his deathbed, the man presented my husband a tin box which he had lugged all the way from Burma and said it contained money,

weeping that he was to die without seeing his family. My husband said he took the box and although the dead man had gifted it to him handed it over to the British wartime authorities, telling them to do what they thought was the needful.

- "My husband was honest to a fault and had no particular cravings for unearned money. His story however made us all grieve for the dead man. (Did the white egrets appear? I interrupted impatiently at this point). "Yes, yes! They did come flying. But they were not the birds that we were expecting. Instead, they were white airplanes. The first time they came they did not unleash their loads of fire and brimstone. As per instructions we ran and jumped into our trenches but the planes simply turned and flew away. The first day gave us a very wrong impression of the war. We could not figure out why the White men were so fussy about airplanes and the trench routine.
- "A few days latter, on May 10, the airplanes returned and shocked us all out of our complacency, pouring on us bombs that exploded like unending thunder claps. Many said there were 18 of them. So perhaps the puran prophesy did come true.
- "It rained bombs continuously from then on for a long time. A lot of familiar landmarks were flattened. A refugee camp too took a load and many unfortunate souls were killed. The spectacle of terror was simply beyond words.
- "One day my husband turned up at our residence again very briefly. He said he had been transferred to Churachandpur and would be proceeding there immediately. He asked us to stay on at Lilong until the fighting lightened and then to try to make it to Moirang. He had asked Uncle Nongthonba in Moirang to help make it possible."

The battles of the WW-II in Imphal also caused a lot of local displacements, but after the war, all returned to their homes to reclaim them.

REASSESSING IDENTITY

Considering all of the most bitter conflicts and conflict related displacements were on account of ethnic identity assertion, and also the fact that much of these issues seem to be headed towards a dead end, there is a crying need in the state today for all to discard yesterday's slogans in facing today's challenges. Ideally, the defining parametres of nationhood, as well as the identity of its citizens should be constitutional, which presumably is the summary of the experience through history, as well as the vision of the future of the nation and its people. Such a constitution must however not be a monolith, to be revered as a sacred and irrefutable with no scope ever of adapting to the changing times and needs.

The proposition is important in the present context of Manipur and the also the nation. In Manipur the question is relevant because of the upsurge of ethnic nationalisms and the consequent conflict situations, and in the country as a whole, because of the upswing of the rightist philosophy of cultural and religious nationalism. Both in their distinct ways undermine the constitution. An article by Amit Choudhury in *Outlook* raises an interesting point. He talked of his experience during his decade long stay in the United Kingdom before moving on to the United States. A decade or two ago, he was of the opinion that United Kingdom was one of the most racial and intolerant countries in the Western world.

Today, despite the strong residue of racism still prevalent, the country has more or less come to terms with the problem, and consequently is one of the most ethnically diverse countries. His analysis of what happened is most interesting. He says it was not on account of a voluntary change of attitude on the part of the racists amongst the Whites Britons, but the aggressive and pro-active posture of the children of the Asian and other immigrant populations on their political status and citizenship that ushered in the change.

To the abuse "go home", the answer became "this is home," not said merely to sting back, but out of a conviction that England was indeed their home, and that they as citizens have a right to claim every guarantee under the British constitution. Choudhury's was a reflection on the plight of the Muslims in India, and how they should abandon the hysterical attitude of the cornered, recoiling in the process deeper and deeper into their shells, and instead go out and claim their place in the nation to the extent that the nation's constitution guarantees every one of its citizens. In the secular, democratic, republic that the Indian constitution defines India to be, all citizens are citizens as per its definition of citizenship, and all of them are equal. Any violation of this guarantee, by anybody, regardless of religion, caste or creed; regardless of who is in power in the government; regardless of any attempt, popular or otherwise, to give nationalism a cultural twist, it will remain a crime. In Manipur's context too, this argument is, we are of the opinion, extremely relevant particularly in any consideration of the people of Manipur's relations with the larger Indian polity, as much as in the settling of the often conflicting inter ethnic relationship in the complex maze of ethnic interests the state has necessarily to negotiate. Perhaps the proactive posture would be to say that like religion, ethnic identity consciousness must remain a private affair, while politics and law must be deciding factors of public life.

The different communities and ethnic groups must by all means be encouraged to retain their ethnicity, for this identity is in their instinct, but when it comes to governance and rights, it must be decided by a common denominator—a general law drawn up with the constitutional philosophy as guideline.

ALIEN PROBLEM

The issue of illegal immigration from Bangladesh and the Illegal Migrants (Determination by Tribunal) Act 1983, in force in Assam legislated basically to deal with the issue has always been a problem area. Many want the Act repealed to be replaced by the Foreigners Act 1946.

The IMDT Act 1983, make it mandatory for complaints to be lodged of the presence of foreigners with the tribunal and then places the onus of proving the alien status of the subject or subjects of the complaint, on the shoulders of the complainant or complainants. This has meant virtually no official identification of foreigners much less deportation, long after the agitation in Assam and some other northeastern states, two decades ago. The Foreigners Act, repealed just about a year ago, on the other hand reverses the procedure and makes the onus of proof of citizenship on the accused. Legality apart, the issue is extremely sensitive. The six year long antiforeigners agitation in Assam, spearheaded by the All Assam Students Union (AASU) and the profiles of its opposition and support bases should testify this.

The then chief minister of Assam, the late Hiteshwar Saikia, of the Congress (I) and the late Sanjay Gandhi, had openly confronted the agitating students then, as well as much after the agitation wound up after the signing of Assam Accord of 1986. Saikia's logic—that of the electoral benefits he stood to reap by patronising the immigrants—was no secret. At one point he had even declared there are no illegal immigrants at all in Assam. But vote bank politics notwithstanding, there is more to the matter than meets the eye.

In the present anti foreigners upsurge for instance, there is a religious tinge to the whole issue and perhaps inevitably so. The campaign makes a clear distinction between Hindu "refugees" and Muslim "illegal immigrants." The former category hence gains domicile legitimacy before the law, the country's as well as international, while the latter is devoid of it altogether. The question then is no longer a question of fixing a cut off date for identification as illegal immigrants to be deported or disenfranchised, as was the demand of the AASU in the 1980s, but of fixing a cut off date and then specifying a screening process solely on the basis of religion. The understanding seems to be, Hindu refugees were forced out of Bangladesh because of state persecution, while Muslim immigrants had come across the border in search of greener economic pastures.

This later aspect of the problem, even if it is based on facts, is bound to create a lot of extra bitterness. But this is not all. There is a subtle interplay of contradicting nationalisms. The present xenophobia in a larger part of the northeast is based less on religious nationalism, and more on linguistic and ethnic nationalisms. At the time of Partition, Assamese linguistic nationalism that feared numerical domination by Bengalis in their own state had led to the gifting away of Hindu majority district of Sylhet to the then East Pakistan. Likewise, it must be noted carefully that the reports of work permits in Nagaland are not to Bangladeshi immigrants alone, but to non-Naga, Indian nationals as well.

POLITICS OF RECOGNITION

In the illegal migration question the basic concern was of the number game of democracy. The more your number the more voice and power you are entitled in the policy making process of the state. But there is another competing interest that has developed in multi-ethnic small states like Manipur. The competition is for recognition under the constitution of India as an independent tribe so as to reap the benefits of the policy of positive discrimination under it. In a span of 20 years, the number of scheduled tribe communities in Manipur has increased from 26 to 29.

The incentive structuring in the India system is such that it has encouraged communities to be labelled "backward" or "tribal". Unwittingly perhaps, it has also been an instrument for division. As for instance, there was once a time most of the southern tribes of Manipur came under the nomenclature of Kuki. Today the Kuki family has splintered. In fact, the Kukis and Paites have fought a fratricidal war already in 1997. To be acknowledged as an independent community however, a certain number is essential. Hence, especially in recent times, population census exercises have become sensitive and far too often controversial.

The latest 2001 census, in particular in Manipur nearly came to blows with extraordinarily abnormal growths recorded in two hill districts. But demography changes have other larger implications. They also must reflect in the constituency delimitation, and in a state like Manipur where there are reserved seats for tribals and general seats, it becomes problematic when tribal constituencies expand. For one thing it results in the disenfranchisement of general voters who get incorporated in the reserved constituencies.

2001 census will indeed go down as another Pandora's box in the state's endless list of such boxes full of troubles. The issue is, how has population grown so haphazardly, with significant to extraordinary rises in some districts, and stagnation or drops in others. If the growth in population is by the natural laws of biological reproduction, the disparity in the growth pattern does seem a little discordant.

Normally, it should have been the valley areas where income avenues are far more in abundance, which should have been at the top of the growth chart. But since this is not so, there must be other factors involved. We can think of two. One, it can be by migration from outside the state, or else by population shifts within the state. Two, it can be by a grossly faulty, dishonest and incompetent census enumeration process. Without making any presumptions on which of these factors is responsible for the present growth imbalance, the responsibility before the state authorities is to establish the truth of the matter before blocking or acting on the proposal for constituencies realignment.

The census report itself should also be able to provide some vital clues. We are sure it has break-ups of the population constituents. If the increases in some of the districts have been because of adult population rise, it would be obvious the second of the two reasons cited would be responsible. Conversely, if the increase is of children under 10 years of age, (the period between the 1991 and 2001 population censuses) the safe assumption would be that the increase is very much by natural population proliferation. Since the increase is also in the number of people of voting age, another way of screening the truth can be by comparing the 1991 census figures with those of the 2001. It should not be difficult to determine whether the number of minors in the 1991 census who would have attained voting age in 10 years, tallies with the increase in the number of persons of voting age recorded in the 2001 census. If it does, then it is a natural growth and if not, there are extraneous factors that have influenced or manipulated the census records. If the increase is natural, then nobody must stand in the way of the proposed delimitation. Representation in the state Assembly must be by the democratic norm of population proportions. If the case is of an unnatural growth in population, then the matter gets more complicated.

One, if the discrepancies indicate a faulty census enumeration, delimitation must not be allowed. Two, if the increase is by migration or population shifts, the issue must be whether the incremental population constitutes of tribal or non-tribal population, and consequently, whether the new constituencies, if at all, should fall in the reserved or non-reserved categories. While proportional representation is sacrosanct, disenfranchisement by unconsidered reservations can be a gross violation of human rights too. It does seem that the matter needs a lot closer scrutiny and there is no time for the government to drag its feet.

On the other hand, if the census enumerations are found to be either dishonest or incompetent, those responsible for committing the blunders in the preparation of a vital document of national and international significance should not go unpunished.

DELIMITATION CAUTIONS

In Nagaland the problem is similar. The vehement protest from practically every section of the Naga population in Nagaland over the proposal for a delimitation of constituencies in the state, should give some pointer to the kind of opposition the same proposal may face in Manipur. In Nagaland, the issue among others was the question of an explosion of population in and around the Dimapur area of the Kohima district on account of sizeable labour immigration.

In Manipur similar problems will be faced particularly in the Senapati district, and in fact may even be more compounded, considering there have been considerable population shifts in the wake of the ethnic turmoil in the state, most notably the Kuki-Naga feud of the early and mid 1990s. Realignment of constituencies, if deemed essential by the population norm, must be done, but keeping in mind the whole exercise can easily be reduced to skating on thin ice.

For one, the delimitation must not be a cause for fresh ethnic strife. Any move to profile freshly created Assembly constituencies on ethnic lines, must be avoided and the population norm must be strictly adhered to. However, since there are two clear-cut officially sanctioned difference between constituencies in the state, one reserved for scheduled tribes and the other open, care must be taken so as not to disenfranchise non tribal population by reserving constituencies with sizeable non-tribal population.

The state already has a big problem with regard to seven Assembly segments of the Outer Manipur Parliamentary seat, in the Thoubal districts. It also needs to be studied carefully whether the disproportionate jump in the population figure of the Senapati district and to a lesser extent in the Chandel district, is because of the Malthusian phenomenon or else by immigration, with two objectives in mind. If there are illegal immigrants, they must not be listed as voters, and if there are legal non-tribal immigrants like the Nepalis, they cannot be disenfranchised. Then again, it also needs to be established if the population shifts the state witnessed, especially during the agitation against the territorial extension of the NSCN (IM)-Government of India ceasefire, are permanent.

The other problem that the delimitation exercise must seek to rectify is to empower marginal communities buried within constituencies dominated by bigger communities. We can think of the Koms, Koirengs, Purums, Moyons, Monsangs, Lamkang, Kharams, Gangtes, Simtes and a number of others, among whom we know there are enough capable leaders, but because of their number, they have little hope of ever sending up a direct representative to the Assembly.

They must be empowered indirectly by constituency structuring wherever possible. As for instance, even if no Kom can hope to be an MLA, the Kom community must be made to command a lobby within the constituency or constituencies they fall in, so that no MLA can ignore their interest. In ethnically diverse and deeply riven society as Manipur, we do not see the delimitation proposal as a simple process. In fact, if not handled sensitively and with tact, the men in charge of this onerous mission, may end up opening yet another Pandora's box, plunging the state deeper into crisis. Or else committing immense injustice.

16

Socio-political Condition of Assam and Role of Media

THE PEOPLE AND THE SOCIETY

Assam has a composite culture of numerous tribes, races each portraying peculiar ethnic identity. As a first step to the study of socio political condition of this great northeastern state of India encompassing an area of 78,438 sq Kms, it is imperative to begin with the basic element of a society, that is, the inhabitants. It will be injustice and unethical to point out a single tribe or race amongst all, as Assamese. Because Assam not only belongs to that community which speaks the official language Assamese. Assam equally belongs to those communities who might not even understand Assamese.

These people even today speak their peculiar dialects or *duans* as locally called. These tribes like the bodo, karbi, chutia, miri, koch, kachari, garo, khamti, singphos, deori, mess, dimasa, laloong, etc, each practicing their peculiar traditions, customs, religious beliefs and language, inhabiting the hilly areas, are the original inhabitants of Assam. In the 12th and 13th centuries *Ahoms* and Muslims came to Assam.

The *Ahoms* are originally conquerors from Thailand who had come to Assam form the east and mesmerized by the virgin beauty of this land, settled down here embracing its language and way of life. In face, the name, Assam, is believed to have been given by the *Ahoms* who ruled Assam for seven hundred years. All these facts serve as an introduction to the diverse yet composite culture of Assam. This is a society that has emerged out of intermingling of diverse races and tribes, yet living peacefully cultivating a feeling of brotherhood and oneness. Assamese, a peace loving community, historically speaking, has always embraced everybody who has come to this land forgetting all religious and communal differences. It is heartening to note that Assam, though infested with violent outfits today, can proudly acclaim its communal unity and peaceful coexistence.

One can witness religions unity of rare variety in Hajo, a small town, 35 kms kilometres from Gauhati, "Serving as the meeting place of pilgrims of three major religions-Hindu, Muslim and Buddhist, Hajo has been most eloquently delivering the message of *sarvadharma samabhava* in its true spirit... the Buddhists from Bhutan, Nepal and Tibet, who believe that Hajo is the place where Lord Buddha attained his *parinirvana,* come to worship *Mahamuni*".—'Folk Culture of Kamrup', by Paresh Baishya. There is the *Haigrib Madhab Mandir* of the Hindus and along with it is *Puwa Macca* of the Muslims. Devotees throng in large numbers all round the year to these places of worship, irrespective of religious boundaries. It is believed that a visit to *Puwa Macca* is eqivalent to a visit to Mecca, and for the fulfillment of wishes one has to offer prayers at both *Haigrib Madhab Mandir* and *Puwa Macca.*

"The Muslims came to Assam in the year 1206. ...in the social sphere there was no difference or social divide

between Hindus and Muslims.....the *Ahom* rulers were so liberal that as an honour to their bravery, did not mind in marrying off their daughters to the Muslims"—*'Drishti Aaru Shrishti"* by Abdus Sattar. This reveals the kind of secularism Assam has always believed in. "*Fatiha* of the *Quran* was translated into Assamese as *Id Stuti* by Maniram Dewan, the great patriot, thus displaying social unity of such high order", says Abdus Satter. Hence, Assam practiced secularism long before the Constitution of India was drafted. Speaking of folk culture mention has to be made of *Bihu,* the festival of Assam. *Bohag Bihu* the festival to welcome the spring and thereby the Assamese new year. *Bihu* is celebrated all over the state by the different communities in their own ways. Teenage children dance to the tune of the *pepa,* the traditional flute, wearing the different ethnic dresses, singing the same love songs but in their peculiar dialects.

Besides *Bihu,* the festival portraying social solidarity, other predominant features of the Assamese society include practice of *Shakti puja,* presence of *naamghars* (the prayer halls one finds in every locality), and *Vaishnavism* (the religion taught by the *Saint Shankardeva,* the great religious and social reformer of the region.).

Christianity though a new entrant (brought in by American Christian Missionaries and popularized among the hill tribes, in the early19th century) is prevalent in the Assamese society. This is an introductory chapter to know the Assamese society closely for a convenient understanding of the present socio—political condition of the state.

POPULATION GROWTH:

As per 1991 population census, the population of Assam, stood at 22.41 million. That is, average density of population per square km is 286 in 1991. According to the Registrar General of India the projected population of Assam stands at 26.37 million as on October 2000. The state which occupy the thirteenth position in terms of population in India has two distinct natural regions, *viz.* the Brahmaputra and Barak Valley. While the former constitutes of 18 districts of plain areas and 2 districts of hill areas, the latter is composed of 3 districts with plain areas.

For administration and revenue purposes, the 23 districts of the state are divided into 48 sub-division and 149 revenue circles. Decadal growth of population of Assam is 24.2 per cent during 1981-91 (taking into account the interpolated population in 1981) as against 23.9 per cent for the country as a whole.

It may be noted here that while between 1901 and 1991 population of the country increased by about 3 times, while the same in the case of Assam rose by about 7 times during the said period. As per projected population of Assam and India also the density have been found to be 336 and 310 per sq km respectively as on October 2000. According to the Election Commission, there has been an increase of more than 30 per cent in 17 assembly constituencies and more than 20 per cent increase in 40 constituencies between 1994 and 1997. Significantly, the all India average growth for a three year period intervening the two intensive revisions in 1994 and 1997, is 7 per cent, the growth in Assam for this period is 16.4 per cent. This increase is mainly due to large scale illegal infiltration from neighbouring Bangladesh.

Annual Average growth rate of population (1971-91); Districts with high growth rate:

- Dhemaji—3.72
- North Cacher Hills—3.48—
- Kokrajhar—2.89
- Bongaigaon—2.52
- Kamrup—2.56
- Dhubri—2.27
- Sontipur—2.29
- Lakhimpur—2.26
- Golaghat—2.32
- Karbi Anglong—2.83

Districts with low growth rate:

- Jorhat—1.44
- Karimganj—1.77
- Sibsagar—1.65
- Dibrugarh—1.62

(There was no census in Assam in 1981. The figures indicated have been worked out on the basis of 1971-91 growth rate) the statistics above clearly show that rate of growth of Muslim population in the state has been much higher than the all Ind: level. Muslim population has grown by 77.42% in 1991 from what it was in 1971. While growth of Hindu population has been nearly 41.89% in this period. Muslim majority districts as per 1991 census are Dhubri, Goalpara, Barpeta and Hailakandi.

Now the list includes the districts of Nowgaon, Karimganj and Morigaon. (courtesy: Governor of Assam's report on Illegal Migration into Assam to the President of India, 1998).

Birth and Death rate:

According to the Sample Registration Bulletin published by the Registrar General of India-

From 1991 to 1999 both birth and death rates were found to be higher in the state than that of the country as a whole.

During the year 1999, the birth rate of Assam was 27.0 per mile while the all India rate was 26.1 per mile. Similarly, death rate of Assam stood at 9.7 per mile while the all India rate was 8.7 per mile. {India rate excludes data for Jammu and Kashmir and Nagaland (rural)}.

(courtesy: Economic survey of Assam—2000-2001).

THE PROBLEM OF ILLEGAL IMMIGRATION:

Political history of Assam since the early 1970's is mostly dominated by the issue of illegal immigration from neighbouring Bangladesh. The unabated influx of illegal migrants from Bangladesh has rendered severe demographic changes to the region, thereby threatening to reduce the indigenous Assamese population to a minority. Movement of population across the border has been a regular practice for over a century now. During the days of British Raj, that is in the late 1860s, migration to this part was encouraged for economic reasons. British initiated tea plantation in upper

Assam. But seeing local people's reluctance to to leave their agricultural fields and work in tea gardens, the British hired labour from east Pakistan (now Bangladesh) and parts of Orissa and Bihar.

Thus came in large number of consumers depending upon the limited agricultural produce. Assamese agriculturists not being very ambitious about increasing productions, stayed contended with cultivating one crop a year. In order to meet the food requirement of additional population of tea garden workers, the British had to hire more such labourer to be employed in agricultural fields.

Gradually immigration of labourers from east Pakistan increased. Unlike Assamese people, the migrants were much more industrious, hard working and ready to be employed in any hazardous work. They gradually encroached vast vacant lands suitable for agriculture. Thus opening up the path of illegal immigration to the north east India. This immigration took a dangerous turn after independence of the country in 1947, thereby inducing a political perspective to the entire issue. "With constitutional reforms, the country started advancing towards democracy, which is a game of numbers.

The Muslim League now came up with its demand for partition, on the basis of religion. This added a new twist to this population movement. During Sir Mohammed Saduua's Muslim League Ministry, a concerted effort was made to encourage the migration of Bengali Muslims into Assam for political reasons. The Victory Lord Wavell wrote in the Victory's journal, 'the chief political problem is the desire of Muslim ministers to increase this immigration into the uncultivated government lands under the slogan of Grow More Food but what they are really after, is Grow More Muslim....... When the demand for partition was raised, it was visualized that Pakistan would comprise Muslim majority provinces in the West and Bang-e-Islam comprising Bengal and Assam, in the East..... Jinnah confidently declared at Gauhati that Assam was in his pocket.

The Cabinat Mission Plan placed Assam in Group C with Bengal. Both the congress high command and the Muslim League accepted the grouping plan but Lokpriya Gopinath Bordoloi vehemently opposed it. He was supported by Mahatma Gandhi. The grouping plan was foiled and Assam was saved from becoming part of Pakistan." *Report on Illegal Migration into* Assam submitted to the President of India (KR Narayanan) by the Governor of Assam, (Lt Gen (RTD) SK Sinha) on November 8, 1998.

After partition of India, it was basically movement of Hindu refugees from East Pakistan. Along with it large number of Muslims crossed the border due to economic reasons. However, Hindu refugee is still continuing in Tripura and West Bengal, immigration is mainly that of Muslims in Assam. "Hindu population in East Pakistan started declining steeply. In 1947 it was 27% by 1971 it got reduced to 14% and by 1991 it was down to 10%", *Assam Governor's report of 1998.*

There has been a great fall in the percentage of indigenous population from 87 per cent of indigenous people in 1901 to 61 per cent in 1951 and a further low of 50 per cent in 1971.

RECENT REPORT ON IMMIGRANTS

The Group of Ministers (GoM) in its report on reforming the national security on May 23, 2001, pointed out, 'The law and order problems of the north-east region have staggered from bad to worse with the influx of an estimated 12 million Bangladeshi since 1971. Politically the Bangladeshi migrants are in a position to influence results of the elections in about 32 per cent of the constituencies in Assam'.

From 1891 till independence, the state's population grew at around 20 per cent each decade. It went up to 35 per cent between 1951 and 1971, and has now touched 53 per cent.

Political encouragement to this influx of immigrants cannot be ruled out even today. The ever increasing pool of immigrant population is serving as a substantial vote bank to the political parties. Though demand for restriction of entry of foreigners to the state is made by political parties time and again, yet clandestine patronage and support is visible.

This unabated influx of illegal migrants from neighbouring Bangladesh raised mass discontent to such a level that people from all walks of life moved into agitation in late 1970s under the leadership of All Assam Students Union (AASU), thus bringing into a new era in Assam politics.

Illegal Migrants (Determination by Tribunals) Act-(IMDT). The IMDT Act was enacted to deal with the issue of illegal immigration into the state. Provisions of this Act to detect, delete and deport illegal migrants from Assam proved inadequate and earned great mass dissatisfaction. It is believed that this Act is standing as a stumbling block in the implementation of the Assam Accord of 1985.

Certain features of the IMDT has given rise to controversy as it stands contrary to the established laws of the country. But before scrutinizing IMDT it is imperative to first know certain features of the established laws of the land with regard to foreigners.

- It was agreed upon by the government of India under the Assam Accord that foreigner who came to Assam on or after March 25, 1971 shall continue to be detected, their names be deleted from the electoral rolls and be expelled in accordance with law. It was decided that steps would be taken for the deportation of such foreigners. The Assam Accord also says that Indian citizenship would be granted to all East Pakistani Muslims who came across illegally between 15 August 1947 and 24 March 1971, with a Special Provision that those who came between 1 January 1966 and 24 March-1971 would be eligible for this, only after a lapse of ten years of being identified as foreigner.
- In pursuance to this provision of the Assam Accord, Act No. 65 of 1985 was enacted by the Parliament incorporating a new provision, namely, Section 6-A into the Citizenship Act, 1955. This section said 'Special Provisions' as to Citizenship of persons covered by the Assam Accord. Under sub-section 1 (b), the term "detected to be a foreigner" has been defined as follows- 'detected to be a foreigner' means detected to be a foreigner in accordance with the provisions of the Foreigners Act, 1946 (31 of 1946) and the Foreigners (Tribunals) Order 1964 by a tribunal Constituted under the said 'Order'.

  That means determination or detection of a foreigner has been left to be governed by the provisions of an existing central legislation, that is, the Foreigners Act, 1946 and the Foreigners (Tribunal) Order 1964.
- Section 9 of the Act provides that as regards the question as to weather a person is or not a foreigner the onus of proving that such person is not a foreigner lies upon such person notwithstanding anything contained in the Indian Evidence Act, 1872.
- The Foreigners (Tribunals) Order, 1964 made under the Foreigners Act, provides for a summary and expeditious proceeding for determination of a

foreigner and his deportation. The burden of proof always lies with the person concerned to show that he is not a foreigner.

SALIENT FEATURES OF IMDT ACT:

- The IMDT Act has sought to classify 'foreigners' into 'illegal migrant' and 'foreigner'. While section 3 (b) of the Act states that 'foreigner' has the same meaning as in the Foreigners Act, section 3 (c) of the Act defines 'illegal migrant' as a person who satisfies the following conditions-
  - He has entered into India on or after the 25th day of March, 1971
  - He is a foreigner
  - He has entered into India without being in possession of a valid passport or other travel document or any other lawful authority in that behalf. On the basis of this a special procedure of detection has been prescribed for illegal migrant who, in fact, is a foreigner and whose detection is always governed by already existing provisions of Foreigners Act. Providence of a Special Procedure more so in the nature of the one under IMDT Act is therefore judicially redundant and stands contrary to the existing laws of the land governing detection of foreigners.
- According to section 8(2) of IMDT; no application shall be entertained by the Tribunal unless the person in relation to whom application is made is found or resides within the jurisdiction of the same police station wherein the applicant has his place of residence.
- Sub-section (3) of section 8 maintains that such application has to be accompanied by affidavits sworn by not less than two persons residing within the jurisdiction of the same police station corroborating the averments made in the application.

- Sub-section (3) also requires that any application filed against any foreign national shall have to be accompanied by such fee being not less than Rs 10 and not more than Rs 100 as may be prescribed.
- Sub-section (2) of section 8-A casts obligation on the applicant requiring that every application made by him under sub-section (1) has to be accompanied by a declaration by yet another person residing within the jurisdiction of the same revenue sub-division.
- Sub-section (2) also says that no person can make more than 10 such applications or more than 10 such declarations.
- Under the provisions of the Foreigners' Act and Order framed there under, the Superintendent of Police in every district was earlier delegated the authority vide various notifications issued under the Act on behalf of the Central Government as per the Foreigners' Act in case of pre-March 25, 1971 migrants, the SP in the state could issue Quit India notices without any prior notice to the foreigners tribunals and the onus to prove that one was not a foreigner always lies on the foreigner. Under IMDT Act, the SP has been barred from serving such notices upon the illegal entrants before he is determined to be an illegal migrant by the Tribunal or the Appellate Tribunal.

  Courtesy: Assam Accord Implementation- IMDT Act—A stumbling Block by Arup Chandra Borbora, Chairman, Gauhati Bar Acieration.

The IMDT is being looked into as highly discriminatory legislation as it is applicable only to Assam and not to any other State. Contrary to any other law where the foreigner has to prove his citizenship, the IMDT entrusts the burden of proof on the complainant that the person against whom the complaint is lodged is a foreigner. "This Act caters for an Appellant Tribunal of two retired High Court Judges, sixteen district Tribunals of two retired district/Additional District Judges with supporting staff..

The border organization of 4000 policemen processes the case of alleged illegal migrants. The efforts of these agencies maintained at a cost of hundreds of crores to the exchequer, extending over a period of 15 years, has led to the identification of only 9,599 illegal migrants. Out of these only 1,454 could be deported. These statistics amply establish the futility of continuing with the IMDT Act in its present form", *Assam Governor's report to the President of India, 1998.*

Proponents of IMDT say that the Act ensures adequate protection of rights of the minorities so that genuine Indian citizens are not harassed in the bid to detect and deport illegal migrants.

But opponents view it as a flawed document encouraging and protecting illegal immigrants. But experience and statistics prove beyond doubt that the IMDT is not adequate to deal with the epidemic growth of infiltrators to this part of the country and in fact the act is serving the interests of certain vested interest groups and political parties whose main stay has been the vast vote bank provided by lakhs of illegal migrants.

Rate of growth of population in Bangladesh is very high. It is the world's most densely populated country with a population density of 969 per sq km. The population of Bangladesh is growing at the rate of 2.8 million per year. Economically the country is very backward and not being able to provide livelihood to its ever increasing population.

The per capita income in Bangladesh is 170 dollars per year. Moreover the hazard of natural calamities like flood and drought are a regular feature. So moving out for greener pasture is obvious.

Coupled with the fact that Indo-Bangladesh has a very porous border. And this is a boon to the very weak Bangladesh economy. From 1993 to September 1998, the BSF tried to hand over 39,746 illegal migrants to Bangladesh Rifles. But Bangladesh accepted only 9,253 migrants and refused to accept 30,493.

Under such circumstances if our laws are also not adequate, the consequence could be disastrous.

POLITICAL DEVELOPMENTS: MAJOR POLITICAL DEVELOPMENTS FROM 1979 UP TO THE PRESENT DAY

Media reports from 1990 up to the present day: Politics—a necessary evil of society. Politics or struggle for power itself influences the society and social problems equally has its impact on political developments. To understand the political scenario of Assam it is essential to look back into the chronological development of events.

The Assam Agitation: (1979-1985): The All Assam Students' Union (AASU) along with the All Assam Gana Sangram Parishad (AAGSP) launched a mass movement in 1979, for the detection of illegal migrants, their deletion from the voters' list and their deportation to Bangladesh. Unabated influx of illegal migrants had always stood as a matter of great social concern. The desire to throw the migrants out of the state was burning in the minds of people. But the spark which lit the fire of agitation was the by—election of 1978 to be held at Mangaldoi. Electorate complained about the presence of 70,000 illegal migrants in the voters' list and government's apathy towards it.

"The people got convinced that illegal migration on a colossal scale had been taking place and this sparked the anti-foreigner's movement in Assam. Government of India forced the 1983 election in Assam on the basis of a defective voter's list. This was done on the plea that there was not enough time to revise the electoral rolls before the election. There was widespread violence during this agitation including the infamous massacre of 1700 Bengali Muslims at Nellie by the Lalung tribe", *Assam Governor's report to* the President of India, 1998. This Assam Agitation which started in 1979 continued to 1985 and gained large scale mass support. The ruling government then was Congress under the Chief Ministership of late Hiteshwar Saikia. Anti-government or rather anti-Congress feelings were mounting. This was the time when anybody who spoke Bengali was treated as a foreigner. This agitation was led by a group of students' leaders headed by Prafulla Kumar Mahanta.

Finally, at the initiative of the AASU and AAGSP, the historic Assam Accord was signed when Rajiv Gandhi came to power in New Delhi in 1985. According to the terms of the Accord, all foreigners who entered Assam on or after March 25, 1971, were to be detected and deported. Along with it the Accord agreed upon fencing of the border with Bangladesh to prevent further immigration. Signing of this Accord, gradually normalized the situation. A new regional party, the Asom Gana Parishad (AGP) was created which brought together many of the prominent leaders of the agitation. Prafulla Mahanta who was chosen leader of the new party, came to power after winning the elections with an absolute majority.

AGP rule from 1985-1990: The AGP came to power in 1985 winning an absolute majority. The party gained wide scale support from all sections of the society. People were moved by these young leaders and their patriotism. Masses attached great hopes to this party.

"The Northeast, particularly Assam, was then a unique story, perhaps the only one in independent history when the national media's sympathy—even admiration- was with the trouble-makers. Most of us on the beat, barring the Calcutta media, never even called them troublemakers. In print, we called them the Assam movement leaders.

In conversation, they were just "boys" ...... the first time such a thing happened in our independent history. If you spoke Bengali, you were an infiltrator" and, therefore, in trouble. But what Mahanta, Phukan and others also proved subsequently was that ethnic hatred was negotiable as long as they had political power.

They forgot the foreigners' issue, deported even fewer infiltrators than the Congress governments had done in the past and failed to bring in even the most basic concessions to their impoverished state from the Centre..... Mahanta has run the most ineffectual, unimaginative and worthless government in Assam in a long, long time and chances are that his own voters are now going to make him pay for it. The very Asamese caste Hindu who treated him and the other student leaders like gods is now set to boot out each one of them ...... Assam, as a consequence, has not only lost a decade, it's even slipping backwards. The only good this has done is driving more and more talented Assamese outside the region". —Shekhar Gupta, *A 'people's movement' that became a cruel joke.*

From 1985 to 1990, the electorate was shocked by the horrendous development of events under the Mahanta administration. Corruption was rampant at all levels of socio-political life. Muscle power became the ultimate buzzword. No improvement has visible in the inflow of illegal immigrants. Industrialization took a backseat. Massive employment under political consideration accounted for excessive burden on the public exchequer, thereby leading to heavy outflow of government funds on unproductive labour under the heads of salary and wages. There was complete anarchy and centralization of power paving very few openings of transparency in government. The insurgents, United Liberation Front of Assam (ULFAs) were given an open hand to operate in the state. Killing and extortion was the order of the day. Particularly the major tea companies, were the target of the insurgents. Tea industry failed to get adequate support and security from the government. Tea company officials were kidnapped, looted and killed.

The Doom Dooma tea company was demanded huge sums of money by ULFA and were threatened to death if it failed to comply with its orders. The company officials were shifted out of Assam immediately. Meeting similar fate another tea company, Brook Bond also closed its auction centre. Complain of tea companies and other such incidents of gross law and order violation in the society and the state government's apathy served a death blow to the Mahanta regime.

On the 27th of November 1990, President's rule was imposed on the state. Together with it came in the massive military operations of the central government to wash away the insurgents. Operation Bajrang was deployed in Assam.

Print media's role was very critical at this juncture. On the one hand AGP government was criticized openly, their activities, various scandals were brought to the forefront, but along with it, a section of the media covertly if not overtly penned ideas clandestinely supporting the insurgents.

The Rs 200 crores Letters of Credit (LoC), scandal was brought to the limelight which reported involvement of ministers belonging to both AGP and Congress. Reports claim it to be the biggest case of corruption in the history of Assam.

As a provision, the government provides credit to the government contractors carry on work. This is done through a letter of credit whereby the amount of payment is being sanctioned by the department that is deputing the work. Only then the money can be withdrawn from the treasury by the contractor. Now the contractors at the patronage of the ministers, produce fake letter of credit with highly inflated sum of amounts. Obviously, the minister concerned stood as a party to the amount received.

Bibliography

Ahmad, E.: *Confronting Empire,* Cambridge: South End Press, 2002.

Ali, T.: *The Nehru's and the Gandhi's: An Indian Dynasty,* London: Picador, 1999.

Ansari, I.: *Communal Riots, the State and the Law in India,* New Delhi: Institute of Objective Studies, 2002.

Balagopal, K.: *Probing in the Political Economy of Agrarian Classes and Conflicts,* Hyderabad: Perspectives Publishers, 1998.

Banerjea, D.: *Central Police Organizations,* Kolkata: Allied Publishers, 2003.

Baruah, S.: *Durable Disorder: Understanding the Politics of Northeast India,* New Delhi: Oxford University Press, 2003.

Chattopadhyay, K.: *Genocidal Pogrom in Gujarat: Anatomy of Indian Fascism,* Kolkata: ICSP Publication, 2006.

Cohen, S.: *India: Emerging Power,* New Delhi: Oxford University Press, 2007.

Das, Dilip K.: *Police Mission: Challenges and Responses,* London: Scarecrow Press, 2007.

Raghavendra K.: *Understanding the Indian State: A Historical Materialist Exercise,* New Delhi: Indian Institute of Public, 2005.

Roy, A.: *The Cost of Living: Narmada Dam and the Indian State,* New Delhi: Oxford University Press, 2006.

Srinivasavaradan, T.C.A.: *Federal Concept: The Indian Experience,* New Delhi: Allied Publishers, 2000.

Tilly, C.: *Collective Violence,* Cambridge: Cambridge University Press, 2004.

Thomas, B.: *Violence in Urban India: Identity, Politics,* Delhi: Permanent Black, 2007.

Verma, J.S.: *The New Universe of Human Rights*, New Delhi: Universal Law Publishing, 1997.

Viswanathan, S.: *Dalits in Dravidian Land*, Chennai: Narayana Publishing, 2002.

Wilkinson, I.: *Religious Politics and Communal Violence*, New Delhi: Oxford University Press, 2003.

Zareer, M.: *From Raj to Rajiv: 40 Years of Indian Independence*, London: BBC Books, 2006.

Index